Representation and Institutional Design

Representation and Institutional Design

Rebekah L. Herrick

LEXINGTON BOOKS
Lanham • Boulder • New York • Toronto • Plymouth, UK

Published by Lexington Books
A wholly owned subsidiary of The Rowman & Littlefield Publishing Group, Inc.
4501 Forbes Boulevard, Suite 200, Lanham, Maryland 20706
www.lexingtonbooks.com

Estover Road, Plymouth PL6 7PY, United Kingdom

British Library Cataloguing in Publication Information Available

Library of Congress Cataloging-in-Publication Data

Herrick, Rebekah L., 1960–
Representation and institutional design / Rebekah L. Herrick.
p. cm.
Includes bibliographical references and index.
ISBN 978-0-7391-5067-2 (cloth : alk. paper) — ISBN 978-0-7391-5069-6 (electronic)
1. Legislative bodies—United States—States. 2. Election districts—United States—States. 3. Representative government and representation—United States—States. I. Title.
JK2488.H47 2011
328.73—dc22 2010052930

™ The paper used in this publication meets the minimum requirements of American National Standard for Information Sciences—Permanence of Paper for Printed Library Materials, ANSI/NISO Z39.48-1992.

Printed in the United States of America

To my partner Lori D. Franklin

Contents

List of Tables and Figures ix

Preface and Acknowledgments xi

1 Institutions and Representation 1

2 Institutional Effects on the Incumbency Advantage 25

3 Institutional Design and Ambition 43

4 Institutional Design and Role Orientation 57

5 Institutional Design and Symbolic Representation 77

6 Institutional Design, Legislators' Information, and Perceptual Accuracy 99

7 Institutional Design and Substantive Representation 115

8 Conclusion 133

Appendix A: State Legislators and Their Districts 151

Appendix B: Descriptive Statistics of Variables 157

References 159

Index 167

Tables and Figures

FIGURES

1.1 Effects of Institutional Features on Incentives, Abilities, and Representation 18

TABLES

1.1 Variations in Who Responded 20

2.1 Relationship of Vulnerability and Candidate Emergence 33

2.2 Institutional Effects on Electoral Vulnerability 36

3.1 Relationships between Institutional Design and Ambition 51

4.1 Influences on Role Orientation—Ordered Logistic Regression 63

5.1 Institutional Effects on Symbolic Representation 85

5.2 Frequency of Types of Communications 91

5.3 Institutional Influence on Modes of Contact 93

6.1 Sources of Information 104

6.2 Institutions and Perceptual Accuracy of District Views 110

6.3 Institutions and Relative Perceptual Accuracy of District Views 111

7.1 Institutional Effects on Service Representation 119

7.2 Institutional Effect on Policy Representation: Bill Cosponsorships 128

8.1 Summary of Significant Effects 137

Preface and Acknowledgments

In a republic it is essential that legislators work to advance their constituents' interest. Several debates surround how legislators should represent their constituents, such as how much congruence there should be between legislators' decisions and constituents' preferences, and what are ideal forms of representation. Instead of engaging in these debates, this book examines how institutional features influence how legislators' represent their constituents. It does so by examining three types of representation, symbolic (being visible to constituents), service (working on individual concerns), and policy (affecting policy consistent with constituents' interests), as well as legislators' incentives to be responsive to constituents.

Each of the three types of representation has an important role in helping the government advance goals. Symbolic representation can help constituents/voters know government policies, and legislators' actions: information needed for "the people" to make reasoned choices at the ballot box. Service representation can help insure constituents' get governmental services and can help legislators know when policies fail. Policy representation involves legislators making policies that advance their constituents' interests. Although each type of representation has an important role, each type also has its failings. Symbolic representation may not be used to educate but to campaign or advertise offering misinformation. Service representation has been criticized for contributing to the incumbency advantage and may result in some constituents being more likely to get government services than others. There are debates too about what is ideal policy representation. For example, serving majoritarian preferences leads to biases that often harm minority rights. Providing insights into these debates is not the goal here, the goal here is to examine how institutional features can enhance or limit each type of representation. Whether each of the different types is good or bad I leave to others to debate.

A central point of this book is that how legislatures are structured, the rules governing how members are elected, and the tools they have available affect their members' incentives to represent and how they choose to represent their constituents. This point brings together two very different traditions, one focusing on the institution and the other on the individual. Much of legislative research has focused on institutions. How are legislatures structured? What affects their structure? How does structure affect outcomes? But much research has also focused on individuals. Who is elected? What affects who is elected? What are legislators' goals? What affects legislators' decisions and behaviors? One problem with bringing these bodies of literature together is that it results in two units of analysis: the institution at one level and the individual at the other. The way I deal with this is by viewing the institution as something that acts on the individual. Or put another way legislators' institutional context affects their behavior. While examining how institutions affect individuals is not new, it has been understudied by scholars.

Countless works have been written to increase our understanding of representation and countless pieces have been written to increase our understanding of how institutions work. What is surprising, however, is the limited number of works looking at modern institutions, which bring these two approaches together. Here I look at how variations in state legislative design affect legislators' incentives to be sensitive to constituents and their representational activities. States vary enough in design and are similar enough in political cultures that comparative analysis can be meaningful. I do not want to overstate the case, as there are limits to these points. For example, state legislative terms range from two to four years, and there are some real differences between states' cultures (California is more liberal than Mississippi). But state legislatures provide a uniquely well-designed set of cases from which to draw comparison. Thus this work takes advantage of the uniqueness of state legislatures to study a highly important but understudied topic of the effects of institutional design on representation.

Few research projects and even fewer book length manuscripts can be written by an individual without the help of others. This project is no different relying on the help of literally hundreds of people. First, I would like to thank the hundreds of state legislators who took their time and trusted me enough to offer their insights and experiences by completing the survey. I also want to thank my sons, Neal and Reece Franklin, and my students Jada Butler, and Will Stewart for helping implement the survey. I am also indebted to Sam Fisher, Lori Franklin, Emily, Herrick, Mark Liotta, and Tracey Osborn, who reviewed drafts of the survey and/or chapters. Finally, I want to thank the OSU Political Science Department, and APSA small grant program for funding the projects, and Oklahoma State University for providing a sabbatical to draft the manuscript.

1

Institutions and Representation

Americans have historically questioned the commitment of elected officials to represent their interests: a concern that remains strong today. According to a 2007 study, only 45 percent of Americans believed that "The government is really run for the benefit of all the people," and only 34 percent agreed to the statement "Most elected officials care what people like me think" (http://people-press.org/reports/pdf/312). The favorability ratings of state governments are also low, barely reaching 50 percent in the fall of 2009 (http://people-press.org/reports/pdf/534.pdf).

A critical issue for any republic is how to insure that policy makers stay connected with and represent their constituents. The founders as well as contemporary reformers have been acutely aware of this problem. Much has been written, some dating back to the classics, about how to structure governments in order to achieve effective representation. Yet few studies have examined numerous institutional features and numerous aspects of representation at the same time. That is the goal of this book. It examines how variation in state legislative features affects how legislators represent their constituents.

REPRESENTATION

Pitkin (1967) defined representation thusly: "[R]epresentation, taken generally, means the making present *in some sense* of something which is nevertheless *not* present literally or in fact" (8–9). This definition is necessarily vague as representation has many conceptualizations.[1] This book examines three types of representation: policy, service, and symbolic.[2] Policy and service representation fall within the category of substantive representation, or working on behalf of the concrete interests of the represented. Policy representation involves legislators' working on policies that advance the interests of their constituents (Jewell 1982; Eulau and Karps 1978). Policy representation is at the nexus of legislators' legislative and representative responsibilities. With policy representation legislators enact policies to advance the interests of their constituents. As one state legislator interviewed for this project[3] put it, "We have a representative democracy. Voters elect officials to study the issues and represent their needs." For representatives to make their constituents present in this manner, they have to know something about their constituents, or be so similar to their constituents that what they would do is automatically what the represented would do. The latter seems unlikely. Most elections in the United States are considered low information races with voters knowing little about the candidates. Even in U.S. House elections, only about 50 percent of the voters can recognize the name of the challenger and less than 20 percent can recall the name (Jacobson 2004, 124). In many elections, incumbents run unopposed or the challenger is not viable. For example, in the last half of the twentieth century, an average of fifty-nine U.S. House incumbents ran unopposed in each election cycle (Davidson and Oleszek 2004, 60). Even if voters select representatives who are similar to themselves, no single individual can resemble the whole complexity of their constituency. Thus the perspective here is that legislators have to try to work on behalf of their constituents. Although voters may have little awareness of legislators' behavior, there still can be electoral consequences for legislators who do not work on constituent needs. For example, legislators who do not work on constituent interests are open to attacks during campaigns from attentive publics who can then sway voters (Arnold 1990).

Substantive representation also includes service representation: legislators acting on behalf of constituents by providing services to individuals (Jewell 1982; Eulau and Karps 1978). A recent survey of state legislators found that 73 percent indicated that "service responsiveness" was an important part of their job (Little and Ogle 2006, 42). Similarly, a legislator from Missouri interviewed for this project stated, "I view my role as being an advocate on behalf of my constituents to the government agencies that they deal with, and helping them to access the benefits of government programs." Legislators are expected to perform services for their constituents and to be an intermediate body between the government and the people; moreover, they get numerous requests from constituents for governmental services.

Another type of representation is symbolic representation (Pitkin 1967; Eulau and Karps 1978; Jewell 1982). Symbolic representation has several conceptualizations, but here it refers to being visible to the district and serving as a symbol of the district to the government and vice versa. Constituents want access to their representative (Fenno 1977, 915), and a recent study found almost 76 percent of legislators felt symbolic representation was an important part of their job (Little and Ogle 2006, 42). Rosenthal (2004, 25) too found that on a 5-point scale the average legislator scored a 4.6 on the importance of communicating with constituents. Legislators who are visible are likely to serve as important role models. Numerous anecdotes suggest politicians are often inspired to public service by meeting a politician when young. As one legislator recalled, "When I was fourteen years old, I helped the Democrat to win this seat. . . . Some twenty-four years later I now hold that same seat. I had no idea at fourteen that I would be serving this same seat." Constituents who have had contact with their representative and feel that person is open to them will also be more likely to contact their representative with policy or service demands.

Symbolic representation may also have an educational function. Congruence between mass and elite opinion can be caused by the masses following legislators' opinions (Hill and Hurley 1999). Legislators often have extra information about policy that they can share with their constituents, to improve constituents' understanding of the legislators' position. This education can be civics or policy related. Rosenthal (1998) argues that this role has been ignored by legislators. Echoing the work of Hibbing and Theiss-Morse (1995), he believes that the public has lost faith in state legislatures in part because the people do not understand the democratic process. He states, "If legislators are to help rebuild public trust and thus maintain the well-being of representative democracy, they will have to devote a lot more than passing attention to the education of citizens" (339). Legislators who are visible to and interested in their constituents should be better able to educate their constituents. One may question whether educating constituents is really symbolic representation since providing information could be seen as a form of service. While the point is well taken, I see this education as a by-product of symbolic representation. When legislators are visible to constituents they are likely to impart some information. Whether the goal of symbolic representation is educating or campaigning is difficult to distinguish since it goes to legislators' motives in contacting constituents. The goals of symbolic representation are likely multifaceted and distinguishing them here is not likely to be fruitful.

Each of these types of representation concerns dyadic as opposed to collective representation. Collective representation concerns the degree to which the legislature as a whole represents the interests of the nation or state. One of the first empirical treatments of collective representation was conducted by Weissberg (1978). He argues that collective representation is important, because it offers some form of representation to districts with representatives who do not work on behalf of their interests. For example, if a Democratic district is represented by a Republican, then the district's voice is being expressed by another representative: likely a Democrat who represents a Republican district. This logic too can be extended to minority voters within a district. Constituents with minority interests in the district may not have their interests articulated by their electoral representative, but by another representative. Although collective representation is important, this book focuses on dyadic representation. Dyadic representation is the relationship between an individual representative and his or her electoral constituents. There is a long historical tradition of thinking about representation from a dyadic perspective. The responsiveness and accountability functions of elections are based on the dyadic relationship. The structure of the U.S. republic is built on the idea that voters in a geographical area select representatives to represent their interests. If representatives fail to satisfy their constituents, they can be voted out of office: a fear of which enhances legislators' responsiveness to constituents' demands. Researchers too have spent considerable time and effort examining the relationship between individual legislators' decisions and their constituents' preferences or interests (see, for example, Miller and Stokes 1963; Holian, Krebs, and Walsh 1997; Gartzke and Wrighton 1998; Burden 2007). Even Weissberg (1978) does not argue dyadic representation is unimportant. Although he argues that an electoral connection is not a prerequisite to accurate representation, he notes that legislators are likely to want to be responsive to voters to keep their positions. Dyadic representation is the critical link in representative democracy and high levels of dyadic representation should increase the odds that the government serves citizens' interests.

WHAT AFFECTS HOW LEGISLATORS REPRESENT THEIR CONSTITUENTS?

The degree to which legislators represent their constituents—be it symbolic, service, or policy—is affected by their incentives and abilities. Their incentives include role orientation, electoral vulnerability, and ambition. Role orientations are individuals' expectations about how they should behave in relation to others (Gross 1978; Wahlke 1978a). They are not absolutes that determine behavior but concern beliefs about how one ought to act in relation to others (Wahlke 1978b). Role orientation is classified as an incentive since legislators who have a role orientation will want to behave in accordance to that orientation for psychological reasons. One role orientation distinguishes between the trustee and delegate approaches to representation (Eulau and Wahlke 1978). With a delegate (mandate) form of representation, legislators believe they should base decisions on constituent preferences. With a trustee (independence) form of representation, legislators believe they should use their own judgment on policy matters, doing what they believe is correct regardless of constituents' preferences. Which of these is preferred depends, in part, on whether constituents' interests are matters of taste or fact (Pitkin 1967). If they are matters of taste, for example, is it better to have more parks or more fine art programs, then only constituents can truly know their preferences and the delegate form of representation is preferred. If, on the other hand, interests are factual, for example, whether inflationary policies will improve or harm one's standard of living, then the constituents' preferences may not be the same as their interests. Constituents could want something that is not in their interest. However, if constituents are rational and know their interests then the trustee and delegate orientation would yield the same results. Governments undoubtedly deal with some issues that are matters of taste and some that are matters of fact, and legislators vary in their trustee-delegate orientation. However, from a practical perspective several scholars (Eulau and Karps 1978; Wahlke 1978a; Jewell 1982, chapter 1) have expressed some limitation with the trustee-delegate dichotomy. These limitations tend to focus on the following:

1) Few constituents have clear issue positions or demands.
2) It is difficult in large heterogeneous districts for districts to have a unified demand or interest.
3) The above suggest that legislators are unlikely to have a clear sense of the district preferences, since few constituents express their demands and there may not be a unified interest.
4) Effective policy representation actually involves both delegate and trustee behavior. Delegates need to use their judgment to evaluate information to determine whether it reflects their district's views. And trustees need to know preferences to determine interests, particularly where interests are matters of taste.

Treating the trustee-delegate distinction as a role orientation helps to account for the limitations associated with treating the trustee-delegate division as a behavior. Role orientation is an expectation about how legislators should behave, but not the behavior itself. Thus even if the conditions for offering delegate representation are not present, legislators may still believe that if the conditions existed they should be delegates. Although the trustee-delegate orientation is most clearly aligned with policy representation, it may affect service and symbolic representation as well. Those who feel a need to represent constituents' wishes/preferences may need to stay in close contact, so that they can gauge those preferences. Although Eulau and Wahlke (1978) warn against assuming that delegates are more engaged with constituents than trustees, it is a common assumption with some empirical support. Delegates tend to engage more with constituents, and they tend to do more casework as well (Halligan et al. 1988; Studlar and McAllister 1996; Ellickson and Whistler 2001; Cooper and Richardson 2006).

Role orientation can also concern the focus of representation (Eulau and Wahlke 1978) or how legislators define their constituents. How legislators define their constituents affects whose interests the legislator is likely to work on behalf of or be visible to. Fenno (1977) assumes "that the constituency a representative reacts to is the constituency he sees" (883). He suggests that members of Congress conceptualize their constituents in the form of concentric circles. The largest circle is the district as a whole or the geographical constituency. When legislators discuss their constituents they often discuss the different economic interests or demographic groups that make up the district. Within this circle there is a circle of supporters. The supporters are the people living in the geographical district that vote for the legislator. The next most inner circle is comprised of those who are primary supporters. These people not only voted for the legislator, but also are strong supporters who likely worked on their campaign and can be counted on for their support. The last group is the intimates or personal constituency. These are the legislators' close associates and family members who may serve as advisors. Based on the above discussion, legislators may focus their representation on either their voters or the district.

While the concentric circles of constituency focus on those residing within the electoral district, some legislators wish to represent a people beyond their districts' boundaries. Several studies have found that some state legislators also wish to represent their states' interests (Wahlke et al. 1962, chapter 13; Smith 2003). Legislators vary in their state/district orientation because they differ in their ambition and in their districts' characteristics. Legislators with progressive ambition and those with small districts whose interests overlap with the surrounding areas tend to have more of a state focus (Smith 2003). Legislators with a state focus likely approach representation in a different manner than those with a district orientation. They work on larger issues and focus less on service and symbolic representation.

Thus far the idea of constituency has been limited to a geographical definition; however, some legislators want to represent a constituency that is not geographically based. Surrogate representation is representation that "rests on shared ideological perceptions or common identity" (Carroll 2002, 51) not on an electoral or geographic relationship (Mansbridge 1999, 2003). These legislators may take a different approach to representation, such as focusing on issues important to those for whom they are surrogates. Even though they do not directly concern an electoral connection, the state and the surrogate orientations both concern dyadic representation. Both involve how a single legislator tries to represent a group of people, not how the chamber as a whole tries to represent a group of people.

Legislators' representational style is also likely affected by electoral considerations. Elections are the glue that connects legislators to their constituents. Over two hundred years ago Madison (2001, 273) wrote: "As it is essential to liberty, that the government in general should have a common interest with the people; so it is particularly essential that the branch of it under consideration should have an immediate dependence on, and an intimate sympathy with, the people, frequent elections are unquestionably the only policy, by which this dependence and sympathy can be effectually secured." Legislators are often assumed to have a mix of three goals: reelection, power, and policy (Fenno 1977). Reelection goals are thought to dominate since legislators can best achieve power and policy goals by staying in office. A common assumption, therefore, is that legislators who are vulnerable will be attentive to constituents. Although this is a common assumption, the empirical research on the effects of vulnerability on legislative behavior is mixed (Wahlke et al. 1962; Fenno 1977; Wright and Berkman 1986; Bickers and Stein 1996; Hill and Hurley 2002; Sulkin 2005; Miler 2007). Some research finds vulnerable legislators offering greater levels of one form of representation or another and some finds no effects at all. Even if vulnerability per se does not affect legislative behavior, elections can still affect representation. Most legislators are concerned about reelection and feel vulnerable even if outside observers do not see them as vulnerable (Jacobson 1987; Rosenthal 1998, 24–25). It is also likely that legislators who actively represent their constituents are secure because of that work (Sulkin 2005, 31–33). Vulnerability is also directly related to accountability. Accountability refers to the power of voters to remove representatives who are not performing their duties adequately. When incumbents are overly safe, few quality challengers will emerge resulting in voters having no option but to reelect. When this occurs, representation can suffer because constituents may be stuck with a legislator who does not effectively represent them.

The electoral connection is likely felt the strongest by legislators with the desire to stay in office. As Schlesinger (1966, 2) puts it, "The desire for election and, more important, for reelection becomes the electorate's restraint upon its public officials." Thus political ambition or politicians' career goals likely affect how legislators represent their constituents. It is generally recognized that legislators can have three types of ambition: static (keep same office), discrete (retire from politics), or progressive (hold higher office) (Schlesinger 1966). Ambition theory assumes members are forward looking and that they behave in ways to reach their future constituents. Thus those with static ambition have strong incentives to represent their current constituents in order to win reelection and keep their job. Likewise, those with progressive ambition need to monitor opinions of current constituents, so that they do not alienate current voters and also to gauge when they should make their run for higher office (Maestas 2003). Those with progressive ambition may also work to represent constituents outside of their current electoral constituency, since they will need these votes in the future. In contrast, legislators with discrete ambition have little incentive to stay in contact or represent their electoral constituency. Indeed, research finds that ambition affects legislators' relationships with constituents (Van Der Slik and Pernacciaro 1979; Herrick and Moore 1993; Smith 2003). For example, those with progressive ambition introduce more varied legislation, are more active on the floor, and have more moderate voting records but are less successful in passing legislation than those with static ambition (Prewitt and Nowlin 1969; Soule 1969; Van der Slik and Pernacciaro 1979; Herrick and Moore 1993). Those with discrete ambition or retiring have the least contact with constituents (Herrick, Moore, and Hibbing 1994) and may shirk in their voting behavior (Rothenberg and Sanders 2000a, 2000b). Smith (2003) too notes that ambition affects state legislators' interaction roles or home-styles. Those with progressive ambition are more likely to be advocates aggressively pursuing policy and interacting through the media as a means to reach voters.

Having the incentive to engage in different types of representation will only result in representation if legislators have the ability to do so. Key to having the ability to engage in representation is having essential resources. Service and symbolic representation require a similar set of resources. Both of these activities require time, money, and expertise. To produce a newsletter that increases visibility, for example, requires the time to write it, money to send it and some expertise in rhetoric and mass mailing. Likewise, to help a constituent gain a governmental service requires time to investigate and expertise in the bureaucratic labyrinth. Thus legislators in institutions that provide greater resources are more likely to engage in service and symbolic representation. Policy representation too requires time but also requires knowledge. To offer effective policy representation, legislators need to know their constituents' interests.

In addition to resources, context can affect legislators' ability to engage in each type of representation. For example, it may be easier for legislators to offer each type of representation when their districts are small. They will simply have fewer people to communicate to, serve, or know. Other district and legislator traits may affect their ability to engage in representation as well (Fenno 1977; Johannes 1980, 1983; Jewell 1982; McAdams and Johannes 1985; Parker and

Parker 1985; Freeman and Richardson 1996; Adler, Gent, and Overmeyer 1998; Ellickson and Whistler 2001; Maestas 2003; Herrick and Fisher 2007). Districts vary in what they expect of representatives depending on what previous legislators have done, the urban rural mix of the district, homogeneity, and education levels. Similarly, legislators vary in their representation based on party, gender, age, and previous experience.

Representation is not a single enterprise but has many unique actions. It can involve working on policies, being visible, or working on an individual's problems. Legislators vary in the degree to which they are active in any one of these forms of representational styles. And this variation likely stems from their role orientation, electoral concerns, political ambition, and abilities.

LEGISLATIVE INSTITUTIONS

Kousser (2005, 3) defines legislative design as "the set of rules governing a democratic body's composition and operation." These rules plus their immediate by-products are what I refer to as legislative features. By immediate by-product I refer to a condition that the rule creates that does not require any other action. For example, rules that set the number of legislators in a chamber has the immediate effect of setting the number of constituents each legislator represents. This would be an immediate by-product. However, whether the district is homogeneous or heterogeneous would not be an immediate by-product, because it would be affected by short-term decisions on how to draw district boundaries. Similarly, institutional features include aspects of elections such as length of term (frequency of elections), ballot access laws, and laws regulating campaign finance, but they would not include the competitiveness of elections since competitiveness is affected by how others react to those rules. Excluded from this definition are informal norms. Although informal norms can affect legislators' behavior, they are simply not the topic of interest here.[4]

Little work has systematically examined how legislative features or designs affect representation in state legislatures. Some books focus on representation (Jewell 1982; Rosenthal 1998) and some examine how one or two features affect the lawmakers' job (Carey, Niemi, and Powell 2000a, 200b; Kousser 2005; Sarbaugh-Thompson et al. 2006; Kurtz, Cain, and Niemi 2007), but none examine how numerous features affect numerous aspects of representation. Yet, examining numerous features at one time is important. Examining only one feature at a time runs a greater risk of finding spurious relationships. It is also important to examine various aspects of representation because a feature that enhances one incentive for representation harms another. For example, professionalism may decrease legislators' electoral vulnerability but also increase their static ambition. Thus it is important to take a systematic examination of how numerous features affect various aspects of representation at once.

State legislatures have the needed variation in institutional features to allow for comparisons. Some of the differences are in size of constituency, length of term, length of session, resource availability, term limits, strength of leadership, rules governing elections, and district magnitude (number of representatives per district). For example, a California senator works year-round, has staff in the district and in the capitol, full-time pay (over $100,000 a year), serves for a maximum of two four-year terms, and represents more people than U.S. House members. By contrast, a senator in South Dakota represents about 20,000 people, represents the same district as two lower house members (multimember districts [MMDs]), has no personal staff (the whole legislature has about sixty staffers), a two-year salary of $12,000, and 35–40 day sessions.[5] While this variation is needed to test for the affects of different institutional features, similarity in other aspects is helpful to control for other conditions that could affect representational styles. The states all function within the U.S. political system and culture, and they have a similar historical lineage (Squire and Hamm 2005). Although there are significant differences between states, they all function within the same federal system constrained by the same federal Constitution. Additionally, although some states have majority Democratic systems and others majority Republican systems, they all have the same two parties vying for power. Thus although variation in political culture varies from state to state, there are more commonalities than you find comparing national governments.

Institutional features can affect legislators' incentives for responsiveness (electoral concerns, ambition, role orientation), their abilities, and ultimately how legislators represent their constituents. To demonstrate this point, the bulk of the book examines four different types of features: professionalism, term limits, election laws, and features affecting dyadic relationships.

Professionalism

Professionalism refers to the levels of resources and capabilities of the legislature. In the 1950s, state legislatures were comprised of part-time legislators who had no personal staff, part-time incomes, met biannually, had weak internal structures and large cumbersome chambers. They simply lacked the resource and procedures to be effective representatives as state legislatures faced new problems and responsibilities (Jewell 1982; Thompson and Moncrief 1992; Rosenthal 1998; Kousser 2005; Little and Ogle 2006, 22–23).

This led many states, particularly large and wealthy states who could afford it (Squire and Hamm 2005) to undergo numerous reforms leading to increased professionalism. Rosenthal (1981, 3) describes the professionalism movement as follows; "legislatures undertook to rebuild themselves practically from scratch. They increased the time they spent on their tasks; they established or expanded their professional staffs, they streamlined their procedures, enlarged their facilities, democratized their processes, enhanced their ethics, disclosed their finances, and reduced their conflicts of interests." There were two major efforts with professionalism: increasing basic resources (such as staff and facilities, pay and days in session) and enhancing, what I term, capacity[6] (having structures that increase the efficiency of lawmaking). As legislatures professionalized the following resources were increased: days in session, pay, and staff. Although most states still limit the number of days a session meets, during the professionalism movement there was a shift away from biennial sessions and toward annual sessions and an increase in the number of days per session. Some states even went to yearlong sessions. Also, although most legislatures have some kind of staff, many still do not provide personal staff or office resources. Professionalism also increased capacity by altering the structure of the legislative process. Although most research on professionalism has focused on the effects of resources, some such as Bowman and Kearney (1988) and Mooney (1994, 1995) have included or discussed what I call capacity as part of professionalism. Part of creating professional institutions involves improving the legislative processes by creating strong internal structures such as leadership and committees and decreasing the size of the legislature.[7]

Although initial research suggested that professional legislatures do not differ from less professional legislatures in policy outputs, legislators in professional legislatures may be more sensitive to constituents. For example, professionalism resulted in higher levels of congruence between constituent opinion and legislators' behavior (Squire and Hamm 2005, 95), and constituents in states with more professionalized legislatures (measured by resources) reported more contact from their legislators (Squire 1993a). A potential reason for the higher levels of representation is that legislators in professional legislatures may be better able to work for constituents because they are more independent of governors and other external sources of information and policy proposals (Thompson 1986). Legislators who served during the reform period indicated that staff increased in importance and provided legislators with better information (Moncrief, Thompson, and Kurtz 1996).[8] Second, these changes enhanced representation by giving legislators the means by which to dedicate themselves to representing their constituents. For example, legislators with full-time incomes can work full-time at being a legislator and not have to have another job. Finally, the institutional changes increased legislators' incentives to be sensitive to constituents. Legislators in professionalized chambers are more likely to identify themselves as professional legislators/politicians. These professionals are dependent on their political position for their livelihood, which consequently increases their reelection concerns and their desires to work for constituents (Rosenthal 1981, 58–59; Thompson and Moncrief 1992). Rosenthal (1981, 58–60) states:

> Amateurs and professionals will behave differently in the legislature. Amateurs will probably care less about satisfying their constituency, because they will be less concerned about winning. As one amateur expressed his strategy a few years ago: "I can afford to do what I feel is right, and if my constituents don't agree with what I do, they can defeat me. I don't need this job, since I'd be better off if I went back and practiced law." Professionals cannot afford to run such risks.

Legislators who see themselves as professional politicians are likely to have unique political ambition and role orientations. Almost by definition they are not likely to have discrete ambition, but either static or progressive. They may also have unique orientations. As professionals with greater capacity and resources they may feel qualified to hold a trustee orientation. They may also hold more of a district orientation so that that they can keep their careers. Even if professional politicians have progressive ambition, however, they still need to focus on their district's interests since these voters will still be needed if they try to move to a higher office.

Although the above suggests professionalism increased legislators' ability and interest in representing their constituents, it also increased their electoral security. By increasing legislators' interest in reelection and providing them with resources that can be used for reelection professionalism decreased incumbent vulnerability (Holbrook and Tidmarch 1991; Weber, Tucker, and Brace 1991; Cox and Morgenstern 1993; Van Dunk and Weber 1997; Berry, Berkman, and Schneiderman 2000; Carey, Niemi, and Powell 2000b). This may weaken legislators' sensitivity to constituents by making them less fearful about losing reelection. However, if legislators in professionalized institutions are less vulnerable because they work hard to win reelection then electoral security is not the cause of being responsive but the effect of being responsive.

Thus in broad strokes professionalism increases the resources for most forms of representation and enhances legislators' incentives to stay connected by increasing their desire to keep their position, but may insulate them from electoral defeat. However, it may be that specific aspects of professionalism work in different directions. For example, increased resources may increase the ability of legislators to engage in symbolic representative behavior, but capacity may focus legislators more on legislating than symbolic representation. The strong committees and leaders associated with greater capacity may also depress the ability of legislators generally to focus on constituents since they can be competing sources of power. Thus in examining professionalism, I do not treat professionalism as a single feature, but as many features. Three of these features (staff, full-time position, and office budgets) are categorized as resources, while another three are categorized as capacity (leadership strength, committee strength, and chamber size). Each specific feature will be examined separately since they too could work in opposite directions.

Election Laws

The second type of feature concerns election laws. The perspective here is that laws that affect the ease with which candidates can run for office may have mixed effects on legislators' incentives and ability to represent their constituents. By mixed effects I mean they have effects that can increase responsiveness as well as those that decrease responsiveness. Generally laws that make it difficult to run for office are expected to increase incumbent security, decrease progressive ambition, and increase district related orientations. These laws too may decrease legislators' ability to represent by making them focus on campaign activities instead of representation activities. The key features examined include frequency of elections (term length), campaign finance laws (contribution limits and voluntary spending limits), redistricting principles (keeping communities together, or helping incumbents), and ballot access laws (filing fees and signature requirements). State legislative terms vary from two to four years. In forty-five of the states' lower chambers and in twelve of the states' upper chambers legislators have two-year terms, other legislators have four-year terms (calculated from *Book of States*). Another set of electoral laws concerns campaign finance. According to the National Conference of State Legislature (NCSL.org), most states (forty-four) have laws regulating campaign contribution limits. These limits can be a dollar limit on how much a type of political actor can give a candidate or party, or they can be outright bans on contributions from a type of political actor. The types of actors whose contributions have been regulated include: individuals, parties, political action committees (PACs), corporations, and unions. States not only differ in whether they have limits or not, they differ in which actors are limited in their contributions. For example, while Missouri has no limits, Colorado has limits on all five actors noted above, South Dakota limits all but PACs and corporations, and North Dakota only limits unions and corporations. In addition to contribution limits, eight states have voluntary spending limits.[9] State legislators who agree to limit the amount of money they spend on elections are offered public funding: four offer full funding and the others partial funding (NCSL.org).

Other electoral features concern ballot access and redistricting. States have tried to limit the number of candidates, particularly frivolous candidates, running for office by requiring some combination of a filing fee and/or a petition signed by registered voters in order for a candidate's name to appear on the ballot. While some states require neither a filing fee nor a petition, others require as much as a $2,000 fee or three hundred signatures on a petition.[10] States also differ in their approach to redistricting. Several states use redistricting commissions in redistricting, some have traditional principles that are to be followed, and some have virtually unregulated redistricting processes (Winburn 2008; Forgette, Garner, and Winkle 2009). The redistricting principles include respecting the core of the prior district, helping to protect incumbents as well as not protecting incumbents, respecting political subdivisions, communities of interests, and compactness (Forgette, Garner, and Winkle 2009). States also differ in the amount of control the legislature has over redistricting. Some states have commissions draw the boundaries, and in some states the courts must okay the plan. However, Forgette, Garner, and Winkle (2009) find that the commissions or use of courts does not affect legislators' vulnerability. Similarly, after examining partisan gerrymandering Winburn (2008, 206) concludes:

> With the growing push for independent commissions, I argue these reformers are stressing the wrong aspect of their proposals. Every proposal for independent commissions that I have seen includes a specific set of rules for the commissioners to follow. These rules usually include the use of traditional districting principles. . . . According to my findings, the rules are the most important components of successful redistricting reform and not necessarily who controls the process.

Thus this book focuses on redistricting principles and not the use of commissions or courts in redistricting.[11]

Electoral features are likely to have mixed effects on legislators' incentives to represent their constituents. Election laws that make campaigning difficult are expected to increase electoral security if they disproportionately affect challengers, increase discrete and static ambition, and district orientations. Electoral features that make campaigning difficult are, by and large, expected to have disproportionately negative effects on challengers. Challengers simply have less of an ability to adjust and cope with extra burdens. Laws that decrease vulnerability of incumbents decrease their incentives to represent their constituents. Legislators who are vulnerable may be particularly concerned about keeping their job and work with an eye toward responding to and being visible to constituents as a way to garner more votes. Electoral laws that make campaigning more difficult could also decrease progressive ambition. Where election laws make campaigning more costly, legislators are likely to think twice before running for a higher office since the costs increase without the benefits increasing. Electoral laws could also increase legislators' district orientations. Election laws that make running for office more difficult may increase legislators need to be sensitive to constituents. Thus they may develop an orientation that focuses on serving their constituents' preferences.

While electoral features may have mixed effects on legislators' incentives to represent constituents, they likely decrease their ability to represent. By making running for office more difficult some features could decrease representation by diverting legislators from representation toward fund-raising or other campaigning activities. Legislators may want to be responsive but are distracted by the need to campaign and simply lack the time to engage in representation. Campaigning has some traits in common with symbolic representation. They both involve increasing legislators' visibility to constituents. However, campaigning is likely more biased toward those whose support is needed and not toward the whole district, and thus is inferior as a form of representation. Since electoral laws may have conflicting effects on resources and abilities their overall affects on the three types of representation may be limited.

Term Limits

A third feature is term limits. Since the 1990s, twenty-one states have enacted limits on the number of terms state legislators could serve. These laws varied, with some states having lifetime bans and others limiting consecutive terms. The limits also vary in length from six to twelve years. For various reasons, six of these states have removed term limits leaving fifteen states with current legislative term limit laws. Term limit laws are not treated as electoral laws because they affect more than electoral considerations. Also they have received so much attention I want to highlight term limits by treating them as a separate category. Also although it may appear as though term limits decrease professionalism, since they lead to less experienced legislators, term limits do not lessen the resources or capacity that define professionalism (Squire and Hamm 2005; Squire 2007). Thus they are conceptually distinct.

Although the effects of term limits on legislators' incentives, abilities, and behaviors have been hotly debated by pundits and scholars alike, the perspective here is that they will have modest negative effects on legislators' incentives, and abilities to represent. The effects are expected to be modest in part because the previous research on the effects of term limits on numerous phenomena have had mixed and weak findings. Term limits are not expected to effect vulnerability because there is not a consistent theory predicting a clear effect. Term limits may increase vulnerability by making the position less attractive which may decrease the effort incumbents put into the job and the costs of running (but see Carey et al. 2006). Conversely, they could decrease vulnerability since quality challengers will wait until the incumbent is term-limited out so they can run in open seats. I expect term limits will hurt the other incentives legislators have to represent constitutions: increase discrete ambition and increase trustee and decrease district orientations. Simply since term-limited legislators are legally prohibited from long service they will not have static ambition, although they may have progressive ambition. They will have less district and delegate orientations because they are freed from the electoral connection. If elections are the glue that connect legislators to their constituents, then by having limited interest in elections these legislators are free to ignore constituents. This may be a significant issue if term-limited legislators are, as was found by Herrick and Thomas (2005), more ideological than others. Ideologues who are unconcerned about elections are likely to be rogue representatives. They may also be less interested in symbolic and service representation since their interest is in policy. Term limits may also decrease legislators' ability to engage in certain types of representation. For example, it takes time for legislators and their staff to develop the knowledge and contacts needed for service representation. Since these legislators have short terms, their start-up costs will have fewer returns.

only in last term, no.

Dyadic Relationships

The fourth type of feature concerns the dyadic relationship between legislators and constituents. Dyadic relationships, the relationship between legislators and constituents, can be made closer or more personal by two features: district size and district magnitude. This includes district magnitude and district/constituency size. District magnitude concerns the number of representatives who represent a single district. Single-member districts (SMDs), districts with one representative, are most common in the United States. There are, however, eleven states that have at least some MMDs in the state legislature (Squire and Hamm 2005). Historically, however, MMDs were more common. It has only been since the 1960s that states have moved toward SMDs, in large part because MMDs were thought to harm racial/ethnic minority candidates. MMDs can be free-for-all races where all candidates' names are put on the same ballot and the top N (number of positions) vote getters win, or they can be position seats where there are essentially N (number of positions) races going on in the district. U.S. Senate seats are essentially position MMDs. Legislators representing SMDs are thought to have strong dyadic relationships since there is a clear one-on-one relationship (Jewell 1982, 120). Also, constituency size can affect dyadic relationships and differ dramatically from state to state. California senate districts average about 850,000 residents while New Hampshire House seats average about 3,000 (Little and Ogle 2006, 141). Close dyadic relationships make it easier for legislators to represent constituents since legislators are likely to know them better. For example, smaller districts make it easier for legislators to know their districts, since they are likely more homogeneous than larger ones. Also, legislators can personally contact and meet a larger share of their constituents. According to a state legislator from Texas "Most contact with constituents is in everyday walks of life: church, grocery store, ball games, charity organizations, service clubs, chamber of commerce, schools." Dyadic relationships may also affect legislators' incentives. Strong dyadic relationships likely insulate legislators from electoral defeat; since there is a close relationship voters are not likely to turn on their representative. This too may decrease the likelihood that challengers run against incumbents. Also, since there is a close relationship legislators may be more likely to have static ambition, not wanting to sever their close relationship. It may also affect role orientations since this close relationship exists legislators may feel a particular obligation to focus on them and do as they wish. It is likely too that constituents from smaller districts will want this from their legislator. Hibbing and Alford (1990), for example, found that constituents in small districts want more contact with their legislators than those in larger districts. While the above suggests close dyadic relationships will increase responsiveness, weak dyadic relationships may increase the need legislators have to engage in service and symbolic representation. Since legislators are less well known where the relationship is weaker, legislators in large districts or with large district magnitude may engage in more symbolic and service representation so that they will be known by their constituents.

So far I have given a brief overview of how the four legislative features are likely to affect legislators' incentives, abilities and levels of representation. Figure 1.1 depicts these expectations. The overview and figures offer a somewhat simplistic view that will be elaborated on in future chapters, each specific feature within each type has its own set of characteristics that may impact how well it fits these expectations. It should be observed too that the incentives and abilities are not only affected by institutional design but are also influences on legislators' representational styles. Also many of the incentives may affect each other. Most notably vulnerability may affect ambition and role orientation; and ambition may affect role orientation.

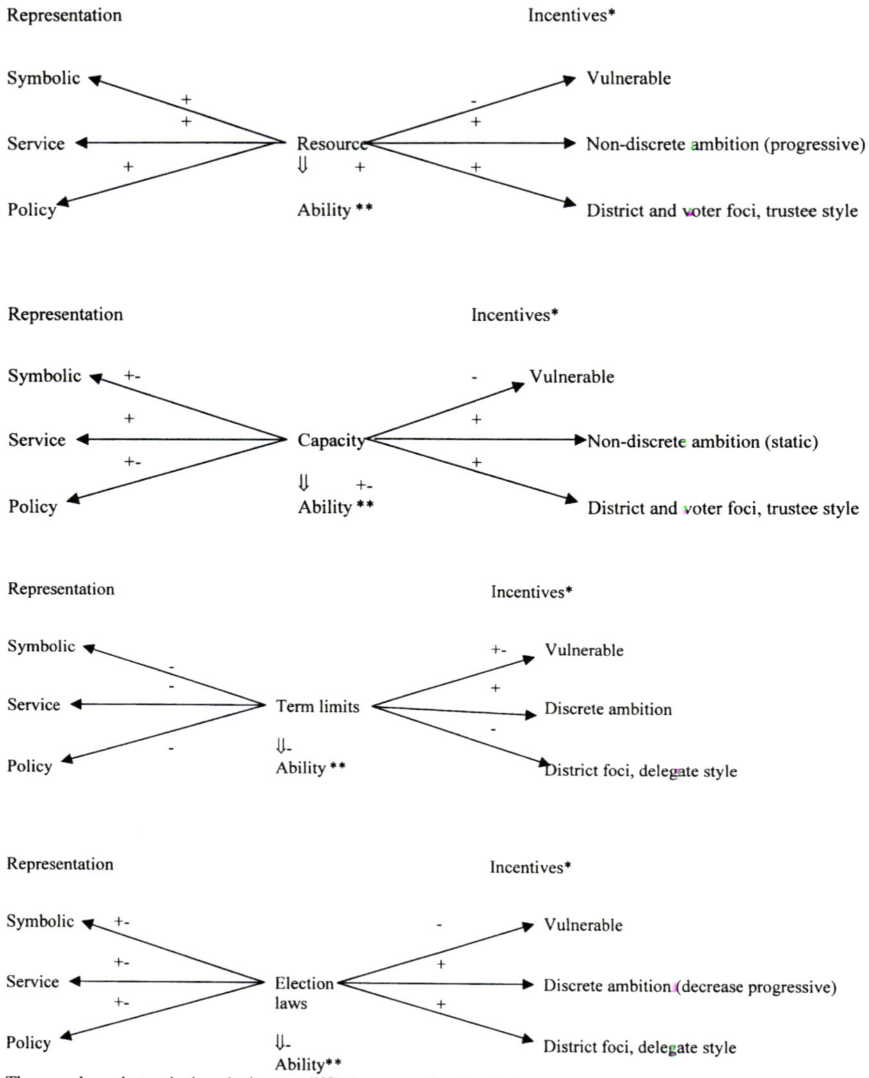

These are laws that make it make it more difficult to campaign by placing restrictions or requirements for campaigns or elections. Features that make it easier for incumbents to win reelection are expected to have the opposite affects.

Figure 1.1. Effects of Institutional Features on Incentives, Abilities, and Representation

Not the most helpful figure

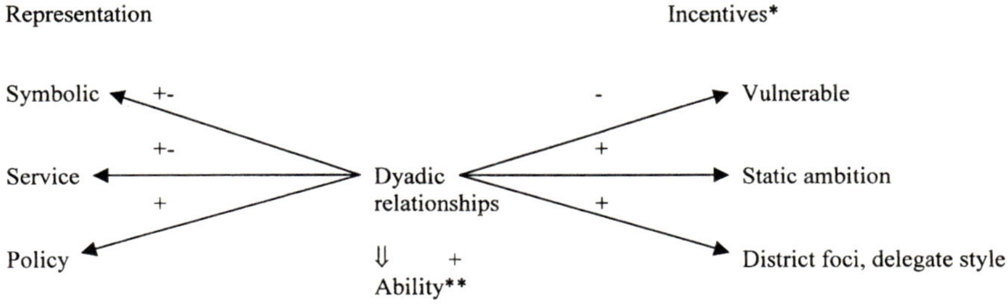

* these incentives are also expected to affect representation.
** ability is also expected to affect representation.

Figure 1.1. ***(Continued)***

To sum up, representation involves several unique behaviors including symbolic, service, and policy representation. These are likely affected by legislators' ability to engage in representational activities, as well as the incentives (ambition, role orientations, and electoral considerations) to engage in these activities. Legislative features are likely to affect how legislators choose to act on their representational duties by affecting legislators' incentives and resources. The effects of a feature could be contextual. The value of resources for an activity may depend on the incentives for that activity. For example, legislatures that offer resources to legislators to contact their constituents but do not provide the incentive for them to use those resources on constituent contact may not increase contact as much as those who provide resources and incentives.

TESTING THE EFFECT OF INSTITUTIONAL FEATURES

In order to test whether institutions affect how legislators represent their constituents, I rely on a survey of state legislators in twenty-six states. It was conducted following the elections of 2008. The states were Alabama, Arizona, Arkansas, California, Colorado, Florida, Georgia, Idaho, Kansas, Kentucky, Louisiana, Michigan, Missouri, Mississippi, Montana, North Dakota, Ohio, Oklahoma, Oregon, South Carolina, South Dakota, Tennessee, Texas, Utah, Virginia, and Wisconsin.[12] One half of the legislators (1831) in these states were randomly selected to receive the survey. A modified tailored design (Dillman 2007) was used in implementing the survey. The subjects were sent a letter informing them that they would be sent a survey. Legislators were then sent a survey followed by a reminder email, then another survey. Finally, they were sent an email with a link to an Internet version of the survey. The response rate was 34 percent. The wording on many of the questions, particularly role orientation, symbolic representation, and service representation were based on, but are not necessarily identical to questions used in the 2002 State Legislative Survey by John M. Carey, Richard G. Niemi, Lynda W. Powell, and Gary Moncrief (ICPSR 20960). Appendix A includes a copy of the survey.

To test for the representativeness of respondents to the survey, data on key characteristics of the legislators were collected on the entire sample (respondents and nonrespondents). These characteristics include: age (year born), gender (0 = male, 1 = female), levels of education (0 = high school or less, 1 = some college, 2 = college, 3 = graduate degree), party (0 = Republican, 1 = Democrat), seniority (year entered), and whether the legislator left his or her chamber at the end of 2008 (0 = still in office, 1 = left). Also data were collected on characteristics of legislators' chambers: chamber (0 = lower chamber, 1 = Senate), levels of professionalism (Squire 2007),[13] term limits (1 = has term limits, 0 = no term limits), and region of the country (0 = northern, 1 = southern states). These data came from votesmart.org, state legislative pages, NCSL.org, and Google searches. There were some missing data, particularly for age and levels of education. Table 1.1 reports both bivariate Pearson correlations and logistic regression analysis with whether or not the subject responded as the dependent variable. Those who responded were coded 1, others were coded 0. Table 1.1 indicates that there were not significant differences between those who responded and those who did not respond in whether legislators were term-limited, their party, gender, age, year entered, chamber, or education levels. However, legislators in southern states, those in professionalized legislatures, and those who left their chamber

Table 1.1. Variations in Who Responded

Variable	*Correlation*	*Coefficient*	*Standard Error*
Democrat	–0.002	0.05	0.12
Female	–0.02	0.00	0.15
Year born	–0.01	0.000	0.001
Education	0.03	0.11	0.08
Left chamber	–0.09***	–0.68	0.18***
Senate	0.02	–0.02	0.13
Professionalism	–0.14***	–4.44	0.58***
Southern states	–0.09***	–0.88	0.13***
Year entered	–0.01	–0.01	0.01
Term limits	–0.02	0.20	0.13
Constant		12.97	19.42
N	1,831 to 1,511	1,394	

Pseudo R^2 = 0.06.
Log likelihood = –875.57.
LR Chi^2 = 107.24 ***(DF = 10).
* <= 0.10; ** <= 0.05; *** <= 0.01 (using a two-tailed test).
Description of variables is in text.

at the end of 2008 were less likely to respond.[14] Even though the relationships were significant, the correlations were quite small: the highest was 0.14.[15]

THE REST OF THE BOOK

The next three chapters examine the effects of institutions on incumbents' incentives to focus on representation. Chapter 2 examines the influence of institutions on incumbents' electoral vulnerability. Electoral vulnerability is related to accountability and may affect legislators' incentives to respond to constituents' needs. Chapter 3 examines how institutional features affect legislators' political ambition. Political ambition is examined because legislators with discrete ambition have little incentive to be responsive to constituents. Chapter 4 examines how institutional features affect another incentive, role orientation. It examines whether legislators' representational role orientations are affected by institutional features. The following chapters examine how institutional features affect aspects of representation. No chapter examines how institutional features affect abilities specifically since there is not an adequate way to measure legislators' ability to engage in the different types of representation, other than looking at levels of representation themselves. Chapter 5 examines how institutional features affect symbolic representation. It does so by examining the amount of time legislators spend keeping in touch with their constituents and by examining different modes of contact legislators use to stay in contact with constituents. Chapter 6 examines two inputs helpful for policy representation. It examines how institutional features affect the accuracy of legislators' perceptions of their constituents' interests, and the sources of information used in making decisions. Legislators who have a better understanding of their district are likely better able to offer high levels of policy representation. Chapter 7 examines the degree to which legislators actually engage in policy or service representation. It does so by examining legislators' cosponsorships and time spent engaging in casework. Chapter 8 summarizes the findings and discusses how each feature affects how legislators represent their constituents. This final chapter notes several broad conclusions from this work: resources to engage in representation are critical to increasing levels of representation; legislators with staff most consistently offer constituents higher levels of representation; professionalism should not be treated as a single reform, because each reform within professionalism had its own effects; professional and citizen legislators offer different styles of representation, notions of surrogate orientation or representation may need some refinement, and term limits generally limit legislators' representational actions. Another key finding is that it is difficult for many features to have strong effects on representation because they have conflicting effects on incentives and abilities. For example, tough election laws make legislators more electoral secure, which should decrease their need to be responsive but at the same time by making elections difficult they increase discrete ambition and increase the time legislators need to campaign distracting them from representational duties.

CONCLUSION

Representative democracy requires representatives who are concerned about and work for their constituents. To do so, they need to have the ability to do so as well as the incentives to do so. This book is an effort to see how variations in legislative features affect legislators' incentives (electoral vulnerability, ambition, and role orientation) to engage in different representational activities and ability to do so. It is expected that by affecting legislators' abilities and incentives to engage in certain actions, legislative design will affect representational styles. To test this theory, this book reports the results of a survey of state legislators. State legislators offer a uniquely valid population since there is considerable variation in legislators' relationships with their constituents and in the institutions in which they work, while still sharing a larger political climate.

This work falls in the broad theoretical framework of neo-institutionalism: arguing that political institutions are important political actors that can affect other political phenomena. Yet this work is also interested in individual behavior by exploring how institutional features affect legislators. Peters (1996) notes that a key problem with neo-institutionalism is the "paradox of constraints." Since individuals create institutions, it is hard to know whether institutions affect individual behavior or whether individual behavior affects institutions. For the purpose of this study, it is assumed that institutions affect behavior. I am not looking at norms but formal rules, most of which were not created by the individuals in office at the time of this study. For example, the movement for professionalism is forty years old and term limit reform is fifteen to twenty years old. Although larger social forces may impact formal rules and legislative behavior, legislative rules often differ dramatically in similar states. Although neo-institutionalism has been criticized for being reductionist (Peters 1996) or asserting the institution is omnipotent, I make no such claim. While clearly this work argues institutions matter, it allows for other factors to affect legislative behavior, such as legislators and their districts' characteristics. It also discusses why a given feature may not have as strong an effect as pundits may expect.

NOTES

1. In her classic, Pitkin (1967) examines how the term representation has been used. She finds three major categories: authoritative representation, stand for (symbolic and descriptive) representation, as well as substantive or act for representation.

2. I do not examine allocation representation, i.e., obtaining resources for the district or pork barreling (Jewell 1982; Eulau and Karps 1978), because my interest is in how legislators interact with constituents, not with all forms of representation.

3. All quotes not otherwise attributed are comments from participants in the survey described later in the chapter.

4. Also it is difficult to separate the effects of norms from individual preferences since individuals, not established rules, determine the norms at a given time.

5. The specifics for these comparisons come from Little and Ogel (2006).

6. The term capability has been used as a measure of efficient decision-making processes and structures. There is just a modest relationship between measures of capability and resources (LeLoup 1978).

7. One might think that large chambers could increase representation in that legislators in larger chambers could have smaller constituencies. Constituency size will be treated as a separate variable.

8. Other important findings were 1) media and lobbyists increased in influence, 2) governors' influence decreased, 3) the job has more pressures, 4) constituent service demands and time requirements increased, and 5) legislators in citizen legislatures saw smaller changes in these areas.

9. Since *Buckly v. Valeo*, 424 U.S. 1(1976) the courts have held that candidates spending money on behalf of their campaign is protected by the first amendment and cannot be limited. However, if the spending limits are voluntary, they are permitted.

10. Source: Richard Winger of *Ballot Access News*.

11. Also, my preliminary findings indicated that commissions had limited effect on legislators' behaviors.

12. These states include the population of states that had had a referenda or initiative vote on same-sex marriages since 2004. It is rare for this many states to have a ballot item on similar legislation in a short period of time. Thus these items provide a unique opportunity to measure state legislative district attitudes. Unfortunately, this pool of states is somewhat biased in that there are no New England or upper Atlantic states. Maine did have a vote on same-sex marriage but did so a year after the survey. However, the results of the marriage ballot items are needed as an indicator of the accuracy of legislators' perceptions of constituent preference and policy representation. Additionally, since I am not interested in overall levels of representation but how features affect representation, the lack of Northeastern states is most important if one argues that they are so unique that the features examined here will have unique effects in these states.

13. Squire's measure is based on the relative level of resources legislators have compared to the resources of members of the House and runs from 0 to 1.

14. Given the large number of missing cases I also reran the analysis without year born in the equation and the results were very similar. This raised the number of cases to 1,625.

15. Defining the population is a bit tricky. Is the population all legislators or is the population comprised of legislators in individual states? If it is the latter, then each state should have the same number of respondents. Because of this, I did weigh the data so that each state would be treated the same. This did not dramatically affect the findings. There were a few cases where a feature went from being significant to just nearing significance or vice versa, but overall the results were remarkably similar.

2

Institutional Effects on the Incumbency Advantage

> My constituents are my top priority. I looked after them and they took good care of me.

Several recent reforms (such as term limits and campaign finance laws) were designed to help increase the vulnerability of incumbents. Incumbents are thought to be so secure that elections no longer fulfill their accountability and responsiveness functions. In other words, incumbents are so secure voters are not able to remove poor representatives, and legislators do not need to take care of constituents to win reelection. Where incumbents are overly secure, it gives voters little opportunity to remove those who are not working in their interests. For example, although legislators involved in scandals lose votes, many if not most are returned to office (Welch and Hibbing 1997; Herrick 2000). Simply, they can survive a 10-point decline in their vote total if they have been winning with more than 60 percent of the vote. Additionally, since the odds of unseating an incumbent are so slim, viable challengers choose not to run. When quality opponents do not run against incumbents, voters have no choice and the elections are meaningless.

Vulnerability can enhance representation by increasing the responsiveness of representatives to their constituents. A key function of elections is to make legislators responsive to their constituents' demands. Legislators who want to win reelection need to serve their constituents. Following from this it is often assumed that legislators who are vulnerable will work to improve their relationships with their voters, so that they can be reelected and keep their job. However, the research on the effects of electoral vulnerability, per se, on legislators' behavior is mixed. This is true whether one looks at the congruence between constituents' preferences and legislators' behavior or whether one looks at casework or contact. On the positive side, vulnerable members of Congress and state legislators have been found to have higher congruence on specific votes (Kuklinski and Elling 1977; Sullivan and Uslaner 1978; Holian, Krebs, and Walsh 1997), offer more pork or transfer payments (Hibbing 1984; Bickers and Stein 1996), and are more likely to advertise (Adler, Gent, and Overmeyer 1998; Bond 1985). In contrast, other works suggest vulnerability has no effect. Gartzke and Wrighton (1998) and Bartels (1991) did not find vulnerable members more likely to vote with constituents' preferences than more secure members. And some research (Johannes 1980; Bond 1985; Freeman and Richardson 1996; Ellickson and Whistler 2001) finds little effect of vulnerability on casework and pork barreling. Fenno (1977) too finds electoral margins unrelated to trips home or to assignment of staff to district.

Several reasons have been offered for these mixed findings. First, part of the reason is that members' perceptions of vulnerability, not objective evaluations affect legislators' behavior. After doing intensive interviews with over two hundred state legislators, Jewell (1982, 47) concludes

> [state legislators] do not feel politically secure, even when they have won by comfortable margins or without opposition. They are always wary of potentially strong opponents and work hard to build a record at the polls and in office that will discourage such persons from running. Those who have strong records of electoral success appear to be just as interested in the constituency and just as attentive to its interests as those who have won by narrow margins—if you can believe what they say in interviews.

margins ≠ Pr(reelection)

This view was echoed by Jacobson's (1987) examination of House members and Rosenthal's (1998, 24–25) examination of state legislators. Both suggest members are concerned about reelection regardless of objective vulnerability.

Other explanations abound. For example, one explanation for the mixed findings is that legislators are responsive for reasons other than reelection. Smith (2003), for example, suggests that legislators interact with constituents not only for reelection, but also for political support more broadly. Yet another explanation comes from Sulkin (2005), who suggests that there are two ways constituent responsiveness could be related to vulnerability. The first view—more common, as noted above—is that legislators who are vulnerable respond by becoming more responsive to constituents. The second is that responsive members are less vulnerable. That is, legislators who are responsive may be rewarded by having relatively easy reelection bids. In her study on uptake[1] she finds some evidence of both. The variation in findings too could be attributed to contextual variation. That is, vulnerability may affect legislators' behavior in some situations but not all. As noted in chapter 1, it is likely that difficult elections consume legislators' time leaving little for legislators to work on official acts of representation.

Although the evidence as to the effects of vulnerability on legislators' behavior is mixed, the effects of institutions on vulnerability still warrant examination. The lack of vulnerability still affects the accountability function of elections. Additionally, the evidence is mixed indicating there is likely some affect of vulnerability on legislators' representational styles.

INSTITUTIONAL EFFECTS ON INCUMBENT VULNERABILITY AND CANDIDATE EMERGENCE

Professionalism is expected to increase legislators' electoral security. Professionalized legislatures provide legislators resources that can be used to reach voters. For example, having resources to communicate with constituents can have electoral value. If nothing else these communications offer legislators the means to advertise themselves and increase their name recognition. Also by increasing legislators' pay and legislative capacity, professionalism increases the value of the job and the willingness of legislators to fight for the job. Much research supports this. The rise of professionalism is associated with the decline of the marginal state legislator[2] (Weber, Tucker, and Brace 1991; Cox and Morgenstern 1993, 1995; Van Dunk and Weber 1997), and the insulation of incumbents from national factors that can affect elections, such as the economy or coattail effects (Berry, Berkman, and Schneiderman 2000). The central factors that increase the incumbency advantage were larger salaries, potential for paid trips home, and staff (Holbrook and Tidmarch 1991; Carey, Niemi, and Powell 2000b).

In general, the resources of professionalism are associated with increased incumbent security. However, professionalism may have a countereffect of increasing the likelihood that an incumbent faces a challenger, or decreasing the likelihood of an uncontested election. Professionalism is widely seen as enhancing the value of the state legislative position. As the value of the position increases so too does the number of people interested in the post. Whether this increase in the likelihood of having a challenger affects vulnerability is less clear. Although professionalism increases the likelihood that an incumbent faces a challenger, some research suggests professionalism decreases the ability of the challenger to do well (Squire 2000; Hogan 2004; Forgette, Garner, and Winkle 2009).

Electoral features too are likely to affect electoral vulnerability. Features that make campaigning difficult are likely to increase security if challengers disproportionately feel their effects. If not, they will increase vulnerability.

As such, it is difficult to predict the effects of campaign contribution laws. On one hand, since money helps candidates win elections, and incumbents have more money campaign finance laws could be expected to increase competition. Generally, incumbents are better able to raise campaign money than are challengers. They have experience raising funds and have already developed contacts; moreover, large donors are more likely to give to those who have already won. Since incumbents generally are better positioned to raise large sums of money from a variety of sources, campaign contribution limits and spending limits should take away their advantage. Challengers, however, have a hard time collecting money from large donors and so should be less affected by campaign finance laws. In fact, campaign contribution limits and campaign spending limits have been found to increase the likelihood that incumbents face challengers and are vulnerable (Hamm and Hogan 2009). On the other hand, it is also possible that campaign funding limits are disproportionately felt by challengers and decrease incumbent vulnerability (Mayer and Wood 1995). Since incumbents are better able to raise money they are likely to be better able to cope with stringent campaign funding laws. Also since they have the perks of office and have already run for the seat they have better name recognition and other traits helpful for winning office. So they start with an advantage that challengers with limited funds cannot overcome.

Another type of electoral law that can affect the likelihood that a challenger emerges and an election is competitive concerns ballot access. These laws either require candidates to pay a fee or get a set number of signatures on a petition to have their name appear on the ballot. Although these laws were designed to prevent nonviable candidates from running, it is feared, that they may also prevent quality candidates from running by adding an additional cost onto the price of running. Research confirms that laws limiting ballot access depress the likelihood that challengers run against incumbent state legislators (Stratmann 2004; Hamm and Hogan 2009). Filing fees have a greater effect on minor party candidates and petition requirements on major party candidates (Stratmann 2004). Ballot access laws also increase the number of uncontested U.S. House elections (Ansolabehere and Gerber 1996). If ballot access laws discourage only frivolous candidates from running, they should have little effect on the vulnerability of incumbents; however, if they prevent quality challengers from emerging, they would be expected to decrease incumbents' vulnerability as well.

Issues concerning the length of legislative terms too have often been thought to affect elections. Most simply, the longer the term, the more vulnerable incumbents are likely to be. As a legislator with a two-year term stated, "It's a catch-22—you need to campaign (i.e., go to tons of events) during the election to win. In the off year you need to do the same thing to let everyone know you haven't forgotten 'em. Then you do it again the next year because if you have an opponent you need to campaign and if you don't, you can't look like you are taking them for granted." U.S. Senators with their longer terms are generally more vulnerable than House members. Their longer terms are thought to increase senators' vulnerability. Presumably House members have to campaign constantly, and senators do not feel the same need to be responsive throughout the term. In looking at the incumbency advantage and the vanishing marginals in state legislatures, Carey, Niemi, and Powell (2000b) and Weber, Tucker, and Brace (1991) find longer terms related to greater vulnerability. However, not all studies find term length to have significant effects. Holbrook and Tidmarch (1991) find little effect of term length on the size of the sophomore surge, and Squire (2000) does not find term length to have a clear effect on the likelihood that a challenger emerges.

Another type of election law concerns redistricting. Since district characteristics can dramatically affect incumbent vulnerability, states can affect incumbent vulnerability by determining district boundaries. When incumbents "fit" their districts, or share important political traits with their constituents, they are more likely to win. When districts are redrawn following the census, it is often assumed that districts will be adjusted in a way that will help incumbents. This sweetheart or pro-incumbent gerrymandering tends to satisfy both parties, which helps pass the districting plans, particularly, in states where one party does not dominate. Redistricting simply affects competition and candidate emergence (Weber, Tucker, and Brace 1991; Van Dunk and Weber 1997). One of the most comprehensive examinations of how redistricting laws affect electoral competition was conducted by Forgette, Garner, and Winkle (2009). They examine the effects of redistricting principles, use of redistricting commissions and the courts[3] on whether elections are uncontested, and on margin of victory. The principles include: respecting the core of the prior district; helping to protect incumbents and not protecting incumbents; respecting political subdivisions, communities of interests, and compactness. Forgette et al. (2009) find that states that have the principle of respecting communities of interests and political subdivisions are less likely to have uncontested elections. They also find that states that prohibit and those that require incumbent protections have more uncontested elections. These counterintuitive findings (that laws that prohibit pro-incumbent gerrymandering are associated with incumbents doing well) may be the results of states with fewer contested elections enacting laws that prohibit pro-incumbent gerrymandering. Neither the role of commissions nor the courts were found to affect the likelihood of an uncontested election. When looking at margin of victory, they find that states with the principle of protecting political subdivisions have smaller margins of victory, and that those that require protecting the core of former districts or incumbents have larger margins of victory. Additionally, Forgette, Garner, and Winkle (2009) find that use of commissions and court-imposed plans do not affect margin of victory.

Features affecting the closeness of dyadic relationships between legislators and constituents are also expected to affect incumbent vulnerability and candidate emergence. Overall, the stronger the dyadic relationship the more likely legislators are to be secure. Legislators with closer relationships with constituents are likely to be trusted by voters and receive their votes. Additionally, the two features examined here have other characteristics that should increase electoral security. Some MMDs have free-for-all elections races where voters pick two candidates from a slate of candidates. These systems result in less predictable elections since a candidate can win with a fairly small share of the vote. Research too indicates that legislators in MMDs are more vulnerable than others (Weber, Tucker, and Brace 1991; Van Dunk and Weber 1997; Carey, Niemi, and Powell 2000b; but see Niemi, Jackman, and Winsky 1991; Squire 2000), and are more likely to have contested elections (Van Dunk and Weber 1997, but see Squire 2000). Additionally, the incumbency advantage grew at a slower rate in states with MMDs than in those with SMDs (Cox and Morgenstern 1995). Small districts, the other feature associated with the dyadic relationship, may also increase security because there are fewer potential candidates. The more people there are in a legislator's district, the greater the odds that one person, all else being equal, will run against the incumbent. Representatives of larger constituencies may also find it more difficult to keep in touch with voters or provide particularized benefits to large segments of their constituencies. Supporting this view is that races in populous states tend to be more competitive than less populous states (Hibbing and Brandes 1983; Lee and Oppenheimer 1997, but see Hibbing and Alford 1990). However, Hogan (2004) offers a different perspective. He finds legislators in large districts are less likely to face a challenger, but that challengers tend to do well. Hogan suggests that the campaign costs in large districts are prohibitive, so that only quality challengers emerge.

The last feature is term limits. How term limits affect candidate emergence and incumbent vulnerability is highly debated. Term limits may decrease vulnerability by decreasing the likelihood that a strategic politician runs against an incumbent. Since incumbents are reelected at very high rates, many potential candidates opt not to run since they have little chance of winning. In term-limited states this may be particularly relevant, because potential challengers can wait an election or two and run in an open seat when the odds of winning are greater. Thus term limits could increase the number of uncontested elections and decrease the vulnerability of incumbents. Term limits may also decrease the value of the job by decreasing legislators' ability to amass power in the chamber and affect policy. This decreased value can result in candidates spending less money on their races, in opening the pool of potential candidates, or in decreasing the number of people who want the job. The decreased value can also limit the effort incumbents spend keeping their post, resulting in increased vulnerability. Finally, term limits have been thought to increase vulnerability, as long-serving members are often very secure. The longer legislators serve the more contacts they have, the larger their war chest, and the larger the perceptions of invulnerability. All this works to make senior members very secure. Thus by eliminating senior legislators, term limits eliminate the most secure members. The empirical evidence on the effects of term limits on candidate emergence and vulnerability is similarly mixed. Some research finds term limits have no effect on vulnerability (Carey, Niemi, and Powell 2000b; Allebaugh and Pinney 2003) or candidate emergence (Squire 2000; Stratmann 2004). However, some research finds term limits increase candidate emergence and vulnerability (Daniel and Lott 1997; Hamm and Hogan 2009). Further complicating the picture, some research finds term limits increase security and the frequency of uncontested elections (Carey, Niemi, and Powell 2000a; Forgette, Garner, and Winkle 2009).

The above literature review leads to the following expectations. Incumbents will be more likely to face a challenger and a tough challenger if any of the following are true: they come from professional legislatures (measured as both capacity and resources); they have longer terms; their states lack ballot access limitations; they have larger district size and district magnitude (MMDs); and there are fewer limits on redistricting. Incumbents will win more easily if any of the following are true: they come from professional legislatures (measured as both resources and capacity); their states have ballot access limitations; they have shorter terms; and there are no limits on redistricting. The effects of term limits and campaign finance laws on candidate emergence and incumbent vulnerability are not clear.

summary

MEASURING THE EFFECTS OF INSTITUTIONAL FEATURES ON CANDIDATE EMERGENCE AND INCUMBENT VULNERABILITY

In order to measure the incumbency advantage and candidate emergence there are four dependent variables. Most of the research examining candidate emergence only focused on whether there was a challenger, and not on the quality of the challenger. Here I am interested in both. While the presence of any challenger leads to a more competitive race than an uncontested election, a low quality challenger is not likely to lead to legislators being vulnerable

?

and to affect accountability or legislators' representational style. Thus I have two variables: one simply measures whether there was a challenger and one measures the quality of the challenger. Both variables are based on a question from the survey described in chapter 1. This question asks legislators about their last election[4] (in most cases this was 2008). This question read: "In your last election bid, which of the following describes your main opponent? If your primary election was more competitive than your general election please answer this question with regard to your opponent in the primary. If you did not have an opponent, go to section III." The first variable, uncontested elections, were coded such that legislators who answered this section were coded 0 as having a challenger, and those who did not answer were coded 1 as uncontested.[5] The second variable measures quality of challenger and is based on the answer to the above question. The options were: Had held an elected position, Was well known prior to election, and Campaign was well funded. A cumulative scale is created where the legislator is given one point for each quality possessed by the challenger. The alpha for the scale is 0.71. The averages for these variables indicate that there is a lack of meaningful competition for state legislative races, much like you find in U.S. congressional races. About 25 percent of the respondents indicated they did not have a challenger and average legislator's challenger had one trait of a quality challenger.

In addition to measuring candidate emergence there are two dependent variables to measure incumbent vulnerability. One of the variables is the size in the vote gap. This is based on the survey question: "What percentage of the vote separated you from your main opponent?" Using this variable to measure vulnerability assumes that each vote has an equal value. However, the picture may be more complex. Each increased vote may not have the same effect: by winning big, legislators are secure whereas by winning small, they are not. To help capture this possibility, a dichotomous dependent variable is created. Legislators who won with a 20 percent or greater vote gap are considered safe and coded 1 and others coded 0. This is consistent with much of the research on vulnerability that codes elections where the incumbent won with 60 percent or more of the vote as safe (Weber, Tucker, and Brace 1991). These variables indicate, as one would expect, that state legislators are secure. The average vote gap was about 45 percent and 60 percent of the legislators had safe seats. There are fairly large correlations between the four measures of incumbent vulnerability (see table 2.1). The correlations range from the 0.40–0.75.

Based on these expectations, there are several institutional features that could affect incumbent vulnerability or accountability. Below, I list these features and indicate how each variable is measured.

Professionalism: To measure professionalism, several indicators are used in lieu of one scale. Using several indicators allows us to see which aspects

Table 2.1. Relationship of Vulnerability and Candidate Emergence

Variable	*Uncontested*	*Quality of Challenge*	*Margin of Victory*
Quality of challenger	–0.41***		
Margin of victory	0.81***	–0.50***	
Safe district	0.42***	–0.40***	0.75***

* <= 0.10; ** <= 0.05; *** <= 0.01 (using a two-tailed test).
Description of variables is in text.

of professionalism have the greatest effects. The different indicators are divided into those that increase capacity with those that increase resources. Capacity includes strong leaders, strong committees, and small chambers. To determine the size of the chamber, I simply use the number of legislators in a legislators' chamber. The measure of leadership strength comes from Martorano (2004). She assigns scores between 0–20 to state chambers based on the powers of the leadership, such as powers of floor recognition, committee assignment, and bill assignment. The measure of committee strength comes from Martorano (2004) as well. It is an 11-point scale based on ability of committees to shape legislation and influence bill passage. The means and standard deviations are 13.24 (SD = 2.95) for leadership, 6.50 (SD = 2.02) for committee strength, and 88.67 (SD = 41.14) for chamber size.

Resources include personal staff (based on whether legislators answered questions on the survey concerning staff);[6] salary in thousands of dollars (Little and Ogle 2006); whether there is an office budget that goes directly to legislators (*Book of States*);[7] and length of session in number of calendar days between beginning and end of session (calculated by author from NCSL.org). Length of session and salary are highly correlated ($r = 0.80$). Because of this, a scale is created using z-scores of the two variables. It measures full-time legislature and ranges from –1.92 to 6.36. Just over 50 percent of the legislators had office budgets and/or staff. The mean for full-time status is 0.02 (1.96).

Limits on Campaign Funding: Two variables measure limits to campaign funding: contribution limits and spending limits. To measure campaign contribution limits, I created an additive scale where each legislator is given 1 point for each type of contribution source (PAC, unions, individuals, and parties) that their state banned from contributing money and 0.5 for each source that had limits.[8] The alpha for the scale is 0.94. These data come from NCSL.org. About 26 percent of the respondents lived in states with no limits; in contrast, 18 percent of the legislators came from states with the highest score of 2.5. To measure spending limits, legislators from either Arizona or Wisconsin (who have voluntary spending limits) were coded 1 and other states (who do not have voluntary spending limits) were coded 0. This measure may be somewhat biased since only two states have spending limits.

Ballot Access Laws: There are two ballot access variables; one for filing fees and one for number of signatures on petitions required for major party primary candidates. The filing fee variable is the actual fee in dollars. I tried using different categories but it did not make much difference in the findings. The petition variable is coded 1 if there is a requirement for a petition signed by constituents, and 0 if not. The dichotomous variable is used in lieu of the actual number of signatures, because the raw score variable is highly correlated to whether or not there are spending limits. Data on ballot access are provided by Richard Winger of *Ballot Access News*. About 27 percent of the states require candidates to have a petition, and about 70 percent of the states require some type of fee, ranging from $10 to $2,000.

Term Length: This variable is simply the number of years for the legislators' term. Term length is either two or four years. About 61 percent of the legislators have two-year terms, and the rest have four-year terms.

Term Limits: The term limits variable is coded 1 if the state has term limit laws in effect at the time of the survey, and 0 if not (source: NCSL.org). Fourteen of the twenty-six states have term limits.

Redistricting Principles: Since Forgette, Garner, and Winkle (2009) do not find redistricting commissions or court review to affect electoral outcomes, they are not examined here.[9] Instead I limit my analysis to districting principles. Forgette, Garner, and Winkle (2009) identified six types of principles: compactness, core of prior district, community of interests, political subdivisions, requiring a pro-incumbent plan, and prohibiting a pro-incumbent plan.[10] Because of the large number of principles and because they fit nicely into one of two categories, I examine the effects of types of principles. One type of principle benefits incumbents in reelection. These include the two principles directly related to incumbency and the principle requiring that core of the prior district is respected. These are coded (0–3) so the direction indicates helping the incumbent. The mean is 1.18, standard deviation is 0.89 and alpha is 0.62. The other category concerns keeping a community or group of people with shared interests together. The remaining three principles are combined into a scale measuring community interests. The mean is 2.11, standard deviation is 0.91 and alpha is 0.57.

District Magnitude: One variable is used to measure district magnitude. MMDs are coded 1, and others coded 0. Four state houses in this data set use MMDs (Arizona, Idaho, North Dakota, and South Dakota). All the MMDs have two members and all but Idaho use free-for-all elections.

District Size: The variable measuring district size uses the census 2006 estimates. These data come from the *Almanac of State Legislative Elections* (Lilley, et al. 2008) and are number of people in thousands. The range was considerable from 7.6 to 975.6.

Control Variables: In addition to these institutional features, other factors have been found to affect incumbent vulnerability. These tend to concern strength of the party in the state/district, levels of education in the district, and previous vote total for the incumbent (Van Dunk and Weber 1997; Squires 2000; Hogan 2004). The variable that measures party strength is the size of the minority party in the chamber measured in percentages. These data come from National Conference of State Legislatures (www.ncsl.org/default.aspx?tabid=16482). District education levels are measured as the percent of district residents who have a college degree as reported in *Almanac of State Legislative Elections* (2008). Previous vote total is also controlled. This variable is the percent of vote legislators received in their previous election as reported in the *Almanac of State Legislative Elections* (2008).[11] Also I control for respondent's sex (women are coded 1, men coded 0), region (southern states are coded 1, others 0) and seniority (number of years legislators have served in their current chamber).[12]

In analyzing these data I did not include legislators who voluntarily retired at the end of 2008, or those that sought a higher office. Appendix B lists the ranges, means, and standard deviations for each of the variables used in the analysis. There are some missing cases because some legislators did not answer every question.

FINDINGS

Table 2.2 reports the results of the analyses. The first column examines what affects whether a challenger emerges. Since the dependent variable was dichotomous, I used logistic regression. The second column examined factors associated with quality of challenger. Since four ordered categories were used to measure quality of challenger, order logistic regression was used to estimate the effects of institutional features on it. The last two columns look at the magnitude of the incumbents' victory. The third column tests the model looking at margin of victory in the most recent election using OLS (ordinary least squares) regression. The fourth column dichotomizes the previous variable treating legislators as safe or not. Since this variable is dichotomous, logistic regression was used. Logistic regression coefficients are difficult to interpret. Therefore, for the three analyses using logistic, including ordered logistic regression, I calculate probabilities for significant relationships. In each case the model had a modest ability to explain vulnerability. The R^2s ranged from 0.07 to 0.30.

Very few institutional features were related to whether or not a challenger emerged. The only variable that had statistically significant relationship was

Table 2.2. Institutional Effects on Electoral Vulnerability

Variable	*Uncontested*	*Quality of Challenger*	*Margin of Victory*	*Safe Seat*	*Reelection Rates*
Leadership strength	–0.005 (0.050)	–0.04 (0.04)	0.80 (0.66)	0.09 (0.05)*	–0.003 (0.002)*
Committee strength	–0.005 (0.081)	–0.01 (0.06)	–0.57 (1.01)	–0.09 (0.07)	
Chamber size	0.003 (0.005)	0.001 (0.004)	0.10 (0.07)	0.01 (0.00)**	0.000 (0.000)
Office budget	1.00 (0.31)***	–0.24 (0.23)	12.41 (3.88)***	0.60 (0.26)**	0.03 (0.01)**
Staff	–0.44 (0.30)	–0.10 (0.23)	–4.36 (3.88)	–0.31 (0.28)	
Full-time	–0.07 (0.11)	–0.18 (0.08)**	–0.75 (1.20)	–0.11 (0.08)	0.007 (0.003)**
Term limits	0.02 (0.38)	0.22 (0.29)	–0.65 (4.87)	0.19 (0.34)	
Size of district	0.001 (0.002)	0.000 (0.000)	0.02 (0.02)	0.004 (0.002)**	0.000 (0.000)
District magnitude	0.11 (0.50)	0.32 (0.38)	–7.00 (6.25)	–1.21 (0.44)***	–0.01 (0.01)
Contribution scale	0.11 (0.15)	–0.18 (0.12)	3.67 (1.96)*	0.34 (0.13)**	–0.004 (0.003)
Spending limits	0.82 (0.69)	1.14 (0.59)*	–8.58 (9.30)	–1.16 (0.66)*	–0.03 (0.01)*
Term length	0.11 (0.20)	0.09 (0.16)	3.22 (2.60)	0.18 (0.18)	–0.01 (0.01)**
Filing fee	–0.001 (0.000)	–0.000 (0.000)	–0.005 (0.005)	–0.000 (0.000)	
Petition	0.50 (0.38)	–0.39 (0.31)	8.38 (4.92)*	0.43 (0.21)*	–0.03 (0.01)**
Community principle	0.12 (0.17)	–0.04 (0.13)	0.45 (2.17)	–0.03 (0.15)	
Incumbent principle	–0.15 (0.22)	0.18 (0.18)	–3.72 (2.95)	–0.44 (0.21)**	0.009 (0.006)
Party strength	0.02 (0.02)	–0.01 (0.02)	0.25 (0.29)	0.01 (0.02)	
Southern states	0.31 (0.54)	0.51 (0.42)	–2.24 (7.01)	–0.46 (0.49)	
Prior vote	0.03 (0.01)***	–0.02 (0.00)***	0.67 (0.09)***	0.04 (0.01)***	
Female	–0.03 (0.29)	–0.58 (0.24)**	4.28 (3.75)	0.23 (0.26)	
Seniority	0.02 (0.02)	–0.06 (0.01)***	0.86 (0.21)***	0.06 (0.02)***	
District education	–0.003 (0.013)	–0.02 (0.01)*	–0.20 (0.17)	0.01 (0.01)	
Constant/Cut 1	–6.27***	–2.72	–51.32***	–4.97***	
Cut 2		–2.04			
Cut 3		–0.87			
R^2/Pseudo R^2	0.15	0.07	0.22 (0.19 adj. R^2)	0.15	0.30
Chi^2	108.04 (22)***	95.13 (22)***		108.04 (22)***	
Log likelihood	–315.01	–616.67		–315.01	
N	552	552	552	552	99

*<= 0.10; **<= 0.05; ***<= 0.01 (using a two-tailed test).
Description of variables is in text.

office budget. Legislators with office budgets were significantly more likely to have an uncontested election (no challenger). The probability that a legislator (everything else at the mean) with an office budget having an uncontested election was 0.29. For a legislator without an office budget the probability was 0.13. This is consistent with the expectation and previous findings that professionalism increases security. None of the other institutional features, however, had significant effects on candidate emergence. Legislators with staff were somewhat more likely to have challengers (less likely uncontested) and those with spending limits somewhat less likely to have challengers. But these relationships just neared but did not meet normal levels of statistical significance.

While the emergence of a challenger is important for accountability, it is equally as important that the challenger is a quality challenger. As with candidate emergence, legislative capacity, district magnitude and size, term length, term limits, and redistricting procedures had nominal effects on the probability that a legislator faced a quality challenger. However, institutional resources were related to whether incumbents face lower quality challengers. Each of the resource variables was negatively related to quality of challenger, and the relationship for full-time status was significant. The probability that a legislator with a full-time position (one standard deviation above the mean on the scale) had a challenger with at least three traits of a quality challenger was 0.11, for a legislator in a part-time legislature (one standard deviation below the mean) the probability was 0.16. The probabilities of having a challenger with none of the qualities were 0.54 and 0.45, respectively.

The direction of the relationships between challenger quality and campaign contribution limits and spending limits differed, but only the spending limits variable had a significant relationship. While contribution limits were somewhat associated with decreased quality of challenger, spending limits were significantly associated with higher quality. For a legislator in state with voluntary spending limits the probability that a quality challenger (had three or more traits of a quality challenger) emerged was 0.29 compared to 0.11 for legislators in states without spending limits. It appears as though contribution limits make raising funds difficult for all, depressing the likelihood that a quality challenger will emerge. In contrast, spending limits even the playing field more successfully and increases the chance that a quality challenger emerges.

When examining incumbent vulnerability measured by vote totals (see the third and fourth columns), office budgets were associated with greater incumbency advantage. Incumbents with office budgets won their most recent election by larger margins. The gap was about 12 points higher for those with office budget than those without. Similarly, those with office budgets were more likely to have safe seats. The probability of a legislator with an office budget having a safe seat was 0.70 compared to 0.56 for one without an office budget. Although legislators with office budgets won by large margins, legislators with staff and full-time status won by slightly smaller margins.

Legislative capacity had stronger relationships with election outcomes than candidate emergence. However, the relationships were not always as predicted. On the one hand, legislators from larger chambers (less capacity) were more secure than those from smaller chambers (more capacity). The probability that a legislator in a chamber with 125 members (roughly one standard deviation above the mean) had a safe seat was 0.66, while it was 0.53 for a legislator in a chamber with forty-five members (roughly one standard deviation below the mean). On the other hand, legislators from states with strong leaders (more capacity) were more secure than others. The probability that legislators with strong leaders (one standard deviation above the mean) had safe seats was 0.69. It was 0.57 for legislators with weak leaders (one standard deviation below the mean). Thus although two measures of capacity had significant effects on vulnerability, capacity, per se, does not have a consistent effect on vulnerability. Smaller chamber size increased vulnerability; strong leaders decreased vulnerability, while committee strength failed to have a significant effect.

Election laws also had inconsistent effects on incumbent vulnerability. Limiting candidate contributions was related to increased incumbent security while spending limits were related to candidate vulnerability. For example, the probability that legislators in states scoring a two on the contributions scale had a safe election was 0.68 compared to 0.52 for a legislator in a state that had no limitations. The probability that legislators in states with voluntary spending limits had a safe election was 0.37 compared to 0.64 for legislators in states without spending limits. Spending limits were also associated with lower margins of victory. Although the association was not statistically significant, the vote gap for legislators in states with spending limits was about eight points smaller than others.

Although filing fees had nominal effects on electoral security, petition requirements for ballot access were associated with legislators having greater electoral security. The voting gap for legislators with petition requirements was over eight points larger. Similarly, the probability that a legislator in a state with petition requirements had a safe seat was 0.71 compared to 0.61 for a legislator in a state without the requirement. This finding indicates that petition requirements not only limit frivolous candidates but may also limit quality challengers. This is somewhat supported by the results in the first two columns. Although the relationships do not meet normal levels of statistical significance, they are in the right direction and neared statistical significance.

The effect of term length was not in the predicted direction, and just neared statistical significance. Longer legislative terms were associated with less incumbent vulnerability, or more security. Legislators with four-year terms won with margins of about 6.5 more points than those with two-year terms.

Although the community redistrict principle variable was not significantly related to electoral outcomes, the pro-incumbent variable was. However, legislators in states that have a pro-incumbent approach to redistricting were less secure. The probability that a legislator in a state scoring a two on this scale had a safe district was 0.55 but it was 0.75 for a legislator in a state scoring zero. This is consistent with Forgette, Garner, and Winkle's (2009) assertion that states with vulnerable legislators were more likely to enact the protectionist principle.

There is some evidence that district size and magnitude were related to election outcomes. But again the direction varied. As predicted legislators in MMDs were less secure than others. The probability legislators in MMDs had safe seats was 0.37 compared to 0.67 for those in SMDs. However, legislators with large constituencies were more secure. The probability that a legislator representing 175,000 (about one standard deviation above the mean) had a safe election was 0.73 compared to 0.58 for a legislator in a district with 20,000. This is not in the expected direction. It was expected that smaller districts would be safer, because the legislator and the constituents would know each other better. However, the findings support the idea that it is too expensive in large districts for challengers to do well. Thus the effect of district size is unrelated to the dyadic nature of the district and more related to the costs associated with campaigning.

As with candidate emergence, these data offer no support for the idea that term limits affect vulnerability. None of the relationships between whether a legislator was term-limited and vulnerability were significant, and their directions varied.

Since most of the previous research on emergence and vulnerability have controlled for previous vote totals, I did so here as well. However, to do so could bias the results, as the effects of the institutional features would have been felt in earlier elections. Thus, I reran the analysis reported in table 2.2 without controlling for previous vote. Generally the findings were similar. There were a handful of cases where a variable went from just reaching normal levels of statistics significance to just missing normal levels, or vice versa. These findings suggest that institutional features can have significant effects on vulnerability. Although most features had fairly modest effects, professionalism (most notably resources) and campaign funding laws did have significant effects. The findings regarding professionalism are consistent with a fairly large body of literature. The findings also suggest that features that make campaigning difficult (including large districts as well as campaign contribution limits) are disproportionately felt on challengers and can contribute to the incumbency advantage, but that voluntary spending limits make it easier for challengers to wage a competitive campaign.

REPLICATION

The findings above examine individual legislators' electoral experiences in twenty-six states. Another way to examine the effects of institutional features on incumbent vulnerability is to use legislative chamber as the unit of analysis and examine whether the features noted above affect reelection rates. A reelection rate variable was created by averaging rates for two time periods. The author calculated reelection rates as the percentage of incumbents who sought reelection and who won between 2007 and 2009. The data become less available with time; however, NCSL.org had reelection rates for 2002 races. Thus I also used these data. To these, I add the rates for chambers that did not have races in 2002 by examining races in 2003 and 2004 (for Senate races in KS, NM, and SC). Most incumbents win reelection. The average reelection rate was 0.96 and the standard deviation was 0.04.

To try to replicate the above conclusions requires removing some variables from the equation. Here there are only ninety-nine cases; so if I included all the features in the model it would be overspecified. To deal with this issue, I eliminate from the model variables that did not have significant bivariate relationships here and did not have significant relationships in the previous analysis. These include committee strength, term limits, filing fee, community principle scale, and staff.[13] Thus initially these results support the findings that these features do not affect incumbent vulnerability.

These results are reported in the last column in table 2.2. These findings reinforce the conclusion that the resources of professionalism, minus staff, increase the incumbency advantage. Chambers offering legislators an office budget, for example, had a reelection rate of just under 3 percentage points higher whereas the standard deviation was only 4 percent. These finding also reinforce the conclusion that spending limits increase incumbent vulnerability. The reelection rate in states with spending limits was just under 3 percent lower. These findings offer stronger support for the somewhat weaker findings earlier that longer terms increased incumbent security. These findings, however, call into question the earlier findings that legislators with strong leadership and states requiring petitions for ballot access had greater security. Here the effects were in the opposite direction. There were also some features that did not have significant effects when individuals were the unit of analysis but did when the state was the unit of analysis: number of members, contribution limits, district magnitude, incumbency principle, and population size.

CONCLUSION

The findings here support the idea that institutional features, particularly professionalism and campaign funding regulations, affect the incumbency advantage or accountability. The main finding is that professionalism; particularly providing an office budget to legislators is significantly related to incumbents' security. In professional legislatures legislators tended to have less qualified competition and won with larger margins. Having said that, however, legislators with staff did not differ from those without staff in their electoral security. This implies that legislators do not use staff for reelection purposes. Second, while legislators with spending limits had higher quality opponents and smaller margins of victory, legislators with contribution limits were more secure. This is likely because contribution limits make it difficult for challengers to raise money. On the other hand, spending limits truly even the playing field by giving both candidates the same amount of money. This finding is particularly important for those interested in increasing competition, because it indicates that contribution limits are not an effective way to increase competition. That contribution limits appear to make campaigning more difficult will be discussed in later chapters. But contribution limits appear to increase the effort legislators spend fundraising, thus resulting in these limits decreasing the time legislators spend interacting with constituents. While resources and campaign funding laws have the greatest effects on incumbent security, there was little evidence that term-limited legislators were more or less electorally secure. This is an important finding given all the debate and discussion concerning term limits. Although term limits increase turnover simply by preventing senior incumbents from seeking reelection, for those seeking reelection, term limits did not affect incumbent vulnerability. There was some evidence that SMDs (single member districts), large district sizes, and large number of members increase incumbent security. But these findings were more modest. These findings suggest that reformers interested in increasing accountability would do well to examine the use of office budgets and understand how they affect the incumbency advantage. They would also be well served by advocating for spending limits and increasing district magnitude.

NOTES

1. Uptake occurs when legislators take up the issues used against them by a challenger after winning reelection. For example, if a legislator was attacked for not being tough on crime he or she would introduce bills that address crime in the next term.

2. Marginal legislators are those who are not electorally secure or tend to face tough reelection bids.

3. The Voting Rights Act requires states with histories of denying minorities the right to vote and with low levels of minority voter participation to have their redistricting plan approved by the courts.

4. Many legislators with four-year terms were not up for reelection in 2008, and Mississippi and Virginia have elections in odd numbered years. In these cases the results would be based on either 2007, 2006, or 2005 elections.

5. In coding this section, legislators who did not finish the survey were treated as missing.

6. This allows legislators to indicate whether or not they believe they have staff. Since some states give staff to some members this is more accurate than coding those in states with a few personal staff as not having staff.

7. Although Kansas legislators are given a budget, these legislators were coded 0 since the money is to hire a secretary during the session and a different variable taps staff.

8. I did not include corporation limits, because the scale's alpha was higher without it and initial analysis suggests that its effects on vulnerability differed from the other limits.

9. Also early analysis here suggests they were marginally correlated to representation, or incentives to represent.

10. Although Forgette, Garner, and Winkle (2009) found that both pro- and anti-incumbent principles were associated with electoral security, with these data this variable was more strongly related to electoral vulnerability than using two separate variables.

11. Some states (Mississippi, Alabama, Virginia) did not have elections in 2008; also some senators with four-year terms did not have 2008 elections. In these cases the next to the last election results were used, as the last election would be the one reported on the survey. For missing cases I used mean substitution.

12. I did not control for whether legislators were still in their chamber, since the only ones gone were those who lost reelection and would be too strongly related to the dependent variables. For most legislators seniority was determined by a question on the survey about year entered. When this data were missing, the year entered was found using legislative web pages and votesmart.org. The year entered was subtracted from 2009 to determine seniority. In the very few cases where data was still missing, mean substitution was used.

13. In the name of full disclosure, filing fees and community principle were significant in one bivariate analysis (I examined three measures of reelection rates) at the 0.10 level.

3

Institutional Design and Ambition

According to ambition theory, "our ambitious politician must act today in terms of the electorate of the office which he hopes to win tomorrow" (Schlesinger 1966, 6). This means that legislators will work to represent those whose support they need to gain the political office they aspire to. There are three types of ambition that are likely to affect legislators' approach to representation: static (the desire to keep the current position as long as possible), discrete (the desire to leave political office), and progressive (the desire to hold a higher political position) (Schlesinger 1966). Legislators with different types of ambition have their own approach to representation. Legislators with static ambition will be sensitive to their current constituents to insure future reelections. Those with progressive ambition will need to keep the voters in their current district happy to garner their votes as well as build support outside of their current district. Maestas (2003, 441) argues, "Progressively ambitious legislators cannot neglect the interest of constituents regardless of how secure they feel in their current office; attempts to move to higher office will thrust them into a highly competitive situation where their current policy record and conduct in office will be carefully scrutinized by their opponent and by voters." The idea that ambition affects legislators' relations with their constituents is supported by the literature. Legislators with progressive ambition travel more to their district, spend more time monitoring their constituents, and get more pork for their districts than others (Parker and Parker 1985; Ellickson and Whistler 2001; Maestas 2003; Herrick and Fisher 2007). Legislators with discrete ambition have little incentive to keep in contact with or work for their constituents. Retiring members of Congress and those exercising discrete ambition often shirk their representational duties; are less likely to vote constituent preferences, are more likely to miss votes (Rothenberg and

Sanders 2000a, 2000b) and also tend to have less contact with constituents than others (Herrick, Moore, and Hibbing 1994).

Not only will ambition affect how legislators represent their constituents in one way or another, but also institutional features are likely to affect ambition. Schlesinger (1966) argues that ambition stems in large part from opportunity structures. That is, one's future career path is affected by the expectations people have of the person's current location. So, for example, someone with a dead-end job is not likely to advance, so a person with that job is unlikely to harbor ambition for a higher post. Legislative positions vary from state to state in their ability to foster different career paths with variation in institutional features resulting in some state legislatures being career legislatures, some springboards, and others dead ends (Squire 1993b; Maestas 2003).

Since Schlesinger's classic was published, research examining variation in ambition predicts that legislators' ambition is a product of legislators' costs and benefits of keeping the same job, moving up, or leaving office (Black 1972; Rohde 1979; Kiewiet and Zeng 1993). These evaluations are based on benefits, likelihood of obtaining the benefits (opportunities), and the risks or costs of trying for an office. There are often several benefits associated with a higher office, such as longer terms (having to run for office less often), more prestige, greater ability to accomplish goals, and higher pay. On the other hand, there can be greater costs to seeking a higher office. A key cost is giving up one's current position. Often legislators have to sacrifice their current position to make a bid for higher office, and if they lose they are unemployed. One way institutional features can affect ambition is by altering the costs and benefits of different career options. For example, term limits may decrease the costs of running for a higher office, because term-limited members are not sacrificing their current position to seek a higher office; staying in office is not an option.

A related way that institutional features can affect opportunity is by affecting electoral vulnerability. Chapter 2 found that institutional features (particularly campaign finance laws and resources) can affect incumbents' electoral vulnerability. This vulnerability, too, can affect the likelihood that legislators have static ambition. Since opportunity is thought to structure ambition, it makes great sense that electoral competition will affect ambition. Legislators who face tough electoral battles often decide that the costs of running are too great, and thus will have less static and more discrete ambition (Kiewiet and Zeng 1993; Rohde 1979). Those too with a greater chance of winning a higher office may have greater progressive than static ambition (Rohde 1979; Kiewiet and Zeng 1993). This chapter examines the degree to which different institutional features affect legislators' ambition.

Before discussing specific features and how they might affect ambition, there are a few controversies surrounding ambition that need to be addressed. First, much of the research has not really examined legislators' desires for political offices as much as they have examined decisions to seek specific offices. This literature examined members of Congress, and it is difficult to get Congress members to be forthright about their political goals. So, instead of examining legislators' goals, the research examined legislators' career decisions assuming those who behaved in a certain way during a time period were expressing their ambition (Rohde 1979; Kiewiet and Zeng 1993, but see Herrick and Fisher 2007; Carey, Niemi, and Powell 2000a). Those, for example, who did not leave office were presumed to have static ambition; those who retired had discrete ambition; and those who sought a higher office progressive ambition. The problem with this approach is that there are undoubtedly members who would like a higher office, work with an eye toward advancement, but never run for higher office. Similarly, there may be those who never really plan for or have as a goal a higher office but stumble upon it. For example, a seat could open up unexpectedly and the individual could be recruited. Although Rohde (1979) assumes that all legislators have progressive ambition in that they would take a higher seat if offered, that may be less true of state legislators. State legislators who would be offered national level offices would have to relocate to Washington, D.C. and work on a different set of issues. Additionally, only those who truly desire a higher office are likely to work for it. That is not to say that opportunity or perceived opportunity do not structure that desire, but that it is the desire or the goal that affects behavior.

A related issue with ambition concerns the stability of legislators' ambition. It is unknown, and likely a variable, as to how often or if legislators' career goals change. The assumption here is that ambition is at least somewhat malleable. That is, legislators' ambition can change due to new experiences. It is expected that institutional design will affect legislators' experiences and perceptions about the desirability of different career moves. Even if ambition is fairly stable institutional design can be related to legislators' ambition, if institutional design affects the type of candidates who seek legislative positions. People with different types of ambition may be more likely to run for a legislature depending on the characteristics of that legislature.

INSTITUTIONAL EFFECTS ON OPPORTUNITY, COSTS, AND BENEFITS

Schlesinger (1966) finds that legislators' opportunity for a career option, that is, the availability of a position, affects their political ambition. One of the more obvious features likely to affect career opportunities is term limits. Term limits essentially deny legislators the opportunity for long-term static ambition and increase discrete ambition. However, whether term limits increase progressive ambition is debated. Many of the reformers calling for term limits thought that term limits would lead to legislators with discrete ambition. They wanted citizen legislators who would serve a short period of time and then go back to a private life. For example, Paul Jacobs of U.S. Term Limits wrote: "If you stay in power for a very long period of time, you're going to be more and more tempted to sacrifice principle on the altar of political convenience" (http://termlimits.org/Press/Common_Sense/cs977.html). However, scholarly research finds that term limits increase legislators' progressive ambition as well as discrete ambition. A couple of examples illustrate this literature. Herrick and Thomas (2005) examine the goals of legislators in fifteen states, finding that legislators in term-limited states had higher levels of progressive ambition than others. Carey, Niemi, and Powell (2000a) too find that although legislators in term-limited states were less likely to seek reelection (even before they were term-limited out); they were also more likely to run for higher office than those in non-term-limited states (see also Powell 2000). The reason term limits is thought to lead to progressive ambition is that term limits decrease the costs associated with making a bid for higher office. Most legislators are electorally secure, so by running for a higher office, they are risking their job. In term-limited states, legislators are not risking losing a career as a state legislator, because that is simply not an option.[1] Term limits are also not likely to prevent people from wanting political careers. History is full of people who have dedicated their lives to governmental service and limiting how long they can hold a given position will not prevent them from wanting public service, it will only affect the nature of their career path. What further complicates the picture is the possibility that term limits will not have a noticeable effect on progressive ambition. This view is supported by research by Moncrief, Powell, and Storey (2007) who found that term-limited and non-term-limited legislators were similar in their career plans.[2]

The dyadic relationship between legislators and their constituents should also affect their ambition. Overall, the closer the relationship between representative and constituent, the more value legislators will feel in keeping that relationship. The relationship may be more personal and fulfilling, thus resulting in static ambition. In addition, each of the individual dyadic features has unique characteristics that could weaken or strengthen legislators opportunities for an office. District size likely affects the pool of competition, and competition for an office affects career opportunities. The number of constituents could affect competition for a legislators' seat and decrease the opportunity for static ambition. This could occur simply because the more people a legislator represents the more likely someone will want the seat. The other way district size could affect opportunity is by decreasing competition. Larger numbers of constituents may be associated with more prestigious positions and have more costly elections decreasing incumbent vulnerability. The previous chapter found modest support for this possibility.[3] District magnitude could have its own set of effects on career opportunities. Those in MMDs may have limited opportunities for advancement. With MMDs each legislator has at least one potential opponent who has represented the same future constituents and thus may be equally qualified. This could depress progressive ambition. However, most states with MMDs have identical House and Senate districts. Thus the opportunity for advancement might be quite large, because the legislator has already won an election in the same district.

Although overall professionalism (usually measured as resources) is believed to decrease discrete ambition (Thompson and Moncrief 1992; Moncrief, Thompson, and Cassie 1996; Rosenthal 1998), the effects on static and progressive ambition are less clear. A couple of points support the belief that professionalism decreases discrete ambition. Being a legislator in a professional legislature is a more attractive position than being a legislator in an amateur legislature. They offer legislators more power and resources to do the job, which increases their influence over policy. They also have large salaries essentially allowing for the position to be a "career." Prior to the professionalization of legislatures, legislators were more likely to retire voluntarily, often citing the demands of their business or the low pay as the reason (Rosenthal 1998, 59–60). Although professionalism is expected to depress discrete ambition, it is less clear whether it increases static or progressive ambition. Legislatures that professionalized by focusing on resources may differ from those who focused on capacity. Maestas (2000, 665–66) states that institutions that provide "resources of time, remuneration, and public exposure" lead to progressive ambition and those that offer "internal career opportunities" lead to static ambition. Thus resources should increase progressive ambition, and capacity should increase static ambition. The fact that chambers with greater capacity can offer legislators the opportunity to have influence and power inside the chamber should stimulate static ambition. Chambers with fewer members offer legislators greater influence and less competition for advancement. Consequently, legislators in smaller chambers should have more static ambition. Also legislators with strong committees, which give legislators the opportunity to have influence in a particular niche, are likely to increase static ambition. Powerful leadership could either increase static ambition, because legislators may want to stay in the chamber, so that they can become powerful leaders, or decrease static ambition by making it difficult for rank-and-file members to have influence.

Electoral costs affect legislators' ambition such that the rules governing elections may also affect the costs and benefits of career decisions. Rules that make it more difficult to run for office should increase discrete ambition and decrease progressive and static[4] ambition. One cost of holding an office is needing to be reelected to keep it. Legislators with short terms have greater costs since they have to frequently stand for reelection. This is likely to lead to less static ambition.[5] Contribution limits should also increase discrete ambition since they increase the costs of running for office. Contribution limits increase the time legislators need to devote to raising the necessary funds to hold office. Or, in lieu of raising funds, it may be more costly if legislators have to spend their own money to campaign. Spending limits too may increase discrete ambition but for different reasons. Although spending limits should make it less costly to run for office by decreasing the amount of time needed to raise funds, they also increase the costs by increasing vulnerability (see chapter 2). Contribution and spending limits may also depress progressive ambition. Contribution limits will increase the costs of the higher bid and spending limits may decrease the ability of legislators to advance.

Redistricting principles may also affect ambition. All else equal, legislators in states with the pro-incumbent redistricting principle should have greater static ambition because their positions should be more secure. Although the results from chapter 2 suggest that pro-incumbent principles are actually associated with greater vulnerability, if they are enacted where legislators want long careers they should still be associated with static ambition, although not a cause of static ambition. The community principles too may increase static ambition: districts may be more easily represented if they constitute more homogeneous communities. Finally, greater ballot access requirements should decrease progressive ambition. Since running for higher office is a greater risk than running for reelection or retiring, legislators who have extra burdens to run for an office may decide the costs of progressive ambition are too great.

Although the focus of this chapter is the effects of institutional features on ambition, other factors likely affect legislators' ambition and these will be used as control variables. One factor often expected to affect legislators' ambition is electoral security. Legislators who are less secure should have less static ambition since the opportunity to hold the office may be less and the costs greater. Electoral security was measured with two variables: the vote gap and the reelection rates variables described in chapter 2. The vote gap variable measured legislators' own vulnerability, and the rate variable measured how the vulnerability of those around them may affect individuals' ambition. Other factors that have been found to affect legislators' ambition include: seniority, age, gender, majority party and minority party strength (Hain 1974; Kiewiet and Zeng 1993).[6] Given the lower response rates of those who left their current office, I also controlled whether legislators left their chamber (coded 1) or not (coded 0). I also controlled for region (legislators in southern states were coded 1, others 0). Descriptive statistics are reported in appendix B.

EXPECTATIONS AND MEASUREMENTS

The above indicates several ways legislative features can affect legislators' ambition, and these form the basis for the following expectations. Most of the institutional variables were discussed in chapter 2, but I note the coding schemes of the variables used to measure an institutional feature with the expectation.

1) Legislators in term-limited states are more likely to have discrete ambition and less likely to have static ambition. Term limits were coded 1 if there were term limits, and 0 if there were not.
2) Legislators with stronger dyadic relationships are more likely to have static ambition.
2a) Legislators with large constituencies are more likely to have discrete ambition. Constituency size is measured by the number of constituents in thousands.
2b) Legislators in MMDs are less likely to have progressive ambition. Legislators in MMDs are coded 1, others 0.
3) Legislators in professional legislatures (resources and capacity) are less likely to have discrete ambition than others.
3a) Legislators with resources are more likely to have progressive and static ambition than others. Three resources are examined. Whether a legislature is full-time is measured with a scale combining salary and days in session. This scale is based on z-scores. Whether a legislator has an office budget is coded 1 if the legislator has an office budget, and 0 if not. Whether a legislator has personal staff is coded 1 and coded 0 if not.
3b) Legislators with greater capacity are more likely to have static ambition than others. Capacity is measured by the number of legislators in a chamber (smaller number more capacity) and the strength of the leadership and committees. These last two variables come from Martorano (2004). The leadership variable ranges from 6–16 and the committee variable from 3–11.
4) Legislative features that make elections more costly foster discrete ambition.

4a) Legislators with longer terms are more likely to have static ambition. Term length is simply the number of years in a term, range 2–4.
4b) Legislators in states with more limits on campaign contribution sources are more likely to have discrete ambition. Campaign contribution limits variable ranges from 0–2.5.
4c) Legislators in states with spending limits are more likely to have discrete ambition. Legislators in states with spending limits are coded 1, and others 0.
4d) Legislators in states with more pro-incumbent redistricting principles are less likely to have discrete and more likely to have static ambition than others (coded 0–3).
4e) Legislators in states with more community redistricting principles are less likely to have discrete and more likely to have static ambition than others (coded 0–3).
4f) Legislators in states requiring signatures for ballot access are more likely to have static ambition (coded 0 and 1).
4g) Legislators in states requiring filing fees for ballot access are less likely to have progressive ambition (coded 0–2000).

TESTING THE EFFECTS OF INSTITUTIONAL DESIGN ON AMBITION

To measure legislators' ambition, the following question was placed on the survey: "Which of the following best describes what you plan to be doing five years from now?" Respondents were given the options: Hold the same or similar office; Hold a higher office; Hold a lower level office; Work for a party or political organization; Hold no political office; Other. Although the question allowed for ambition types not normally discussed, for example, desire for non-electoral office or lower level office, most legislators were able to answer the question and 98 percent of the respondents' ambition fit within the typology. For the remainder of the book, legislators who said they plan to hold the same or similar office were coded as having static ambition (47 percent); those with higher office progressive (20 percent); and others will be treated as having discrete ambition. It should be noted that this was the last question on the survey and several chose not to respond. For this chapter, these were treated as missing cases. Each of the independent and control variables was discussed in previous chapters, and appendix B lists the descriptive statistics.

Table 3.1 provides the results of a categorical logistic regression with discrete ambition as the reference group. Overall, the model did a modest job explaining ambition. The pseudo R^2 was 0.20. There was support for the general idea that institutional design affects legislators' ambition. Term-limited

Table 3.1. Relationships between Institutional Design and Ambition

	Static		*Progressive*	
Variable	*Coefficient*	*Standard Error*	*Coefficient*	*Standard Error*
Leadership strength	0.04	0.06	0.16	0.07**
Committee strength	−0.09	0.08	−0.05	0.10
Chamber size	−0.01	0.01**	−0.01	0.01*
Office budget	−0.22	0.33	−0.22	0.41
Staff	0.20	0.30	−0.20	0.38
Full-time	0.13	0.11	0.40	0.13***
Term limits	−1.21	0.40***	−1.21	0.50**
District size	−0.000	0.002	0.004	0.002*
District magnitude	0.56	0.45	1.00	0.62
Contribution limits	−0.32	0.16**	−0.40	0.20**
Spending limits	−0.93	0.71	−1.99	0.89**
Length of term	−0.28	0.22	−0.60	0.27**
Community principle	0.18	0.19	0.08	0.23
Incumbent principle	0.29	0.27	0.70	0.34**
Petition requirement	−0.51	0.46	−0.94	0.56*
Filing fee	0.0005	0.0004	−0.000	0.000
Vote gap	0.000	0.003	0.006	0.004
Reelection rate	−5.55	4.98	−6.09	6.75
Seniority	−0.10	0.02***	−0.06	0.02**
Majority party	−0.17	0.23	−0.58	0.29**
Age	−0.04	0.01***	−0.10	0.01***
Gender	0.96	0.31***	1.08	0.37***
Southern states	1.13	0.67*	0.67	0.82
Gone	−0.95	0.36***	−0.79	0.46*
Minority party strength	0.02	0.02	−0.001	0.027
Constant	9.81	5.33*	12.27	7.16

Log likelihood = −486.71.
LR Chi(43) = 239.12.***
Pseudo R^2 = 0.20.
N = 582.
* <= 0.10; ** <= 0.05; *** <= 0.01 (using a two-tailed test).
Description of variables is in text.

legislators were more likely to have discrete ambition, but were neither more nor less likely to have progressive ambition. The probability that a term-limited legislator had progressive ambition was 0.13; it was 0.41 for static ambition and 0.46 for discrete ambition. For non-term-limited legislators the probabilities were 0.19, 0.60, and 0.21, respectively. Other work has found that term-limited legislators had greater progressive ambition. It may be that these different findings have to do with the length of time since term limits were enacted. It is logical to expect that immediately after term limits were enacted those with political ambition had not adjusted their career path plans and those with progressive ambition still sought those jobs. However, as time has gone on those with political ambition have adjusted their career paths and term-limited positions have become more of a dead-end job and less of a stepping stone. Relatedly as legislators were term-limited out the competition for higher seats were likely to rise, as it will increase the number of potential candidates with similar qualifications. This too may decrease the progressive ambition of term-limited legislators.

There was mixed support for the idea that features thought to increase legislators' relationships with their constituents (district size and magnitude) affected political ambition. Legislators in MMDs tended to have less discrete ambition; however, the coefficients just neared but did not reach normal levels of statistical significance. Legislators from larger districts were more likely to have progressive ambition and less likely to have discrete ambition. Legislators in districts with 175,000 residents (about one standard deviation above the mean) had a 0.23 probability of having progressive ambition, a 0.49 probability of static and a 0.28 probability of discrete ambition. This compares to 0.14, 0.55, and 0.30 respectively for legislators in districts with 20,000 (about one standard deviation below the mean). It is likely that seats with fewer constituents are seen as dead-end positions and that those who seek and hold the office do not want political careers. Since it is harder to win in larger districts (see chapter 2), those with the strong desire for a political career are more likely to run and win in those districts. These findings suggest that although district population affects ambition, these effects are unrelated to the nature of dyadic relationships. Instead it is related to the value of the position.

There was limited support for the idea that professionalism decreased discrete ambition. Although the direction of the variables (for resources and capacity) varied, those that were significant were in the predicted direction. There was some evidence that legislators in chambers with capacity were less likely to have discrete ambition, although they were not more likely to have static ambition per se. As predicted, those from large chambers (less capacity) had significantly less static and progressive ambition than discrete ambition. Legislators in chambers with 125 members (about one standard deviation above the mean) had a 0.39 probability of having discrete ambition, a 0.46 probability of static, and a 0.15 probability of progressive ambition. The probabilities for those with forty-five members (about one standard deviation below the mean) were 0.20, 0.61, and 0.19, respectively. Although legislators with strong leaders were less likely to have discrete ambition, they were most likely to have progressive ambition. Those with strong leaders (scoring about one standard deviation above the mean) had a 0.25 probability of discrete ambition, a 0.52 of static, and a 0.23 of progressive ambition. The probabilities for those with weak leaders (one standard deviation below the mean) were 0.34, 0.54, and 0.12, respectively. Legislators in chambers with strong leaders apparently want to stay in office but would like an office where they can have greater influence.

There was evidence too that legislators with greater resources, at least full-time positions, were less likely to have discrete ambition and more likely to have progressive ambition. Legislators with near full-time positions (one standard deviation above the mean) had a 0.21 probability of discrete ambition, a 0.51 of static ambition, and a 0.28 of progressive ambition. For those in part-time legislatures (one standard deviation below the mean) the probabilities were 0.37, 0.53, and 0.10, respectively.

Electoral laws had noticeable effects on ambition. Although legislators in states with filing fees for ballot access and the community reelection principles did not differ from others, legislators with longer terms, campaign financing laws, petition requirements for ballot access and in states with pro-incumbent redistricting principles did. The relationship of term length on ambition, offers some mixed support for the expectation that tougher elections encourage less static ambition. Although legislators with longer terms had less progressive ambition they also had more discrete ambition than those with shorter terms. The probability that a legislator with a two-year term had progressive ambition was 0.22. It was 0.54 for static and 0.24 for discrete ambition. The probabilities for a legislator with a four-year term were 0.11, 0.50, and 0.39, respectively. As predicted contribution limits and spending limits were associated with discrete ambition. The probability that a legislator in a state with numerous contribution limits (2 on the scale) had progressive ambition was 0.15; it was 0.34 for static and 0.51 for discrete. For a legislator in a state with no limits the probabilities were 0.21, 0.59, and 0.21, respectively. Legislators in states with spending limits had a 0.05 probability of having progressive ambition, a 0.54 for discrete, and a 0.41 for static ambition. The probabilities in states without spending limits were 0.18, 0.28, and 0.54, respectively. Apparently, the difficulty of running where there were contribution and spending limits encouraged legislators to leave politics. They also discourage progressive ambition apparently making it more risky to run for a higher office.

Also there was evidence that redistricting and ballot access laws can affect ambition. Legislators in states with more pro-incumbent principles, which make campaigning easier, had less discrete and more progressive ambition. However, there was not much difference in static ambition. The probability that a legislator with a 2 on the pro-incumbent principle scale had progressive ambition was 0.24; it was 0.53 for static and 0.23 for discrete. For a legislator scoring a 0 the probabilities were 0.10, 0.51, and 0.39, respectively. Petition laws were associated with discrete ambition not static ambition. Legislators in states with petition requirements for ballot access had a probability of 0.11 for progressive ambition; it was 0.49 for static and 0.39 for discrete ambition. For legislators in states without these requirements the probabilities were 0.19, 0.54, and 0.26, respectively.

Also, several of the control variables were significantly related to legislators' ambition. Legislators who were older, had more seniority, and were male were more likely to have discrete ambition. The effects of age and length of service are intuitive. However, with this population women had greater progressive and static ambition than did men. This clearly demonstrates that the old model of gender effects on ambition—at least for those in office—has come to pass, as women do not express greater discrete ambition than men. Southern legislators were less likely to have discrete ambition. Interestingly, being in the majority party discourages progressive ambition over discrete ambition.

CONCLUSION

These findings indicate that institutional design affects legislators' political ambition in a manner generally consistent with ambition theory. By affecting opportunities, and costs of different offices, institutional features can at least have some effect on legislators' ambition. Term limits that clearly decrease future static ambition were associated with greater discrete ambition, although it was not associated with progressive ambition. Although having close dyadic relationships, per se, did not appear to have clear effects on ambition, legislators representing larger districts had higher levels of progressive ambition. Because of the difficulty in gaining these seats, those who have them likely have the desire to be a politician. Similarly, giving legislators greater resources, particularly making the position full-time increases legislators' progressive ambition. Legislatures with greater capacity, with the exception of committee strength, had members who had less discrete ambition. Working in a chamber that has power and effective structures encourages legislators to want to be politicians. Electoral features that make campaigning difficult increase discrete ambition. Difficult campaigns make running for office most costly and the investment more costly. As a consequence, where there are contribution or spending limits legislators have more discrete ambition than in other situations. Conversely where there are pro-incumbent redistricting principles legislators have less discrete ambition.

How ambition affects representation has not be examined here, but based on previous research legislators with static and progressive ambition tend to be more attentive to their constituents than others. Based on this research those wanting attentive representatives would be well advised to advocate for stronger leaders, small chambers, full-time legislators, the repel of term limits, and removal of campaign funding, spending limits, and petition requirements.

NOTES

1. The form of term limits may affect progressive ambition. In most states, term limits apply to one chamber only, such that a legislator in the lower chamber would be limited to the number of terms in the lower chamber but then could run for a higher office. In Oklahoma, the term limit is for both chambers. Thus Oklahoman legislators who are term-limited out of the lower chamber could not run for the higher chamber. The first form of term limits is likely to lead to higher levels of progressive ambition; these legislators would have the greatest opportunity (as well as benefits) to run for higher office. However, since only Oklahoma has this form of term limits, it is difficult to test for this possibility.

2. They asked the question, When you leave your current chamber what do you plan to do? This question obviously does not take into consideration static ambition. So it essential was testing levels of discrete and progressive ambition.

3. It could be that the number of seats in a chamber in relation to the number of potential higher seats could affect ambition. The greatest competition for a state House member wanting to move up would be other House members. I tested this possibility and found little evidence.

4. The effects on static ambition may be muted. Although they increase the costs of seeking reelection they may also make the position more secure. Thus the increased costs may be offset by greater likelihood of reelection.

5. It may be that it is the relative length of the term that affects progressive ambition. These higher costs of short terms may only increase progressive ambition if the higher office has longer terms than the current one. That is if a higher office has longer terms than a legislators' current position, the legislator is more likely to have progressive ambition since the higher office has the added benefit of fewer elections. I examined this possibility and did not find any effects of relative length being more significant than simply length.

6. Legislators' ages were calculated by subtracting the year legislators were born from 2009. The year born was determined by the following question: "In what year were you born?" Seniority was measured by subtracting the year members entered from 2009. The year entered variable was taken from the survey. The question read: "When did you enter your current legislative chamber?" Majority party was coded 1 if the legislator was in the majority party, and 0 otherwise. This was determined by comparing legislators' party identification from votesmart.org with party composition coming from NCSL.org. If there was a tie, the legislator was coded 0.5. Legislators were coded 1 = female and 0 = male for the gender variable. This data too came from the survey: "What is your sex?" Where legislators did not answer personal question, the answers were taken from votesmart.org, legislative webpage, or google searches. In the very few cases where there was still missing data, means were substituted. The competitiveness of the minority party was coded as the percent of seats held in the legislator's chamber by the minority party.

4

Institutional Design and Role Orientation

This chapter examines the effect of institutional design on role orientation. Wahlke (1978b) defines a role as a person's "perceptions of his relationships to the things and persons in the universe around him" (26). Legislative role orientation therefore concerns how legislators define their position, including their relationship to society or their relationship to those they engage in as legislators. It concerns the expectations legislators have for their position and how they should perform their duties. There are two broad types of representational role orientations: style and foci (Eulau and Wahlke 1978). *Style* concerns whether legislators prefer a trustee or a delegate approach to decision making. Legislators must decide how they best represent constituents' interest—either by acting as trustees using their own judgment to make legislative decisions or by acting as delegates by following the constituents' preferences. *Foci* concerns how legislators define their constituents. Constituents can be residents of the district, a subset of the district, the entire state, or a particular demographic group regardless of where they live. The fact that legislators differ in their focus has implications for representation. Legislators will focus on serving the interests of their focus, perhaps at the cost of representing other constituencies.

There are three general ways institutional features can affect role orientation. First, institutional features may affect the types of people who run and win. For example, people with a trustee orientation may be more likely to run and win where there are more professionalized legislatures since these legislatures afford members the resources to collect independent information. Second, institutional features may affect legislators' experiences with others including with whom they interact. Legislators who interact with constituents, for example, are likely to have role orientations that focus more on constituents than elites, and vice versa. As discussed throughout the book, several theories indicate that what people see affects what they think about (Mooney 1991a, 1991b; Miler 2007). Third, institutional features may affect legislators' freedom to focus on a particular type of constituent. For example, legislators who have more difficulty campaigning may have less freedom to focus on the interests of the state as opposed to the district or the voter, or they may feel more constrained by constituent preferences. An assumption behind these ideas is that legislators' role orientations are at least somewhat changeable. They will change while in office depending on their experiences and context. Even if not changeable, institutional features may also affect role orientations by affecting who runs for office. Legislators in positions that are seen as service positions may have orientations more directed toward serving the district than the state or may have orientations more consistent with a delegate than trustee role.

ROLE ORIENTATION: STYLE

A key legislative role orientation concerns style, or the trustee-delegate dimension. Should legislators act on the basis of their own preference or should they defer to constituents' preferences? Discussions and treatments of the trustee-delegate dimension are very common; however, the utility of the dimension has been questioned (Eulau and Karps 1978; Wahlke 1978a; Jewell 1982). In reality it is difficult to see how legislators could be pure delegates. Since few constituents have clear issue preferences or demands and even fewer share them with legislators, constituents simply may not have preferences for legislators to follow. It is also difficult in large heterogeneous districts for districts to have a single or consistent preference ranking across the range of issues related to the district. Another issue is that effective policy representation actually involves following constituents' wishes and using one's own judgment. Delegates need to use their judgment to evaluate information to see whether it reflects the districts' views, and trustees need to consider districts' preferences in determining their interests (Jewell 1982, chapter 4). These limitations, however, do not negate the possibility that when a situation arises where the district's preferences are clear and the legislator's preference differ that some will see their role as doing what the district prefers and some will see their role as doing what they prefer. The roles also appear to have some meaning as the congruence between constituent preferences and legislators' behavior is stronger for those who self-identify as delegates than those who identify as trustees (Jones 1973; Kuklinski and Elling 1977; but Gross 1978).

There are questions as to whether legislators with a delegate orientation are more involved with their district/constituents or just have different methods of resolving conflict between constituent preferences and their own preferences. By definition, the latter seems more accurate (Eulau and Wahlke 1978, 17). Those who tend to base decisions on their own judgments often feel the constituent demands they hear are unreliable, believe they were elected because voters trust their judgment, or feel a need to be leaders (Jewell 1982, 105–9). This however does not mean that they are otherwise disengaged from serving or being visible to the district. And Eulau et al. (1978) did not find that trustees were less focused on representing their district than others. However, more recent research in other settings indicates delegates interact more with constituents than do trustees. Studlar and McAllister (1996), looking at the Australian federal legislature, find that delegates engage in high levels of casework, although they are not unique in their travel to the district. Halligan et al. (1988) find that in Australia and Canada legislators who are delegates as well as those focused more on the district than state are more likely to engage in casework. Katz (1997) finds that members of the European Union who have an agent (delegate) orientation receive more contact from constituents. In U.S. state legislatures, those with delegate orientations do more casework and have more office hours (Ellickson and Whistler 2001; Cooper and Richardson 2006). Interestingly, however, research also finds that delegates tend to have less accurate perceptions of constituents' opinions (Hedlund and Friesema 1972).

It is likely that the strength of legislators' role orientation will vary from legislator to legislator. Because of this, some researchers employ a three-prong typology: trustees, politicos, and delegates (see, for example, Kuklinski and Elling 1977; Eulau et al. 1978). Politicos are representatives who are situated somewhere between trustees and delegates, with their orientation changing with context. My preference is to see it more as a continuum with some legislators at one extreme, others at the other extreme, and most at various points in between: using a continuum simply allows for greater variation. A multipoint scale has also been used by more recent scholars (Cooper and Richardson 2006).

One way institutional features could affect legislators' style orientation is by affecting the type of person who seeks and obtains a legislative position. Because term limits make it impossible for an individual to make a career out of serving in the legislature, term limit supporters hoped that term limits would limit the incentives career politicians have to seek office. They hoped term limits would result in legislators being elected who were more concerned with their constituents and less concerned with their own political careers. There is some empirical evidence suggesting that term limits are related to legislators' motivations to serve. Herrick and Thomas (2005) find that term-limited state legislators are more policy-driven than others. However, policy-driven legislators may be more trustee than delegate, especially if they want to affect a specific policy rather than serve a group of constituents. And some term limits supporters, such as George Will (1993), anticipated this effect. Additionally, term-limited legislators have little incentive to be responsive to constituents to win future elections and thus are likely to be trustees. Simply put, the electoral connection is weaker since legislators' livelihood might be less dependent on the elected position. This view too is supported by research that finds that term limits lead to legislators having a trustee role orientation (Cooper and Richardson 2006; Carey et al. 2006; Powell, Niemi, and Smith 2007).

Election laws are also expected to affect legislators' trustee-delegate orientation. Laws that make elections more difficult or incumbents more vulnerable should increase the delegate style. These legislators will simply see a greater electoral value to serving constituents' wishes. Legislators with long terms of office are expected to have more of a trustee style, because elections are less frequent. This frees them from the constant campaigning done by legislators with short terms who invariably have to start campaigning almost immediately after they won an election. Also, since voters' memory of legislators' actions tend to be short-lived those with longer terms are more likely to see voters' memory of controversial votes fade before the next election.

If legislators' concern for reelection affects their role orientation, then campaign finance laws should affect their role orientation. Legislators with strict contribution limits have to spend more time raising money. Assuming they are not raising money from a large pool of varied constituents, spending time on fund-raising may distance legislators from their constituents, resulting in a trustee orientation. Legislators with spending limits, on the other hand, have tougher reelections, since they make it easier for strong challengers to emerge and thus these legislators should have more of a delegate orientation. Since ballot access laws increase electoral security, they likely incrase the trustee orientation. The effects of redistricting principles may be more tenuous. Principles that require communities and interests to be kept together should make it easier to have a delegate orientation. It will be easier for districts with a common community to have a set of preferences, which makes it easier for legislators to be delegates. This effect may be muted as these principles may also make incumbents less electorally vulnerable. Conversely, principles that protect incumbents are likely to make elections easier and could enable legislators to be more like trustees. However, if as suggested by chapter 2 pro-incumbent principles are more likely to be enacted where incumbents feel less secure, these principles may be associated with legislators having a delegate orientation. Thus contribution limits and ballot access laws should be associated with the trustee orientation, and spending limits should be associated with the delegate orientation. The effects of the redistricting principles are less clear.

Increased professionalism (resources and capacity) of legislatures too may increase the trustee orientation. First, potential legislators with a trustee orientation may be more likely to run for professional positions. Since professional legislatures are full-time, only those desiring a career out of politics are likely to want to seek such a post. As such, these career politicians may believe that their legislative skills and policy knowledge put them in a superior position to make decisions compared to the population at large. This predisposition may be reinforced in professionalized legislatures. Professionalism alters the nature of the job which, in turn, could alter legislators' role orientation. Since professionalized legislatures are designed to give legislators extra capacity and resource—including information—to make policy, it is reasonable to assume that professionalized legislators will believe that they have greater knowledge and understanding than the average constituent. This view is consistent with the trustee role.

Features that strengthen the relationship between legislators and constituents should produce more of a delegate orientation. Legislators from highly populated districts are expected to be more like trustees. These districts are more likely to be heterogeneous, which makes it difficult to gain a clear sense of the preference rankings by constituents. Consequently, legislators are more likely to take on the trustee role. In contrast, in less populated and more homogeneous districts it is easier for legislators to discern the popular preference, and thus these districts are likely to have more delegate-oriented legislators.

Legislators from MMDs too may be more likely to be trustees. The legislator-constituent relationship is weaker in these districts since there is not a one-on-one relationship between constituent and representative. According to Jewell (1982, 120), "Single-member districting makes the legislator more directly responsible to constituents. This fact may make some legislators more sensitive to demands from the district—more likely to be delegates. The form of districting clearly affects the focus of representation." The limited research on the effects of district magnitude on role orientation suggests legislators from MMDs are more likely to be trustees (Jewell 1982, 1983; Cooper and Richardson 2006).

Based on the above, legislators with term limits, with long terms, with contribution limits (but not spending limits), with more ballot access requirements, in professionalized legislatures (measured as resources and capacity), with large constituencies, and with MMDs are expected to have more of a trustee orientation than others. The effects of redistricting are a bit tenuous but legislators in states with pro-incumbent principles should be more trustee and those with community principles more delegate in their orientation.

In addition to these institutional features several other factors affect role orientation (Wahlke et al. 1962; Gross 1978; Jewell 1982; Katz 1997). These factors will be control variables in the analysis. Two of these relate to the previous chapters: ambition and electoral vulnerability. Legislators in safe districts may feel freer to do what they believe is best without fear of electoral defeat. Thus vulnerable legislators may have more of a delegate orientation and secure ones more of a trustee orientation. Similarly, legislators with discrete ambition may have a more trustee approach. The measures of institutional features, ambition, and electoral vulnerability were discussed in the previous chapters. However, here ambition is a series of dummy variables, with discrete ambition as the reference group. Also, because of the large number of missing cases, I did a median substitution for missing cases (missing = static ambition). I also controlled for legislators' gender, seniority, education level, political experience, age, party identification, if the legislator was in the majority party, and if the legislator had left the chamber.[1] I also controlled for percentage of district that has a college education, is rural, how ideologically diverse the district is, the size of the minority party in the legislature, and region (southern states).[2]

TESTING FOR RELATIONSHIPS BETWEEN INSTITUTIONAL DESIGN AND ROLE ORIENTATION

To see whether institutional features affect role orientation, the survey had a series of questions concerning how legislators resolve certain types of conflict. One question tapped the trustee-delegate orientation: "When there is a conflict between what you think is best and what you think the people want, do you think you should follow your conscience or follow what the people in your district want?" Respondents were asked to use a 7-point scale with "always district" coded 1 and "always conscience" coded 7.[3] Because so few people selected 1 or 2, those categories were combined into one category, leaving six categories. Consistent with previous work (Jewell 1982, 111–12; Rosenthal 1998, 11) legislators were more likely to self-identify as trustees. The mean was 3.7. Since the dependent variable is categorical data I used Ordered Logistic Regression. Appendix B has the descriptive statistics for all the variables.

The results are reported in table 4.1, column 1. Much of the research on role orientation has had low R^2s, and the results here are no different. The pseudo R^2 was only 0.04, however institutional features affect role orientation. There was mixed support for the expectation that legislators with greater resources were more like trustees than others. While legislators with an office

Table 4.1. Influences on Role Orientation—Ordered Logistic Regression

Variable	*Trustee-Delegate Style*	*District-State Foci*	*District-Voter Foci*	*Surrogate Foci*
Committee strength	–0.05 (0.06)	–0.07 (0.05)	0.05 (0.06)	–0.11 (0.07)*
Leadership strength	–0.05 (0.04)	0.06 (0.04)	0.06 (0.04)*	–0.11 (0.04)***
Chamber size	–0.01 (0.00)***	–0.012 (0.004)***	–0.000 (0.003)	0.004 (0.004)
Office budget	0.45 (0.22)**	–0.37 (0.22)*	–0.55 (0.22)**	0.05 (0.26)
Staff	–0.46 (0.20)**	–0.60 (0.21)***	0.20 (0.20)	–0.11 (0.24)
Full-time	–0.03 (0.07)	0.002 (0.067)	0.04 (0.07)	–0.01 (0.08)
Term limits	0.11 (0.27)	–0.13(0.27)	–0.64 (0.27)**	0.62 (0.32)*
District size	0.001 (0.001)	–0.02 (0.15)	0.000 (0.001)	–0.00 (0.00)
District magnitude	0.04 (0.32)	0.34 (0.32)	–0.13 (0.32)	–0.22 (0.38)
Contribution limits	–0.06 (0.10)	0.03 (0.11)	0.03 (0.11)	–0.29 (0.12)**
Spending limits	0.76 (0.50)	–1.44 (0.50)***	0.41 (0.49)	1.66 (0.57)***
Term length	–0.33 (0.14)**	–0.02 (0.15)	0.21 (0.14)	–0.18 (0.17)
Community principle	0.04 (0.13)	–0.31 (0.13)**	–0.03 (0.13)	0.16 (0.15)
Incumbent principle	0.22 (0.18)	0.64 (0.18)***	0.28 (0.18)	–0.48 (0.21)**
Petition requirement	–0.41 (0.29)	0.09 (0.30)	0.15 (0.30)	–0.46 (0.34)
Filing fee	–0.000 (0.000)	0.0005 (0.0003)	–0.000 (0.000)	–0.00 (0.00)
Vote gap	–0.002 (0.002)	–0.000 (0.002)	–0.000 (0.002)	0.000 (0.003)
Reelection rate	0.69 (3.43)	0.72 (3.41)	–0.50 (3.33)	1.20 (4.01)
Progressive ambition	–0.57 (0.24)**	–0.35 (0.24)	0.28 (0.24)	–0.25 (0.29)
Static ambition	–0.47 (0.19)**	–0.28 (0.19)	–0.12 (0.19)	–0.36 (0.22)
Legislator's education	0.10 (0.11)	0.12 (0.11)	–0.13 (0.11)	0.17 (0.13)

(*continued*)

Table 4.1. (*continued*)

Variable	*Trustee-Delegate Style*	*District-State Foci*	*District-Voter Foci*	*Surrogate Foci*
Southern states	–0.03 (0.45)	–0.83 (0.45)*	0.06 (0.44)	1.27 (0.52)**
Gone	0.08 (0.26)	0.32 (0.26)	0.43 (0.25)*	0.82 (0.32)***
Majority party	0.07 (0.16)	0.33 (0.16)**	0.05 (0.16)	–0.35 (0.19)*
Party strength	0.02 (0.01)	0.02 (0.01)**	–0.02 (0.01)	–0.02 (0.02)
Ideological heterogeneity	0.16 (0.06)**	0.12 (0.06)**	0.11 (0.06)*	0.12 (0.07)
Rural	–0.006 (0.003)**	–0.006 (0.003)**	0.000 (0.003)	–0.001 (0.003)
District education	0.006 (0.010)	0.01 (0.01)	0.01 (0.01)	0.01(0.01)
Party ID	–0.19 (0.16)	0.11 (0.16)	0.06 (0.16)	0.53 (0.19)***
Seniority	0.02 (0.01)	0.03 (0.01)**	0.01 (0.01)	–0.03 (0.01)*
Previous experience	–0.08 (0.16)	–0.27 (0.16)*	–0.24 (0.16)	0.09 (0.19)
Age	–0.02 (0.01)**	0.006 (0.008)	–0.00 (0.01)	0.000 (0.009)
Female	–0.07 (0.21)	–0.36 (0.20)*	–0.01 (0.21)	–0.06 (0.25)
Cut 1	–4.32	–2.00	–0.54	2.09
Cut 2	–3.56	–0.37	0.75	
Cut 3	–2.69	0.77	1.49	
Cut 4	–1.74	2.13	2.44	
Cut 5	0.17	3.27	3.25	
Cut 6		4.81		
R^2	0.04	0.05	0.03	0.08
Chi^2 (DF)	72.27 (33)***	106.22 (33)***	57.24 (33)***	67.93 ***
Log likelihood	–970.34	–1,002.04	–955.98	–381.49
N	589	598	593	611

* <= 0.10; ** <= 0.05; *** <= 0.01 (using a two-tailed test).
Description of variables is in text.

budget had more of a trustee orientation, legislators with staff had significantly more of a delegate orientation. The probability that legislators with office budgets were delegates (scored a 1 or 2) was 0.18, and the probability they were trustees (scored 5–6) was 0.43. This compares to 0.25 and 0.32 for those without office budgets. For legislators with staff the probability of being a delegate was 0.24 compared to 0.33 of being a trustee. For those without staff the probabilities were 0.17 and 0.44. It may be that instead of offering information on policy that could distance legislators from their constituents, staff may serve as a link between legislators and constituents and advocate for constituents. That having legislative staff likely helps keep legislators close to their constituents is supported by findings throughout the book, including a finding that staff spends much time keeping in touch with constituents.

There was some support for the expectation that legislators in chambers with greater capacity were more likely to be trustees than others. Although neither strong committees nor strong leadership were related to legislators' trustee orientation, legislators in larger chambers (less capacity) had more of a delegate orientation. The average legislator in a chamber with forty-five members (standard deviation below the mean) had a 0.14 probability of being a delegate and a 0.49 of being a trustee, compared to 0.28 and 0.29 for the average legislator in a chamber with 125 members (roughly one standard deviation above the mean).

There was little evidence that tough electoral laws increase the delegate orientation. Most electoral laws, ballot access laws, campaign finance laws, and redistricting principles variables were not related to legislators' trustee-delegate roles. And although term length had a significant relationship with role orientation, it was not in the predicted direction. Legislators with longer terms had more of a delegate than a trustee orientation. The average legislator with a two-year term had a 0.17 probability of being a delegate and a 0.45 probability of being a trustee, compared to 0.28 and 0.29 for a legislator with four-year terms.

Term limits and features believed to affect legislators' relationships with their constituents did not significantly affect legislators' role orientation. None of these coefficients even neared statistical significance.

The control variables had a few interesting relationships. One important finding was that legislators with progressive and those with static ambition expressed significantly lower levels of a trustee orientation than did those with discrete ambition. This is consistent with the notion that those leaving office offer a most distant form of representation. Also consistent with other work are the findings that legislators of ideologically homogenous and rural districts are more likely to be delegates.

Although many features did not affect legislators' delegate-trustee role orientation, those that did—particularly aspects of professionalism—had significant relationships with legislators' views toward representation. However, the professionalism reforms did not work in a monolithic direction to increase the trustee orientation. Although legislators from smaller chambers and those with office budgets had more of a trustee orientation, those with staff had more of a delegate orientation.

ROLE ORIENTATION: FOCI

While style is one form of role orientation, other orientations concern the foci of legislators' attention. Legislators vary in how they define or conceptualize their constituency and foci refer to which set of constituents legislators prioritize. Here, I examine three such role orientations: seeing constituents as the district as opposed to the state, seeing the voter as opposed to the district, or having a special nongeographical constituency. These are consistent with research on legislators' perceptions of their constituents (Wahlke et al. 1962, chapter 13; Fenno 1977; Mansbridge 1999; Smith 2003).

First, I examine the state-district orientation. With the exception of professionalism, the expectations for this orientation mirror those of the trustee-delegate orientation analysis. Close or costly elections increase legislators' reelection concerns and therefore increase their district orientation. Term limits free legislators from electoral concerns, weaken district focus, and strengthen state focus (Powell, Niemi, and Smith 2007). Features that strengthen the relationship between the district and the legislator should increase the district orientation and weaken the state orientation. The expectations regarding professionalism do not mirror the expectations of professionalism on the trustee-delegate orientation. Although professionalism gives legislators the ability to step away from their constituents and gain extra knowledge, professionalism also increases legislators' desires to keep their jobs and as a consequence increases their need to focus on the district as opposed to the state. The specific expectations therefore are that legislators with term limits, longer terms, fewer campaign contribution limits, tougher ballot access laws, spending limits,[4] in legislatures with less professionalism, with larger districts,[5] and with MMDs will have more of a state orientation than others. The effects of redistricting principles again are hard to predict. This research is exploratory as little research has been done on the effects of institutional features on the state-district role orientation; therefore, these expectations have little empirical support from previous research.

To measure whether legislators had more of a state or district orientation, legislators were asked the following question: "When voting on bills, do you feel you should be more concerned with the needs of the district or the needs of the state as a whole?"[6] Respondents were asked to use a 7-point scale with always district coded 1 and always state coded 7. Legislators differed substantially on their state-district orientation. The distribution was: 1 = 5.25 percent, 2 = 15.41 percent, 3 = 20.82 percent, 4 = 20.34 percent, 5 = 16.39 percent, 6 = 9.32 percent, and 7 = 3.44 percent. As with the earlier analysis, ordered logistic was used. Column two in table 4.1 reports these findings. The pseudo R^2 was small (0.05).

Institutional features affected the state-district orientation. Professionalism, particularly resources, increased legislators' district focus. As with the earlier analysis there is evidence that legislators with staff were more focused on their district. The probability for legislators with staff having a state orientation (scoring 6 or 7) was 0.09, compared to 0.14 for one with no staff. For district orientation (scoring a 1 or 2) the probabilities were 0.36 to 0.14, respectively. Also consistent with earlier findings, legislators from larger chambers had more of a district focus. Legislators with about 125 colleagues had a 0.25 probability of having a district orientation and a 0.07 of having a state orientation. For those with twenty-nine colleagues the probabilities were 0.11 and 0.17, respectively. Also legislators with office budgets had less of a state orientation. The probability of a legislator with an office budget having a state orientation was 0.09 compared to 0.21 for a district orientation. For those without office budgets the probabilities were 0.13 and 0.15, respectively.

Election laws had mixed effects on legislators' state-district orientation. Although contribution limits were not related to legislators' role orientation, legislators with spending limits were more focused on the district. As was to be expected, legislators in states with spending limits were less likely to have a state orientation. The probability of a legislator with spending limits having a state orientation was 0.03 compared to 0.46 for a district orientation. For legislators without spending limits the probabilities were 0.11 and 0.17. Both of the redistricting principles affected legislators' state-district orientation. Legislators in states with more community principles were more likely to have a district focus and those with more pro-incumbent principles more of a state focus. The probability of a legislator in a state with one community principle having a district focus was 0.13, and it was 0.22 for a legislator in a state with three such principles. For having a district focus the probabilities were 0.15 and 0.08. On the other hand, a legislator in a state with one incumbent principle had a 0.20 probability of a district focus compared to 0.06 for a legislator in a state with three such principles. The probabilities for having a state focus were 0.10 and 0.28, respectively. Although several election laws were related to legislators' state-district orientation, term length, contribution limits, and ballot access laws were not related to the state-district orientation.

As with the trustee-delegate orientation, neither district magnitude nor term limits were related to whether legislators had a state or district orientation. However, the relationship between district size and state orientation neared statistical significance. Legislators from small states were somewhat more likely to have a state orientation. Although this is not the predicted direction, there is a plausible explanation. Smith (2003) notes that the interests in small districts often overlap with those in neighboring districts expanding legislators' focus.

A handful of the control variables also had significant relationships with legislators' state-district orientation. Although neither ambition nor electoral vulnerability was significantly related to a state orientation, they were in the expected direction and the ambition variables neared statistical significance. Other controls that increased state orientation were: legislators in the majority party, where the minority party was strong; legislators who were senior, men, and legislators who represented ideologically diverse and urban districts.

These findings support earlier research that professionalism and election laws affect legislators' orientations. However, some features associated with the delegate style were not associated with the district focus. This was particularly true for office budgets. Although legislators with office budgets use their own judgment in making decisions, they are highly focused on districts' interests when making decisions. Legislators with staff and those in large chambers, on the other hand, were more likely to be delegates and focus on the district. The fact that factors varied in their relationships with the trustee-delegate orientation and the district-state orientation indicates that these are distinct orientations. Legislator can be trustees who focus on the district, or they can be delegates who focus on the state. The correlations between legislators' trustee-delegate orientation and state-district orientation was 0.27 (p = 0.00), indicating modest overlap.

Voter Orientation

The next role orientation is more directly related to elections; being orientated more toward representing voters than the district as a whole. Whether legislators use support at the polls as a way to define their constituents depends on the primacy of elections. Legislators facing tough reelections have less leeway to focus on the district as a whole, but they must pay more attention to the voter casting a positive vote on Election Day. Features likely to affect electoral vulnerability and thus the primacy of elections have been discussed in earlier chapters, but I want to offer a quick review. Legislators with term limits who are presumably less election focused should have less of a voter orientation than non-term-limited legislators. Campaign finance laws affect legislators' vulnerability and the difficulty of running and thus should affect voter-district orientation. Since contribution limits increase electoral security, legislators in states with more limits should have more of a district and less of a voter orientation. And since spending limits increase vulnerability, legislators with spending limits should focus more on the voter than on the district. Legislators with shorter terms should see a greater need to represent the voters, because they face the voters more frequently. Legislators in states with pro-incumbent redistricting principles should be less focused on the voter if they are more electorally secure. As with the other foci role orientations the predicted effects of the redistricting principles are ambiguous. Principles that focus on keeping communities may make the distinction between voter and district less meaningful, particularly if the district is homogeneous. The pro-incumbent principles should make legislators more secure but are also enacted where they are less secure. Finally, legislators in states with tough ballot access laws, who are presumably safe, should also be less focused on the voter.

Legislative professionalism and weak dyadic relationships are expected to increase legislators' focus on voters. Although legislators in professional legislatures are more electorally secure, they are also highly concerned about winning reelection (Rosenthal 1998). Additionally, features that strengthen the dyadic relationship make it easier to represent the district may increase the district, as opposed to the voter, orientation. Since small districts are assumed to be more homogeneous, it is likely difficult for those representing small districts to distinguish voters from the district. Also, since the dyadic relationship between legislator and district is presumed weaker in MMDs than in SMDs, those in MMDs may have more of a voter focus. Additionally, legislators from MMDs are more electorally vulnerable.

To measure the degree to which legislators have a voter orientation, the following question was placed on the survey: "When voting on bills, do you feel you should be more concerned with the needs of the people who voted for you or the needs of your district as a whole?"[7] Again a 7-point scale was used with 1 indicating district. Not too surprisingly, legislators are more likely to report focusing on the district than the voter, but some are focused on the voter. The breakdown of responses was 1 = 27.1 percent, 2 = 28.3 percent, 3 = 15.7 percent, 4 = 15.0 percent, 5 = 6.9 percent, 6 = 4.3 percent, and 7 = 2.64 percent. Because of the small number of cases coded 6 and 7, these were collapsed, leaving a 6-point variable. The district-voter orientation is distinguishable from the other orientations discussed. The bivariate Pearson correlations were –0.03 ($p = 0.42$) between trustee-delegate and voter-district orientations and 0.05 ($p = 0.22$) between voter-district orientation and state-district orientation.

The third column of table 4.1 reports the ordered logistic findings. First, the model explains very little of the variance and few of the control variables had significant coefficients. Again, the R^2 was small (0.03) and ambition and previous vote total did not affect legislators' voter-district orientation, but, more importantly, only three institutional features affected this orientation and not all were in the expected direction. First, legislators in term-limited states, as predicted, were less likely to focus on voter than district preferences. The probability that legislators in term-limited states had a district orientation (scored 1 or 2) was 0.64 compared to 0.48 for legislators in non-term-limited states. The probabilities for having a voter focus (scoring 5 or 6) were 0.09 and 0.16, respectively. Second and unexpectedly, legislators with an office budget had more of a district focus than those without an office. The probability that a legislator with an office budget had a district focus was 0.60 compared to 0.48 for a legislator without an office budget. The probabilities for having a voter focus were 0.10 and 0.17, respectively. Third and expectedly, legislators in states with strong leaders were more likely to have a voter orientation. Legislators with strong leaders (about one standard deviation above the mean on the scale) had a 0.48 probability of having a district orientation and a 0.15 probability of a voter orientation. These compare to 0.59 and 0.11 for those with weak leaders (one standard deviation below the mean). Although not quite reaching normal levels of statistical significance, there was some evidence that legislators with longer terms and pro-incumbent principles had more of a voter orientation. The findings concerning pro-incumbent principles strengthen Forgette, Garner, and Winkle's (2009) argument that pro-incumbent protections are enacted where incumbents are less secure.

Legislative features had limited influence on the district-voter orientation. Part of the reason that there were not more significant effects may be that there was little variation in the scale. However, these findings reinforce the view that professionalism has the strongest effects on role orientation, although not always as predicted, followed by election laws.

Surrogate Orientation

Another role orientation concerns whether legislators have a surrogate orientation.[8] Some legislators see a particular group or interest, such as an ethnic/racial minority, as needing a voice. This orientation is not related to a geographical or electoral relationship to the legislator but stems from a shared or empathetic experience between the legislator and a particular group. The need to represent a non-electoral constituency, Mansbridge (1999, 523) suggests is strongest when a representative shares the experiences with a constituency that is underrepresented. For example, congresswomen often feel a need to be surrogate representatives for women (Carroll 2002) and gay, lesbian, and bisexual (GLB) legislators feel a need to represent GLB citizens (Herrick 2009). Two common stimuli for surrogate representation are that minority representatives receive political pressure to work on certain issues and that they see a need for the policy work. For example, some congresswomen have been pressured by interest groups and their parties to be visible on women's issues (Swers 2002), and others become surrogate representatives because they recognized the need for women's issue legislation and no one else was working on the issues (Carroll, 2002). Institutional features are not likely to affect legislators' shared experiences but may increase legislators' leeway to be surrogate representatives. One way to increase leeway is by having easier reelections. Legislators who have tough reelections are unlikely to have the leeway to work on a cause that is not tied to their electorate. There may also be institutional features that focus members' attention making it more difficult for legislators to select which issues to focus on. For example, legislators in chambers with strong committees may be limited by norms and rules to work on issues of their committees. In large chambers, too, legislators may feel less of a need to be surrogate representatives as there are others who may represent specific constituencies. Also, close dyadic bonds may make it more difficult to have a surrogate orientation. In multimember districts it may be easier for legislators sharing a district to allow one of them to focus on a subconstituency. Too in larger, more heterogeneous districts, legislators may be less able to work on one set of district issues and may find a niche to focus on. Based on this reasoning the following features are expected to increase the likelihood a legislator has a surrogate orientation: term limits, contribution limitations, no spending limits, no pro-incumbent redistricting principles, community redistricting principles, ballot access requirements, amateur chambers, and MMDs. Legislators with shorter terms may also be more likely to have surrogate orientation. However, since these legislators are expected to work more on reelection, this expectation is somewhat debatable.

To test these expectations, a survey question asked: "Please list any constituencies you feel a particular responsibility to represent. If none, please state so." The most common responses were: seniors, children, disabled, poor, education, agriculture, and business. The concern here was not with which particular groups legislators were surrogates but whether or not they felt a need to be a surrogate representative. Legislators were coded 1 if they listed a group, and 0 if not. Fifty-seven percent were coded as having a surrogate orientation. This measure does not take into consideration whether or not the legislator has shared experiences/interests with the groups, only that they feel a need to represent this group. It is not feasible to check if each legislator has some shared interest with the groups they identified. This was a unique role orientation. The correlation between trustee-delegate orientation and surrogate orientation was 0.08 (p = 0.05), and it was 0.02 (p = 0.61) between state-district and surrogate orientation. The correlation between the voter-district and surrogate orientations was 0.02 (p = 0.66).

The last column in table 4.1 reports these findings. The model did a modest job predicting which legislators had surrogate orientation. Although three election laws had significant relationship with whether a legislator has a surrogate orientation, they were not in the expected direction. Legislators in states with spending limits were more likely to have surrogate orientation and those in states with contribution limits were less likely. The probability that a legislator in a state with spending limits had a surrogate orientation was 0.88 compared to 0.57 for a legislator in a state without spending limits. Legislators in states scoring a two on the contribution limits scale had a 0.55 probability of having a surrogate orientation compared to 0.68 for legislators in states with no limits. Also, legislators in states with more pro-incumbent redistricting principles were less likely, not more likely, to have surrogate orientation. The relationship between petition requirements and surrogate orientation neared statistical significance. Legislators in states with petition requirements for ballot access (who were more secure) were less likely to have surrogate orientation. These findings raise the specter that those with surrogate orientations have the orientation as a way to help campaign supporters. For example, it is likely that those who are surrogates for business interests get electoral support from business interests, that those who are surrogates for seniors get electoral support from seniors, and so on. It may be that there are two types of surrogate orientations: one based on shared experiences and one based on needing a group's support, even if many members are outside of the representative's district. Whether this form of representation advances the public good is unknown, but it certainly warrants further research.

Professionalism was expected to decrease legislators' freedom to have surrogate orientation and each of the relationships was in the predicted direction and two were significant. Legislators in states with stronger leaders were less likely to have a surrogate orientation. The probability that legislators from a chamber with weak leaders (one standard deviation below the mean) had a surrogate orientation was 0.67, compared to 0.51 for those in chambers with strong leaders. Similarly, legislators from chambers with weak committees were more likely to have a surrogate orientation. The probability that legislators in chambers with strong committees (one standard deviation above the mean) had a surrogate orientation was 0.78 compared to 0.70 for those from chambers with weak committees.

There were no significant relationships between features affecting the dyadic relation and surrogate representation. Neither district magnitude nor district size was related to whether legislators had a surrogate orientation.

Finally, term-limited legislators who are assumed to have greater independence from their districts were more likely to have a surrogate orientation. The probability that term-limited legislators had surrogate orientation was 0.68, and it was 0.53 for non-term-limited legislators.

Although several control variables significantly affected surrogate orientation, the coefficients for the election and ambition variables were not significant. However, the relationship between static ambition and surrogate orientation neared statistical significance, indicating some tendency for those with static ambition to be less likely to have a surrogate orientation.

CONCLUSION

To summarize, although individual legislative features have modest relationships with legislators' role orientations, collectively they have significant effects on legislators' orientations. Each of the role orientations was affected by several features, particularly those related to elections and professionalism. Several electoral features were examined and those related to redistricting principles were strongly related to the different role orientations, there was some evidence too that campaign contribution limits and spending limits affect orientations. Professionalism has many features, and they worked in different ways. Most notably, legislators with staff had orientations more directly related to the district, and those with office budgets were associated with trustee but not state orientations. Some features that increase legislators' leeway to see beyond the district and the voter, most notably term limits, increase the likelihood that legislators will have role orientations that are less reelection focused. Legislators who were less electorally secure were more likely to have a surrogate orientation.

The findings give us greater understanding of role orientation and the effects of institutional designs. Orientations do appear to be affected by context. Legislators may arrive at a legislature with a particular orientation but it may change depending on their experiences, otherwise legislative design and seniority would not affect orientations. The findings also suggest that the different orientations are unique. There were weak to moderate relationships between the different orientations. Because of this the effects of the institutional features varied by type of orientation. Most noticeably although office budgets were associated with legislators having more of a trustee than delegate orientation (less sensitive to district preferences) office budgets were also associated with legislators focusing more on the district than the state (more sensitive to the district).

For reformers wanting to affect legislators' role orientation, the findings offer the following suggestions. Reformers wanting more trustee styles should advocate for smaller chambers, office budgets, fewer staff, and longer terms. Reformers wanting legislators with a state focus should advocate for smaller chambers, no staff, no spending limits, pro-incumbent principles, and no community redistricting principles. Reformers wanting a district and not a voter focus should support office budgets, large chambers, strong leaders, and term limits. Finally, reformers wanting fewer legislators with surrogate orientations would want strong leaders, strong committees, campaign contribution limits, no spending limits, no term limits, and pro-incumbent redistricting principles. The findings also raise the prospect that vulnerable legislators are more likely to be surrogate representation for key electoral interests. Whether this advances substantive representation is not examined here, but it is expected to be a variable depending on whose interests are being represented and how legislators behave as surrogates.

This and the previous two chapters have examined how several features affect legislators' incentives to be responsive to constituents. While many features had minimal effects on legislators' incentives, some had effects likely to increase responsiveness, some likely to decrease incentives and some had mixed effects. Those that had minimal or mixed effects may have muted effects on the different types of representation. First, I will summarize the features related to professionalism. Staff had more consistent positive effect on incentives increasing the delegate and district orientations. Office budgets seem to increase legislators' incentives to be responsive by increasing their district (not state) orientation, but also decrease incentives by making them electorally secure and increasing their trustee orientation. Full-time status too had mixed effects although it decreased discrete ambition it also increased electoral security. One word of caution in interpreting the effects of vulnerability on responsiveness, with regard to professionalism, the lack of vulnerability is likely a product of legislators wanting political careers and being hypersensitive to reelection concerns. Thus the apparent mixed effects of full-time status and office budgets on legislators' incentives may be more a sign of hypersensitivity. Legislators in states with strong leaders appear to be more secure, which should decrease responsiveness. However, these legislators were also less likely to have discrete ambition (more progressive), less surrogate and more voter orientations; all of which should decrease sensitivity to the district. Small chambers should increase responsiveness since they increase vulnerability, and delegate and district orientations, but this is offset by small chambers' positive effect on discrete ambition. Committee strength appears to have no affect on incentives, except they are associated with legislators being less likely to have surrogate representation. This summary makes it clear that professionalism is made up of features that have real effects but that all the features do not work in a consistent manner with regard to being responsive to constituents.

Next, I'll summarize the effects of electoral features on legislators' incentives to be responsive. Spending limits had mixed effects. Since they increase vulnerability and district orientation they would be expected to increase responsiveness, however, since they increase discrete ambition they would be expected to decrease responsiveness. Campaign contribution limits have more consistent negative effects on responsiveness incentives, by decreasing vulnerability and increasing discrete ambition and surrogate orientation. Short terms (frequent elections) may increase responsiveness somewhat. Short terms increased progressive ambition and trustee orientation. Pro-incumbent districting principles too have mixed effects. On one hand, they increase vulnerability and progressive ambition, which should increase responsiveness. But on the other hand, they increase a state orientation. Requiring petitions for ballot access laws likely decrease legislator's sensitivity to constituents, they decreased vulnerability and increased discrete ambition. Filing fees had no significant effects and community principles increased legislators' district orientations. These findings generally suggest that electoral laws have mixed effects; those that increase vulnerability, which should increase responsiveness, also increase discrete ambition, which should decrease responsiveness.

Term limits and dyadic relationships also had mixed effects on incentives. While term limits increased discrete ambition and surrogate representation they also increased district (as opposed to voter) orientation. District magnitude only had one significant effect: legislators from single member districts had greater electoral security, which should decrease sensitivity to constituents. Small districts, however, tended to increase responsiveness. Legislators from small districts had less security and were more discrete than progressive ambition.

These results suggest that many of the features will have muted effects on representation since they increase some and decrease other incentives for legislators to be responsive. However, incentives are only one piece of the equation and the features may also increase legislators' abilities to affect representation. Based on the first chapter dyadic relationships, and professionalism (less so with capacity) should increase legislators' ability to be responsive while term limits and laws that make campaigning difficult should decrease their ability to be responsive.

NOTES

1. Party identification comes from votesmart.org or legislators' web pages, coded 1 = Democrats and 0 = Republicans. Level of education was coded 0 = high school or less, 1 = some college or associate degree, 2 = college degree, 3 = graduate degree. Previous experience is measured from the survey item, "Did you hold an elective position in government prior to your current chamber?" with yes answers coded 1 and no 0. If legislators did not answer these questions, the information was found elsewhere, for example, votesmart.org or legislative web pages. In the few cases where missing data remained, legislators were coded at the mean, or median. The other variables were discussed in previous chapters.

2. Ideological difference is based on a series of questions from the survey. "How would you describe your political views and those of others in your district?" Respondents were asked to use a scale of 1–7 (conservative) to indicate the views of Republican primary voters and Democratic primary voters. The difference in responses in absolute figures is used as an indicator of ideological variation in the district. How rural the district is comes from 2000 census data (factfinder.gov) and is in percentages. Percentage of the district that has college degree comes from *Almanac of State Legislative Elections* (2008).

3. This question wording comes from Carey et al.'s (2002) survey *The 2002 State Legislative Survey* (ICSPR 20960).

4. Although the community redistricting principle is discussed with election laws, these laws may also increase the dyadic relationship between legislators and their districts.

5. It may also be that small districts result in more of a state focus because the districts' interests are more likely to extend into other districts.

6. This question wording comes from Carey et al.'s (2002) survey, *The 2002 State Legislative Survey* (ICSPR 20960).

7. This question wording comes from Carey et al.'s (2002) survey, *The 2002 State Legislative Survey* (ICSPR 20960).

8. This is usually treated as a type of representation; however, treating it as a role orientation is consistent with the previous treatments of the foci role orientation. It concerns the focus of a legislator's representation.

5

Institutional Design and Symbolic Representation

> The most important service, in my opinion, is being available—making certain that all know that I am accessible.

The previous chapters examined how various institutional features affect legislators' incentives (electoral vulnerability, ambition, and role orientations) to be sensitive to constituents needs. Finding that while a few features had generally positive effects on these incentives many increased some incentives and decreased others. This chapter moves away from looking at incentives and looks instead at variation in representational behavior, particularly symbolic representation. It is expected that not only will the incentives to be responsive affect symbolic representation but that institutional features will too by affecting their ability to engage in symbolic representation. Some features may also have unique effects on the value of symbolic representation to legislators.

Symbolic representation is defined here as legislators' efforts to be visible and stay in contact with their constituents. This is an important type of representation in and of itself. It may indeed help constituents better know and understand their representative, legislature, and state policy and the knowledge legislators have of their constituents. As Jewell (1982, 77) observes:

> Effective representation requires that legislators become thoroughly familiar with the needs and interests of the district, a requirement that cannot be met by waiting passively for mail or phone calls. It is equally important that the legislator explain his activities and decisions of the legislature to the constituents. . . . The legislator who is not an effective communicator not only risks defeat at the polls; he may unknowingly misrepresent the district because he fails to understand its needs and evaluate the demands that reach him.

Legislators who engage in more symbolic representation have a heightened awareness of their constituents' interests. Using cognitive psychology, Miler (2007) argues that legislators are "cognitive misers," using easily accessible information to make decisions. This literature suggests that people are most likely to be cognitive misers when there are "demands for their time and attention and must make decisions under considerable time pressure" (601). All of these are indeed conditions that exist for legislators. Miler also suggests that three conditions affect accessibility of information: frequency, salience, and familiarity (602). That is the frequency of legislators' contact with a subconstituency, in her case, the importance of the subconstituency and the legislators' familiarity with the subconstituency increases the likelihood that legislators will think about the group when making decisions. As such, legislators who have more contact with constituents are more likely to consider constituents when making decisions as it undoubtedly affects frequency and likely affects familiarity.

I limit my discussion of symbolic representation to direct contact between individual private citizens and the legislator or his/her staff. It does not include contact with representatives of interest groups, such as lobbyists. Although lobbyists can inform legislators as to constituent interests, meeting with lobbyists is not symbolic representation in that it does not increase legislators' visibility with constituents. Also, I do not examine media use by legislators. The media filter messages, thus limiting the ability of legislators to control their contact. Also, media markets and district traits primarily dictate legislators' use of the media. In metropolitan areas legislators cannot rely on the mass media since there are many other legislators and numerous news stories to compete with, while in larger geographical areas there are too many news outlets for legislators to try to use the media (Jewell 1982). Furthermore, I do not examine campaign activities, since this project is interested in legislators' behavior as legislators, not as candidates. The degree to which legislators can separate contacting constituents for electoral purposes versus representational purposes may be debatable, however, there is a legal difference and legislators undoubtedly have some understanding of a difference.

Symbolic representation helps members achieve reelection and policy goals. Previous research finds that legislators who engage in greater contact with constituents are rewarded at the polls (Serra and Moon 1994; Box-Steffensmeier, Kimball, Meinke, and Tate 2003). Thus legislators who are vulnerable or otherwise particularly focused on reelection may engage in greater symbolic representation. Also, when legislators contact their constituents, they build a reservoir of goodwill and trust that gives legislators greater leeway to cast unpopular votes or work on issues of little interest to constituents (Fenno 1977; Parker and Parker 1993; Parker and Goodman 2009). A legislator from Kansas stated, "It has been my experience that with open, honest, and direct discussion with constituents it is possible to gain continued trust and respect as an elected official. This is very important (trust and respect) when it comes to issues that tend to divide a community. While we may not always agree, we have learned to respectfully disagree." Legislators' time frame may affect the effort they put into symbolic representation. If legislators engage in symbolic representation to advance their goals, those who have shorter time frames may see less value in symbolic representation since they will not have long-term value. Conversely, the value of this work will be greater if members plan to stay in politics and garner long-term value from symbolic representation. Also features that increase legislators' reelection concerns or make working on district interests more difficult may increase the value of, or need for, symbolic representation and subsequently increase it.

The general effects of electoral features are more nuanced and confusing than one might originally expect. Features that make campaigning difficult may increase the value of symbolic representation since it helps legislators win elections. That is they can use contacting constituents as a way to reach voters. However, features that make elections difficult also tend to depress incumbent vulnerability decreasing legislators' electoral concerns and the value of symbolic representation. As a legislator from Colorado put it, "Because my district elects me by such a large margin, I don't have to expend as much time on communication." Features that make elections difficult may also increase discrete ambition decreasing the long-term value of the symbolic representation. They may also distract legislators from symbolic representation or other legislative duties and focus them more on campaigning, thus decreasing the ability of legislators to engage in symbolic or other forms of representation. Thus one needs to look at each feature to try predicting its effects.

First, overall, short terms are expected to increase symbolic representation. They are presumed to increase legislators' reelection concerns. Those with two-year terms cannot put off electioneering since another election is always approaching. This suggests that legislators will engage in symbolic representation as a means to keep in touch with voters/constituents throughout their term. Those with short term also have more progressive ambition, which too should increase their sensitivity to constituents and increase their symbolic representation. However, in part because they are focused on reelection throughout their term they are more secure, which may depress symbolic representation. Also muting the positive effects of short terms on symbolic representation is that those with short terms were more likely to have trustee orientation. Despite these last two points short terms are expected to have a positive effect on symbolic representation.

Campaign contribution limits are expected to have weak negative effects on symbolic representation. The effects are expected to be weak since their incentives and abilities do not consistently lead toward more symbolic representation. Since they restrict legislators' ability to campaign by limiting the contributions of large donors, legislators may see greater electoral value to symbolic representation. However, other factors more clearly point to contribution limits depressing symbolic representation. Since contribution limits increase legislators' electoral security, and increase discrete ambition they likely decrease legislators' incentives to engage in symbolic representation. Also campaign contribution limits may limit the ability of legislators to engage in symbolic representation. Limiting the ability of legislators to raise large sums of campaign dollars from individual sources increases the time legislators spend raising money and decreases their ability to engage in symbolic representation. During debates on the campaign finance reform in Congress, a common refrain was that contribution limits increase the time it takes to raise campaign funds. Thus, legislators with severe contribution limits may have to divert their attention from symbolic representation to fund-raising.

The effects of spending limits are generally expected to increase symbolic representation. They will increase the value of symbolic representation by limiting their ability to spend money on their campaigns and increasing their vulnerability and district orientation. Also, since spending limits are accompanied by campaign funding legislators can spend less time fund-raising and more time engaging in their legislative responsibilities, such as symbolic representation. These effects however may be muted since spending limits also increase discrete ambition.

Redistricting principles should have modest effects on symbolic representation. On one hand, principles that help create districts with a shared community or interest should make it easier for legislators to get to know their district. Since these districts are easy to know, they may decrease the need legislators have to stay in contact, and their legislators may feel less need to work at keeping in touch. On the other hand, they increase legislators district orientations thus legislators have some incentive to keep in touch with their constituents.

Pro-incumbent redistricting principles should be associated with modest increases in symbolic representation. Although they are expected to make incumbents safer, which would decrease their incentives to engage in symbolic representation, chapter 2 found that they were associated with greater vulnerability, which should be associated with greater responsiveness. Also although legislators from states with these principles had high levels of progressive ambition, which should increase symbolic representation, they also, not surprisingly, had a state orientation, which should decrease it.

Tough ballot access laws, particularly petitions, are generally expected to decrease symbolic representation. Petition requirement decrease vulnerability, and increase discrete ambition. Paying the filing fee make it just that much more costly to run a campaign and likely distracts legislators from engaging in symbolic representation and somewhat increase legislators' state orientations.

One institutional feature likely to abridge the value of symbolic representation to legislators is term limits. Term-limited legislators have less incentive to keep in contact with their constituents, since the benefits of the contact will be short-lived. Simply since they had high levels of discrete ambition the policy or electoral value of symbolic orientation will be short-lived. They also were more likely to have a surrogate representation, which could distract legislators from representing the whole district. Research too indicates that legislators in term-limited states are less committed to district activities and spend less time working on pork barreling, conducting casework, and contacting constituents (Carey, Niemi, and Powell 2000a, chapter 3; Carey et al. 2006, Powell, Niemi, and Smith 2007). The only caveat to this expectation is that term-limited legislators had district as opposed to a voter orientation.

Features strengthening the dyadic relationship between legislator and constituent may have muted affects on symbolic representation. Strong dyadic relationships may make contact easy and increase the efficiency of symbolic representation. In SMDs, there is a one-on-one relationship in which a member who contacts and works for the district may be more clearly rewarded for it. In MMDs, legislators may be tempted to free-ride on others' work (Snyder and Ueda 2007). In MMDs, if one member stays in contact with constituents, all the representatives of the districts may feel the benefits, since constituents may not distinguish between specific legislators. Research is replete with accounts of voters/constituents having low levels of information about their legislators or being unable to distinguish the actions of one legislator from all legislators. There are a couple of counterarguments to this expectation. It may be that legislators in MMDs have to engage in more symbolic representation to achieve their goals. If voters have a hard time distinguishing between their representatives, legislators may need to work extra hard to have their name known and to build trust. That they are more electorally vulnerable too may increase their need to engage in symbolic representation.

Legislators with small constituencies may be somewhat more likely to engage in symbolic representation. There may be greater efficiency in engaging in contact in small districts. There is simply greater bang for the buck in smaller districts. To reach a sizeable proportion of the population may not be cost-effective in large districts. The marginal benefits of such work are smaller for representatives of larger districts (Atlas, Hendershott, and Zupan 1997). Reaching 1,000 in a district with 5,000 voters reaches a significantly larger share of the population than reaching 1,000 in a district with 500,000 voters. Additionally, constituents in smaller districts may expect more personalized contact from their representatives (Hibbing and Alford 1990; but Oppenheimer 1996). Looking at the U.S. Senate, there is some evidence that constituents in smaller states (whose senators had smaller constituencies) have significantly more contact (in the form of mail, speaking with staff, or with their senator) with their senator, and are more likely to contact their senator (Hibbing and Alford 1990; Oppenheimer 1996). Oppenheimer (1996) also finds that although generally constituents have more contact with members of the House than of the Senate, this is not the case in small states where the constituency size of both is similar. Senators in smaller states also spend more money on district staff, thus reflecting greater emphasis on constituent contact (Atlas, Hendershott, and Zupan 1997). These effects may be somewhat offset by economies of scale. The time it takes to create a web page or write a newsletter is the same whether it is read by one constituent or a million. Economies of scale are expected to affect the mode of symbolic representation more so than the amount of symbolic representation and will be examined later. Second, it may be easier to reach constituents in smaller districts, and therefore these representatives need to expend less energy in communicating with their constituents. Additionally, the earlier chapters found that legislators from small districts had more discrete than progressive ambition decreasing their need to be responsive but were less electorally secure, which should increase their need to be responsive.

Professionalism is expected to result in greater symbolic representation. Although the effects of the different aspects of professionalism on vulnerability varied, it is expected that they are generally less vulnerable because they work hard to prevent quality challengers and have resources to fight for reelection. Thus their low levels of vulnerability are not expected to decrease sensitivity to constituents. Generally, legislators with resources had less discrete ambition and more district focused orientations, which should increase responsiveness and symbolic representation. The effects on the trustee-delegate orientations were mixed: legislators with office budgets are more likely to have a trustee orientation, and those with staff are more likely to have a district orientation. Capacity too decreased legislators' discrete ambition, but had mixed effects on their delegate and district orientations. Not only does professionalism lead to incentives to engage in symbolic representation but also they make it easier for them to do so. Legislative features that increase legislators' resources should increase symbolic representation. It simply makes sense that having resources to engage in an activity will increase that activity. As Jewell (1982, 9) writes:

> How a legislator represents his district depends to a large extent on the resources at his disposal. . . . However eager he may be to maintain communications with his district, the legislators with a large number of constituents cannot answer

> many letters without a secretary and cannot send out many newsletters without the postal frank. The legislators with professional staff members can deal more effectively with constituency service requests, especially if he can afford to locate staff members in the district office.

Empirical research, too, supports the idea that legislators with resources engage in more symbolic representation than others. Parker (1980) finds one reason that the amount of time legislators spent in their district increased over the years was because of increases in congressional travel allotment. Maestas (2003) finds that legislators in more professionalized legislatures have spent more time monitoring constituent opinions in part because they have resources to do so. Consequently, since legislators in professional legislatures have resources—such as staff, budgets, and a full-time position—to actively engage in symbolic representation they will do so.

Related to resources is capacity. Efficient chambers should make it easier for legislators to reach their constituents. They may provide the means to advertise and claim credit. Committees, as noted by Mayhew (1974), offer legislators the opportunity to take positions, to advertise, and to take credit. Also, good strong legislative leadership can yield a more efficient lawmaking process, giving legislators more time to engage in their non-lawmaking responsibilities. The process of consensus building, too, may be more efficient in smaller chambers, thus increasing legislators' time to contact constituents. One caveat to this is that legislators in chambers with high capacity may focus more on their lawmaking than representational roles. They may have greater pressures on them to focus on lawmaking and come to see it as the greater part of their job.

Based on the above, I expect the following legislative features to increase legislators' symbolic activities: no term limits, spending limits, short legislative terms, fewer community redistricting principles, fewer ballot access requirements, and professionalism (resources). The effects of capacity, dyadic relationships, campaign contribution limits, and pro-incumbent redistricting principles are more ambiguous.

EXPLAINING VARIATION IN AMOUNT OF SYMBOLIC REPRESENTATION

There are two measures of levels of symbolic representation. Both are based on the amount of time legislators spend contacting their constituents. Time is an appropriate indicator of legislators' commitment to and work on symbolic representation, since time is a limited resource for legislators (Fenno 1977). On the survey (described in chapter 1) respondents were asked, "When the legislature is in session approximately how many hours a week, on average, do you spend on the following activities? If zero leave blank." One of the activities was "Keeping in touch with constituents." In answering this question, respondents were given the following options: 1–4, 5–8, 9–16, or more than 16 hours. Legislators were also asked, "When the legislature is NOT in session, approximately how many hours a week, on average, do you spend on the following activities? If zero leave blank."[1] They were then given the same options to indicate how much time they spend keeping in touch with constituents. This leads to two variables: one for when the legislature is in-session and one for when it is out-of-session. Each variable was coded 1–4 with 4 indicating more time. The means (roughly 2)[2] indicated that most legislators spent a fair amount of time keeping in contact. They spent an average of 5–8 hours a week keeping in contact, regardless of whether they were in-session. The independent variables have all been discussed in previous chapters. Since these variables are ordinal, ordered logistic regression is used.

Although the primary focus of the chapter is on how institutional features affect symbolic representation, I also examine the degree to which certain incentives: electoral vulnerability, ambition, and role orientation affect symbolic representation. These incentives are measured by variables discussed in chapters 2–4 and include: vote gap, reelection rates, static ambition, progressive ambition, trustee-delegate role, state-district role, voter-district vote, and surrogate role orientation.

Previous research on legislators' contact with constituents suggests several control variables that should be included in the analysis (McAdams and Johannes 1985; Parker and Parker 1985; Johannes 1980, 1983; Jewell 1982, Freeman and Richardson 1996; Adler, Gent, and Overmeyer 1998; Ellickson and Whistler 2001; Maestas 2003; Herrick and Fisher 2007). I controlled for the following legislator characteristics: gender, party identification, if the legislator had left the chamber, seniority, levels of legislators' education, and if the legislator had previous political experience. I also controlled for the following district traits: percentage rural and percentage college educated. Following from the previous chapters, I also controlled for minority party strength and region (southern states). All of these variables have been discussed in previous chapters.

Table 5.1 reports the findings. These findings suggest that it was easier to explain variation when the legislature was not in-session. The pseudo R^2 was noticeably larger when the dependent variable measured contact when the legislature was out-of-session than in-session (0.16 compared to 0.05). This implies that legislators had less latitude in their symbolic work when the legislature was in-session, perhaps because they all are busy with lawmaking. Many institutional features were related to symbolic representation in the expected

☆ ambition as an intervening variable

Table 5.1. Institutional Effects on Symbolic Representation

Variable	*Time Keeping in Touch (In-Session)*	*Time Keeping in Touch (Out-of-Session)*
Leadership strength	−0.02 (0.04)	0.08 (0.04)**
Committee strength	−0.12 (0.06)**	−0.01 (0.06)
Chamber size	−0.001 (0.004)	−0.004 (0.004)
Office budget	0.59 (0.24)**	0.44 (0.24)*
Staff	0.01 (0.22)	−0.13 (0.22)
Full-time	−0.02 (0.08)	0.17 (0.08)**
Term limits	0.04 (0.29)	0.07 (0.29)
District size	0.002 (0.001)*	0.001 (0.001)
District magnitude	−0.49 (0.34)	0.51 (0.35)
Contribution limits	−0.10 (0.11)	−0.25 (0.11)**
Spending limits	0.40 (0.53)	−0.86 (0.52)*
Term length	−0.20 (0.15)	−0.33 (0.15)**
Community principle	−0.03 (0.14)	−0.04 (0.14)
Pro-incumbent principle	−0.17 (0.19)	0.14 (0.19)
Petition requirement	−0.53 (0.32)*	−0.56 (0.31)*
Filing fee	−0.001 (0.000)***	−0.000 (0.000)
Vote gap	−0.001 (0.002)	−0.000 (0.002)
Reelection rate	−2.26 (3.55)	−3.12 (3.53)
Progressive ambition	0.13 (0.25)	−0.31 (0.26)
Static ambition	0.37 (0.20)*	−0.13 (0.20)
Trustee	−0.09 (0.06)	−0.14 (0.06)**
State orientation	−0.06 (0.06)	−0.07 (0.06)
Voter orientation	0.02 (0.05)	0.05 (0.05)
Surrogate orientation	0.20 (0.17)	0.34 (0.17)**
Seniority	−0.004 (0.014)	−0.008 (0.014)
Rural	0.001 (0.003)	0.001 (0.003)
Legislator education	−0.13 (0.12)	−0.21 (0.12)*
Time not in-session	0.02 (0.01)***	0.06 (0.01)***
Party ID	0.31 (0.17)*	−0.16 (0.17)
Constituency education	−0.004 (0.011)	−0.03 (0.01)**
Southern states	0.38 (0.47)	1.13 (0.47)**
Gone	0.45 (0.27)*	0.17 (0.28)
Previous experience	−0.25 (0.17)	−0.11 (0.17)
Female	−0.07 (0.22)	0.18 (0.23)
Minority party strength	0.002 (0.014)	0.04 (0.01)***
Cut 1	−8.54	−6.30
Cut 2	−5.34	−3.10
Cut 3	−3.87	−1.30
Cut 4	−1.80	0.47
Pseudo R^2	0.05	0.16
Chi^2 (DF)	81.00 (35)***	257.82 (0.35)***
Log likelihood	−724.01	−688.93
N	565	566

* <= 0.10; ** <= 0.05; *** <= 0.01 (using a two-tailed test). Description of variables is in text.

use some scales so
less ind. vars necessary

ways. First, legislators with greater resources spent more time contacting their representatives. Legislators with office budgets spent significantly more time contacting their constituents. Those with an office budget had a 0.16 probability of working 1–4 hours when in-session compared to a 0.25 probability for legislators without office budgets. The probabilities of working more than 16 hours were 0.13 and 0.07, respectively. When the session was over the probabilities for working 1–4 hours were 0.14 and 0.20, respectively, and 0.14 and 0.10 for working more than 16 hours. Those in full-time legislatures also spent more time contacting constituents, with the difference significant when the legislature was out-of-session. Those with full-time positions (one standard deviation above the mean) had a 0.12 probability of working 1–4 hours compared to 0.21 for those with part-time jobs (one standard deviation below the mean). The probabilities of working more than 16 hours on symbolic representation were 0.16 and 0.09, respectively. It is likely that those in more part-time legislatures have to work when out-of-session and have less time to engage in symbolic representation. Rosenthal (2004, 24) notes that because many legislators have to supplement their legislative salaries they do not feel they have enough time to do their legislative job. Although legislators with staff did not differ from others in the amount of time they spent on symbolic representation, legislators' staff spent much time on symbolic representation. The survey also asked about the amount of time staff spent "keeping in touch with constituents." The mean was 2.70 on the 4-point scale, but the most common response was 4. Since staff spent much time on symbolic representation, and legislators with staff did not significantly lessen the time they spent on symbolic representation, overall staff increased the amount of contact that legislators—or their offices—had with constituents.

Although the amount of resources was associated with legislators spending more time "keeping in touch," the effects of capacity were mixed. On the positive side, when the legislature was out-of-session, legislators in chambers with strong leadership spent more time keeping in contact with their constituents. Legislators in chambers with strong leaders (one standard deviation above the mean) had a 0.14 probability of working 1–4 hours compared 0.20 for those in chambers with weak leaders. The probabilities were 0.14 and 0.09 for working more than 16 hours, respectively. On a negative note, the number of legislators was not related to symbolic representation and legislators in chambers with strong committees were less engaged in symbolic representation, but this was just significant during the session. Legislators in chambers with strong committees (one standard deviation above the mean) had a 0.24 probability of working 1–4 hours on symbolic representation compared to 0.16 for those in chambers with weak committees (one standard deviation below the mean). The probabilities of working 16 hours were 0.08 and 0.12, respectively. This is likely because legislators in strong committee systems have to spend more time doing committee work and have less time on symbolic representation during the session.

There was also evidence that electoral laws affect symbolic representation. As expected legislators with longer terms spent less time on symbolic representation than those with shorter terms. Those with four-year terms had a 0.22 probability of working 1–4 hours on symbolic representation compared to 0.13 for those with two-year terms when they were out-of-session. The probabilities for working 16 hours were 0.08 and 0.15 respectively. Also as anticipated, legislators in states with more limits on campaign funding were less active in symbolic representation. Legislators in states scoring 2 on the contribution limits scale had a probability of 0.19 of working 1–4 hours compared to 0.12 for legislators in states with no limits, when the session was over. The probabilities for working more than 16 hours on symbolic representation were 0.10 and 0.16, respectively. It is likely that these legislators were raising money instead of engaging in symbolic representation. What was less expected was that legislators with spending limits spent significantly less time on symbolic representation when out-of-session, although they spent slightly more when in-session. The probability of legislators in states with spending limits working 1–4 hours was 0.30 and it was 0.16 for those in states without spending limits. The probabilities for working more than 16 hours on symbolic representation were 0.06 and 0.12, respectively. Ballot access laws also decreased symbolic representation. Legislators in states with larger filing fees spent less time when the legislature was in-session and those with petition requirements spent less time when out-of-session. Finally, redistricting principles, as anticipated, did not affect symbolic representation.

It was anticipated that features affecting the dyadic relationship would have modest effects, since dyadic relationships increase the easy but decrease the need of symbolic representation. These expectations were supported. Neither district magnitude nor size had significant effects on the amount of time legislators spent on symbolic representation.

The findings also indicate that legislators' vulnerability, ambition, and role orientations are related to symbolic representation. Legislators with static ambition spent more time on symbolic representation, and legislators from states with smaller reelection rates spent somewhat more time engaging in contact when the session was over. Role orientation also affected contact. Although the voter-district orientation had nominal relationships with contact, legislators with less of a trustee (more of a delegate) orientation spent more time on contact, with the relationship being significant when legislature was out-of-session.

Legislators with more of a state and less of a district orientation also spent less time engaged in contact, but the relationships were not statistically significant. Legislators with a surrogate orientation spent more time on symbolic representation, with significant effects on out-of-session contact.

One concern with legislators' spending time on nonlegislative matters is that it takes time away from legislating (Thomas 1992). Therefore, to see if this is the case, I examined the amount of time legislators spent legislating and the time they spent meeting with lobbyists, controlling for time spent contacting. To control for time spent contacting, I created an additive scale with the two measures of contacting. To measure the amount of time legislators spent legislating, the same series of questions that were asked about legislators' time "keeping in touch" were also asked about time spent studying legislation and meeting with other policy makers. The legislators were asked about their time spent both in- and out-of-session. The four items were combined to create a scale ranging from 2–16 (alpha = 0.63). The same series of questions was asked about time spent meeting with interest group representatives. The in-session and out-of-session responses were combined into one scale ranging from 1–8 (r = 0.35). In these analyses, if the contact variable is negative and significant, it indicates that legislators who engaged in symbolic representation were distracted from legislating. The results (not shown) suggest that legislators who spent more time keeping in touch with constituents also spent more time legislating and meeting with lobbyists. Since there was a strong relationship between symbolic representation and other activities, this means that these legislators either overestimated their time or work much harder than others. Because of these potential biases, I reran the equation reported in columns one and two from table 5.1 while controlling for variations in the time legislators spent lawmaking and meeting with lobbyists. The results of these analyses (not reported) support the previous findings. The only differences were that district size and petition variables went from reaching normal levels of statistical significance, when in-session, in the original analysis to just nearing statistical significance in the latter. Also district magnitude went from not being significant when out-of-session, to being significant such that those in MMDs spent more time engaged in symbolic representation.

These findings can be construed to suggest that features that enable legislators to stay in contact (resources) as well as those that increase the need (district size and magnitude) increase the effort legislators put into contacting their constituents. On the other hand, features that focus members on other activities, such as strong committees, decrease the contact. The effect of any one feature is fairly modest. However, collectively these features had a significant effect on the time legislators spent on symbolic representation.

These findings also demonstrate that the incentives (ambition, vulnerability and orientation) effect symbolic representation, and that most features that had conflicting incentives and abilities were not significantly associated with symbolic representation.

Interactions

It is possible, as was noted in chapter 1, that resources have their greatest effects on representation when legislators have greater incentives to represent their constituents and vice versa. To see whether resources and other features interact to affect legislators' symbolic representation, I created and tested several interaction variables. Since having an office budget was the main resource that affected the amount of time legislators spent on symbolic representation I focus on it. Also since term length, district size, petition requirements, and filing fees had significant effects on symbolic representation; I create interaction variables by multiplying the office budget variable by each of these variables. Large interaction variables would indicate that the legislator had an office budget and more of the other feature. To test for the effects of the interaction, I reran the equations from table 5.1 inserting each interaction variable individually. Also since trustees were significantly less likely to engage in symbolic representation and those with surrogate representation more so, I also created interaction variables for these role orientations.

What is amazing about these findings, not shown, is the uniformity of the insignificance. Only one of the interaction variables even neared significance. Legislators with office budgets and surrogate orientation were more likely to engage in symbolic representation when the session was over than were those with office budgets but without a surrogate orientation.

These results indicate that resources alone will suffice to encourage symbolic representation without creating additional ways to encourage it. That is not to say that incentives are not important. It is just that reelection and other incentives are strong enough or uniform enough such that legislators will use resources on symbolic representation.

MODES OF CONTACT

Not only might legislative features affect levels of symbolic representation, but they might also affect modes of symbolic representation or the means used by legislators to reach their constituents. The type of contact legislators use for symbolic representation affects the nature of that contact. Some forms, such as newsletters, are less personal and offer a one-way flow of communication, while others, such as meetings, are more interactive. Although legislators may solicit constituents' opinions in newsletters, there is not a direct give and take. However, when legislators meet with constituents, constituents have the opportunity to converse with their representative. Using the same body of literature cited above, it would make sense that those who spend the most time on contact will also be the most likely to use each mode of contact. There are a few caveats to this. I expect that legislators in more populous districts will rely more on less personal communications such as newsletters and web pages while those in smaller districts will rely more on personal contact such as meetings. Additionally, I expect that resources—particularly staff—are more important for modes that are labor intensive (such as newsletters) or require special skills (such as maintaining a web page).

Here I examine institutional affects on three different modes of symbolic representation or contact: newsletters, meetings, and electronic communications. Meetings are one of the best ways for legislators to communicate with their constituents (Jewell 1982, chapter 3; Rosenthal 2004). In meetings legislators can explain their activities and positions directly to constituents, and, in turn, constituents can express their concerns directly to legislators. One of the limitations of using meetings with groups or organizations is that organizational boundaries differ from legislative boundaries. Most organizations or branches of organizations are by city, county, or state, not by legislative district. Another problem is that typically audiences are small. However, the meetings are still important, as one legislator from Arizona noted, "Many events are simply *not* well attended. I found it very difficult to get people out of the house—although those in attendance were very appreciative of the opportunity to share their stories and ask questions. So, I always felt scheduling meetings with groups was valuable use of time." Attending meetings is most likely used by legislators in less professionalized legislatures and by those who have small constituencies because they require few resources and tend to reach relatively few constituents. To estimate the number of meetings legislators attend, respondents to the survey were asked, "In your average *month this year*, how many local meetings or speaking engagements did you have with groups in your district such as but not limited to: school, business, social service, gender, race/ethnic, or church groups?" The average legislator went to about 11.8 meetings (the standard deviation was 16).[3]

Newsletters are another common way for legislators to communicate with constituents. They are vehicles used by legislators to tell constituents what legislation they have been working on, what they have done for the district, and generally explain what they have been doing (Jewell 1982, chapter 3). This helps legislators fulfill their educational responsibilities. Additionally, many legislators use them as a way to encourage constituents to contact them, either by using surveys or providing contact information for the legislator or other public service providers. Because legislators need a budget and staff to produce and mail newsletters the level of available resources will have a significant impact on the use of newsletters. To determine which legislators used newsletters, respondents to the survey were asked, "Do you have a newsletter you send to your constituents?" Of those answering the question, 43 percent sent a newsletter to their constituents. Legislators who sent a newsletter were coded 1 for the newsletter variable and others were coded 0.

Electronic or virtual communications provide efficient ways to communicate. Electronic newsletters, emails, and web pages do not incur the expense of printing or postage of a newsletter. They are also very popular. For example, a legislator from Kentucky stated, "Email is becoming more and more the best way to communicate with constituents." Similarly, legislators in Minnesota and Wisconsin in 2002 reported that they received significantly more email messages than phone calls, office visits, faxes, or letters combined (Alperin and Schultz 2003). These legislators, however, also reported that email was considered the least effective means of communication. Although the quality of communication coming from constituents in emails may be less than phone calls, the use of emails by legislators may be more professional. A potential value of e-communication is that it may increase the ability of legislators to educate their constituents (Rosenthal 1998, 339–40). I expected that e-communications are used more by legislators in rural areas and large populations where it might be difficult for legislators to visit with constituents. Additionally, e-communications are expected to be used where legislators have staff to help develop and maintain the communication sites. To determine who relied on electronic communications, the number of electronic methods was estimated by asking respondents: "Which of the following do you use to communicate with constituents? Legislative web pages, blogs, mass email or text messaging, and Facebook or similar site." Most legislators used some form of e-communication. Only 22 percent of the legislators used no e-communication method, 32 percent used only one, 33 percent used two, 11 percent used three, and 2 percent used all four. Table 5.2 reports a breakdown of the different types of e-communications.

Table 5.2. Frequency of Types of Communications

E-communication Type	*Used Communication (%)*	*N*
Mass email	53	592
Web page	62	592
Facebook	16	590
Blog	10	589

In estimating which features were associated with the different modes of symbolic representation, I used the same controls as in the previous analysis, except I added age when examining use of e-communication. Table 5.3 reports the findings concerning the modes of legislators' contact with constituents. Column one reports the results of logistic regression, predicting the probability that legislators sent a newsletter. The findings offer much support for the expectations. Since newsletters are expensive but allow legislators to reach a large number of constituents, it was expected that legislators with large constituencies and significant resources would use newsletters. Consistent with that expectation, legislators with staff, office budgets, full-time positions, and those with large constituencies were more likely to have sent a newsletter. The probability that legislators with staff sent a newsletter was 0.49 compared to 0.32 for those without staff. The probability for those with office budgets was 0.48 and 0.34 for those without. The probability for those with full-time positions (one standard deviation above the mean) was 0.57 compared to 0.28 for those with part-time positions (one standard deviation below the mean). The probability a legislator with 175,000 constituents (about one standard deviation above the mean) sent a newsletter was 0.55 compared to 0.32 for a legislator with 7,500 constituents (smallest district).

Also, legislators with greater incentives to offer symbolic representation were more likely to send newsletters. Legislators who were more electorally vulnerable, measured by vote gap and reelection rates, were more likely to send newsletters, as were those who had higher levels of static and progressive ambition. Also legislators with longer terms and term limits were significantly less likely to send newsletters. The probability that term-limited legislators sent a newsletter was 0.31 compared to 0.49 for legislators that were not term-limited. The probability that legislators with a two-year term sent a newsletter was 0.53 compared to 0.24 for legislators with a four-year term. Also, those in states with more pro-incumbent redistricting principles were less likely to have sent a newsletter while those with community principles were more likely to have sent a newsletter. The probability for legislators in states with no pro-incumbent principles was 0.64 compared to 0.27 for legislators in states with two such principles. The probability for those in states with no community principles was 0.26 compared to 0.48 for those with three principles. Greater ballot access requirements, which increase incumbent security, also decreased the use of newsletters. The probability for legislators in states with petition requirements was 0.26 compared to 0.47 for those in states without these requirements.

Capacity also affected the use of newsletters. However, greater capacity was associated with being less likely to send newsletters. Legislators in

Table 5.3. Institutional Influence on Modes of Contact

Variable	*Newsletter*	*E-contact*	*Meetings*	*Meeting (IRR)*
Leadership strength	−0.14 (0.05)*	−0.01 (0.04)	−0.01 (0.01)	0.99
Committee strength	−0.09 (0.05)*	0.07 (0.06)	0.03 (0.02)	1.03
Chamber size	0.01 (0.00)**	−0.007 (0.004)*	−0.002 (0.001)	1.00
Office budget	0.61 (0.31)*	−0.23 (0.25)	0.08 (0.09)	1.10
Staff	0.69 (0.29)**	0.36 (0.22)	0.10 (0.08)	1.11
Full-time	0.31 (0.11)***	0.07 (0.08)	0.05 (0.03)*	1.03
Term limits	−0.77 (0.37)**	−0.71 (0.29)**	0.00 (0.11)	1.01
District size	0.006 (0.002)**	0.001 (0.001)	0.000 (0.000)	1.00
District magnitude	−0.13 (0.47)	0.54 (0.35)	0.15 (0.13)	1.14
Contribution limits	0.09 (0.14)	0.03 (0.11)	−0.07 (0.04)	0.93
Spending limits	−0.89 (0.72)	−0.16 (0.52)	0.06 (0.19)	1.09
Term length	−0.66 (0.20)***	−0.24 (0.16)	−0.14 (0.06)***	0.88
Community principle	0.32 (0.18)*	−0.04 (0.14)	0.02 (0.05)	1.03
Pro-incumbent principle	−0.79 (0.25)***	−0.10 (0.20)	−0.08 (0.07)	0.92
Petition requirement	−0.93 (0.41)**	−0.64 (0.32)**	−0.23 (0.12)*	0.82
Filing fee	−0.000 (0.000)	0.0005 (0.0003)	0.000 (0.000)	1.00
Vote gap	−0.003 (0.003)	0.000 (0.002)	0.000 (0.001)	1.00
Reelection rate	−15.40 (5.30)***	−4.73 (3.61)	−2.25 (1.27)*	0.16
Progressive ambition	0.60 (0.33)*	0.60 (0.27)**	0.13 (0.09)	1.10
Static ambition	0.32 (0.26)	0.35 (0.20)*	0.20 (0.07)***	1.22
Trustee	0.04 (0.07)	0.03 (0.06)	0.01 (0.02)	1.00
State orientation	−0.10 (0.08)	−0.06 (0.06)	−0.02 (0.02)	0.99
Voter orientation	−0.07 (0.07)	−0.00 (0.06)	0.06 (0.02)***	1.05

(*continued*)

Table 5.3. *(continued)*

Variable	*Newsletter*	*E-contact*	*Meetings*	*Meeting (IRR)*
Surrogate orientation	0.23 (0.22)	0.17 (0.17)	0.06 (0.06)	1.04
Hours not in-session	–0.001 (0.009)	0.02 (0.01)**	0.02 (0.00)***	1.02
Party ID	0.45 (0.22)**	–0.08 (0.17)	0.12 (0.06)**	1.15
Seniority	–0.01 (0.02)	–0.02 (0.01)*	–0.005 (0.005)	1.00
Rural	–0.01 (0.00)**	–0.004 (0.003)	–0.002 (0.001)	1.00
Legislator education	0.02 (0.16)	0.14 (0.12)	0.04 (0.04)	1.03
Constituency education	0.01 (0.01)	0.04 (0.01)***	–0.000 (0.004)	1.00
Southern states	0.95 (0.61)	0.08 (0.48)	0.30 (0.17)*	1.32
Gone	0.04 (0.38)	–0.04 (0.29)	–0.08 (0.11)	0.93
Previous experience	0.35 (0.22)	–0.02 (0.17)	–0.03 (0.06)	0.98
Female	–0.17 (0.30)	0.02 (0.22)	0.07 (0.08)	1.07
Age		–0.02 (0.01)***		
Minority party status	–0.01 (0.02)	0.01 (0.01)	0.007 (0.005)	1.01
Constant/Cut 1	16.71***	–6.85	3.79***	
Cut 2		–5.24		
Cut 3		–3.26		
Cut 4		–1.17		
R^2	0.24	0.08	0.06	
Adj. r^2				
Chi^2 (DF)	182.30 (35)***	114.91 (36)***	235.51 (35)***	
Log likelihood	–285.65	–704.58	1,765.50	
N	551	547	554	

* <=0.10; ** <=0.05; *** <=0.01 (using a two-tailed test).
Description of variables is in text.

chambers with strong leaders (one standard deviation above the mean) had a 0.36 probability of sending a newsletter, compared to 0.47 for those with weak leaders. The probability for a legislator in a state with strong committees was 0.34 compared to 0.46 for one in a state with weak committees. The probability that legislators in chambers with 125 members (roughly one standard deviation above the mean) sent a newsletter was 0.53 compared to 0.28 for those in chambers with 45 members (roughly one standard deviation below the mean).

Column two reports the ordered logistic regression for the number of e-communications used by legislators. E-communications allow legislators to reach a larger number of constituents with fewer resources than sending newsletters. As one respondent to the survey put it, "I use autodialer calls to announce regular town meetings and hold two meetings a month. I also use an e-newsletter. The calls are very effective and much cheaper than U.S. postage and printing." Since e-communications are less cost-prohibitive than newsletters, fewer institutional features affected who used them, but four features had significant relationships. Consistent with the idea that professionalism increases the ability of legislators to engage in symbolic representation, legislators with staff (just neared statistical significance) and those from smaller chambers used more e-communications than others. The average legislator with staff had a 0.16 probability of using no e-communications and a 0.11 of using three. For the average legislator without staff the probabilities were 0.22 and 0.07, respectively. Those from large chambers had a 0.23 probability of no e-communications and a 0.07 of three and those from small chambers the probabilities were 0.15 and 0.12. And, consistent with the expectation that elections encourage symbolic representation, legislators with term limits and those in states with petition requirements for ballot access used fewer forms of e-communications. The average legislators with term limits had a 0.26 probability of no e-communications and a 0.06 of three communications. A non-term-limited legislator had a 0.15 probability of no e-communications and a 0.12 probability of three. And legislators with signature requirements had a 0.27 probability of no e-communications and a 0.06 of three, while one with no signature requirements had a 0.16 of no e-communications and 0.11 of three. Also, legislators with static and progressive ambition were more likely to use e-communications and those in states with smaller reelection rates were somewhat more likely to use e-communication.

Column three reports negative binomial regression coefficients for the number of meetings.[4] Since meetings are count data, negative binomial is the preferred method; however, it is difficult to interpret the coefficients. Thus, column four reports the incidence rate ratios (IRR). The IRR is the factorial change that a one-unit change in the independent variable has on the number of meetings attended by a member (www.ats.ucla.edu/stat/Stata/output/stata_nbreg_output.htm). Compared to e-communications and sending newsletters, resources were not expected to have much effect on the frequency with which legislators attended meetings. Attending meetings are relatively cheap. There was mixed support for this expectation. Although legislators with staff and office budgets attended more meetings than others, the differences were not statistical significant. However, legislators with more full-time status attended more meetings than those with part-time status. The IRR was 1.06 (standard deviation = 2). Full-time positions undoubtedly give legislators more time to attend meetings with constituents than those who need a second job.

There was mixed evidence that electoral incentives affected the number of meetings attended by legislators. On the one hand, legislators in states with lower reelection rates attended more meetings, as did those with progressive and static ambition and with a voter role orientation. On the other hand, legislators with longer terms and those in states with signature requirements, both thought to decrease electoral concerns attended more meetings. Legislators with four-year terms attended meetings at a factor of 0.76 of that of a legislator with a two-year term. Legislators in states with petition requirements attended meetings at a factor of 0.82 of those without such requirements. The coefficients for term limits, capacity, and district magnitude and size were small and not statistically significant.

Several features affected legislators' modes of communication. Legislators used their resources as efficiently as they could to reach their constituents. Legislators were more likely to use less personal forms of communication when they had large districts and resources. Those with large districts reached a smaller share of their constituents by pressing the flesh than did those with smaller constituencies, so they engaged in forms of contact that could blanket their districts. Those in term-limited states and those in states with petition requirements and pro-incumbent redistricting principles were less likely to use any form of contact, and those with short terms were more likely to send out newsletters. This indicates that the electoral connection increases symbolic representation, presumably by increasing legislators' incentives to stay connected with would-be voters. Legislators need resources to be visible to constituents. Those with staff, office budgets, and full-time positions also engage in more types of symbolic representation.

CONCLUSION

The goal of this book is demonstrating that legislative features affect how legislators represent their constituents. Prior to this chapter, I demonstrated that legislative features can affect legislators' incentives for representation, but this chapter examined reported behaviors. It is consistent with the other chapters in that it suggests that institutional design, particularly professionalism, does indeed matter. However, the findings also show that since each feature can have conflicting effects on incentives and abilities to be responsive some features have limited effect of symbolic representation. The findings show that legislators in legislatures offering resources to engage in symbolic representation (such as leadership, staff, budgets, and full-time positions) and incentives to engage in more symbolic representation do so. Another significant finding here, as well as throughout most of the book, is the importance of staff. Legislators with staff engaged in more types of representation than those without staff. Additionally, although staff engaged in symbolic activities, legislators with staff remained as active as other legislators in symbolic representation. The findings also suggest that institutional design can affect the ways legislators engage in symbolic representation. Institutions that provide resources increase the likelihood that legislators send newsletters or use e-communications to keep in touch with constituents. Legislators, too, who have smaller constituencies are better able to meet personally with constituents.

NOTES

1. These questions were based on questions used in the 2002 survey of state legislators (Carey et al. 2002). However, I wanted greater precision in measuring time and allow for differences in work when the legislature is in-session as opposed to out-of-session.

2. The medians and modes were also 2.

3. There was one outlier who reported attending 300 meetings. This mean included the outlier without the outlier; the mean is 11.3.

4. Because of the extreme outlier, I reran the analysis without cases where the respondents indicated more than 101 meetings. The conclusions remained unchanged.

What about the content of the communication? Is it factual? Misleading? etc.

6

Institutional Design, Legislators' Information, and Perceptual Accuracy

> Legislators believe they should act in the interests of the constituency and with the views of their constituents in mind. Even if they were in their last term of office, they would feel this way because this belief is rooted in our representational culture (Rosenthal 1998, 26).

Legislators want to work on the interests of their constituents and are likely to act in accordance to what they believe constituents want. Although legislators may want to act in the interest of their constituents, to do so requires that they understand their constituents' interests. Yet, the degree to which they accurately perceive their constituents is up for debate (Miller and Stokes 1963; Hedlund and Friesema 1972; Erikson, Luttbeg, and Holloway 1975; Uslaner and Weber 1979), indicating the very real possibility of misrepresentation. Determining constituent interests is not easy: constituents often do not indicate their preferences; some constituents are more likely to express their preferences resulting in biased information; and many districts are heterogeneous, thus lacking a clear set of interests. One way legislators may be better able to act in their constituents' interests is by using a variety of sources of information to figure out what, if anything, is the district's preference. Furthermore, although congruence between public preferences and policy outputs is critical for a democracy, minorities need representation and protection as well. That is, after all, one of the primary advantages of a republican system of government over direct democracy. There are also issues of what is the public's interest in situations where the minority has intense preferences and the majority weak preferences. In this chapter, I do not explore how legislators balance these issues but rather examine the types of information legislators use in making decisions. Do legislators try to serve their constituents by basing decisions on information from constituents; do they use information from interest groups that might speak for segments of the population; or do they rely on other legislators who have their own sources of information? The various sources of information used by legislators suggest different styles that legislators have in representing their constituents. This chapter also examines the accuracy of legislators' perceptions of their constituents' preferences. It is presumed that legislators who have more accurate views of their constituents are better able to offer accurate policy representation. In examining sources of information used by legislators and accuracy of legislators' perceptions the key issue concerns the effects of legislative features on these.

INSTITUTIONS AND INFORMATION SOURCES

There are many ways legislators can get information about constituents' interests. One way is from the constituents themselves. As discussed in the previous chapter, legislators expend considerable time and energy engaging in contact with constituents. They also receive considerable contact from constituents. Legislators surveyed for this book, on average, received 240 contacts from their constituents each week. This contact offers a way for legislators to get information from their constituents about their concerns and interests. However, legislators are often skeptical about the quality or representativeness of this information (Jewell 1982). For example, constituents of higher socio-economic status or those with the most intensive views may be more likely to contact their representative about policy preferences. Another source of information is the pool of other legislators. Legislators are busy people who use the information that is most easily accessible when making decisions (Mooney 1991b; Miler 2007). Several models of congressional decision making acknowledge the importance of cue taking from colleagues (see Kingdon 1989). Legislators are around each other and can be used as easy conduits of information. In fact, the dissemination of information from colleague to colleague has been institutionalized through the use of parties, committees, and legislative study groups. Many legislators also represent similar constituencies and may understand policy implications on other members' districts. A third source of information is interest groups and their lobbyists. Because lobbyists can filter and synthesize information, legislators with close contacts with interest groups or lobbyists may find the information coming from organizations more accessible and instructive than that coming from constituents. There is no presumption that one source offers more accurate information about constituents' interests than any other. For example, interest groups may have good accurate information about constituent policy preferences while the information coming from constituents may be biased by the types of people who offer policy demands.

Little has been written about how institutional features affect the sources of information used by legislators, at least in the context used here. However, it is the expectation that features which make legislators more distant from their constituents will decrease the use of constituent-derived information and increase the use of elite sources. Elite sources are powerful political actors such as lobbyists and other policy makers; similar to what Mooney (1991a) has called insider sources. These political actors have professional experiences similar to legislators' experiences, and these actors have frequent contact with legislators. They contrast with outsiders or those "whose professional experience is least like that of a legislators, those who know little about legislative life and have little on-going contact with legislators" (447). Using communication theory, Mooney (1991b) argues that sources of information that are similar to or have close proximity to legislators in their experiences are better able to communicate their positions to legislators. Moreover, such sources of information will be used more often. According to Mooney, information sources are most likely to be used by state legislators when they have professional experiences similar to those of legislators' experiences or when they are elite insiders. Following from the above, legislative features that separate legislators from their constituents should decrease their use of constituents as sources of information and increase the use of elites as sources of information. Based on this, I have the following expectations.

1) Term-limited legislators rely more heavily on constituent-derived information than information from elite sources. Since term-limited members are limited in how long they can be in office they are likely to have experiences similar to the people and less likely to have them similar to political insiders. Citizen legislators' experiences are expected to be similar to that of their constituency, in contrast to professional politicians who can be considered a ruling class separate from rest of society. However, if term-limited legislators are less engaged with constituents while in office they may be less likely to listen to constituents.

2) Legislators in professionalized legislatures rely heavily on elite sources of information. Professional legislatures are more institutionalized and more bounded than amateur legislatures (Rosenthal 1998, 65–67). That is, they are more separate from the rest of society.

2a) Legislators with resources rely heavily on elite sources of information.

2b) Legislators in chambers with high levels of capacity rely heavily on elite sources of information. This may be particularly true for legislators in chambers with strong committees. Legislators in strong committees develop great specialization and knowledge; therefore, legislators will be a great source of information. Also the relationship between lobbyists and members may be greater where committees are strong. The oft-cited iron triangle is thought to be strongest between committee members and groups.

3) Features increasing legislators' electoral concerns increase their use of constituent-derived information. This book has taken the approach that elections increase legislators' contact and concern for constituents. There is, of course, the view of many pundits that elections make legislators sensitive not to their constituents but to "special interests" who offer campaign resources. If this is the case, then we will expect to find that legislators who have tough elections to be beholden to groups for information, unless there are campaign donation limits or spending limits.

3a) Legislators with shorter terms rely more heavily on constituents than do others. Since legislators campaign by reaching voters, those who run for reelection more frequently will spend more time with constituents.

3b) Legislators in states with significant campaign contribution limits have less reliance on groups for information. Legislators with more contribution limits and spending limits may spend less time listening to lobbyists. Lobbyists, as representatives of interest groups, may have little to offer legislators in the area of campaign help (that is, fewer campaign resources to offer).

3c) Legislators in states with campaign spending limits have less reliance on groups for information. This is based on the same reasoning as expectation 3b.

3d) Legislators in states with more community redistricting principles rely more on constituent-derived information. Since these legislators should have more homogeneous districts, they may see this information as more reliable.

3e) Legislators in states with more pro-incumbent districting principles rely more on constituent-derived information. This is based on the finding from chapter 2, which indicated that these legislators are less electorally secure, but the effects of these principles have not been clear throughout this work.

3f) Legislators in states with tough ballot access laws, petition requirements, and filing fees are less likely to use constituent-derived information, since they are more electorally secure.

4) Features that increase legislators' dyadic relationship with their districts increase legislators' use of constituent-derived information.

4a) Legislators with smaller constituencies have greater reliance on constituent information than those with larger constituencies. Legislators with smaller constituencies are more likely to know a higher percentage of their constituents and thus have a better sense of the quality of information coming from constituents. Smaller districts may also be more homogenous, increasing the ease with which legislators can filter information coming from constituents.

4b) Legislators in MMDs are more likely to rely on other legislators than those in SMDs. Legislator in MMDs may rely on other members as there is at least one other member with the same constituents. This legislator may be a quick source of information about the district.

I used three variables to test the above expectations. The variables stemmed from a series of questions from the survey: "How often do you use the following sources of information in considering whether or not to support legislation? If you do not receive a type of information please select never." The options were: almost always, often, roughly half of the time, rarely, and never. The sources of information were: constituents, other legislators or their staff, and organized interests. "Never" was rarely chosen so legislators reporting never are treated as rarely using a source. These variables were coded so that the larger number indicates greater use of the source. The three variables therefore are: use constituents as sources of information, use other legislators, and use interest groups. Since these are ordinal data ordered logistic regression is used. The independent variables are the institutional features. These have been described in previous chapters. The controls include role orientation, vote gap, reelection rates, ambition, party identification, political culture (southern states), levels of legislator initiated contact,[1] minority party strength, gender, seniority, percentage of district that is rural, and whether the legislator left.

The model did not do a very good job explaining how heavily legislators relied on the different types of information (see table 6.1). The pseudo-R2s were small (0.04 to 0.08). There was mixed support for the expectation that legislators who rely on constituents for information, as opposed to elite sources, would be in institutions that increase legislators' contact with constituents while institutions that foster elite contact would use elite sources of information. On one hand, term-limited legislators were less, not more, likely to use constituent based information than were non-term-limited legislators. However, term-limited legislators were also less likely to rely on any source of information. For example, while term-limited legislators had a 0.29 probability of relying heavily on constituents (scoring a 4), a 0.38 of relying on groups (scoring a 3) and 0.47 of relying on other legislators (scoring a 3), the probabilities of non-term-limited legislators were 0.43, 0.48 and 0.57, respectively. Apparently, term-limited legislators are independent decision makers using their own sources of information.

There was mixed support for the expectation that legislators in professionalized chambers rely more heavily on elite sources of information. Legislators with office budgets, like term-limited legislators, relied less heavily on each of these sources. The probability of legislators with office budgets relying heavily on groups was 0.39 and 0.51 for use of legislators. The probabilities for those without office budgets were 0.49 and 0.56, respectively. Legislators with staff were more likely to listen to groups. The probability of a legislator with staff relying heavily on groups was 0.47 compared to 0.40 for a legislator without staff. Staff is often delegated as the contact person for lobbyists

Table 6.1. Sources of Information

Variable	*Use of Constituents*	*Use of Groups*	*Use of Lawmakers*
Leadership strength	0.08 (0.04)*	–0.03 (0.04)	0.00 (0.04)
Committee strength	0.16 (0.06)***	0.09 (0.06)	0.14 (0.06)**
Chamber size	–0.002 (0.004)	–0.001 (0.004)	0.002 (0.004)
Office budget	–0.23 (0.26)	–0.55 (0.25)**	–0.42 (0.25)*
Staff	–0.07 (0.23)	0.37 (0.22)*	–0.01 (0.23)
Full-time	0.09 (0.08)	0.10 (0.08)	0.08 (0.08)
Term limits	–0.60 (0.31)*	–0.55 (0.29)*	–0.70 (0.29)**
District size	–0.001 (0.001)	–0.001 (0.001)	0.000 (0.001)
District magnitude	0.03 (0.37)	0.10 (0.36)	0.61 (0.36)*
Term length	–0.09 (0.16)	–0.04 (0.16)	–0.05 (0.16)
Contribution limits	–0.03 (0.12)	–0.03 (0.11)	0.11 (0.12)
Spending limits	–0.60 (0.59)	–0.78 (0.54)	–1.19 (0.55)**
Community principle	–0.24 (0.15)*	–0.13 (0.14)	–0.26 (0.14)*
Pro-incumbent principle	0.21 (0.21)	0.26 (0.20)	0.20 (0.20)
Petition requirement	–0.44 (0.34)	0.32 (0.33)	0.01 (0.33)
Filing fee	0.000 (0.000)	0.000 (0.000)	–0.000 (0.000)
Vote gap	0.003 (0.002)	–0.001 (0.002)	–0.004 (0.002)
Reelection rate	–1.01 (3.96)	3.78 (3.73)	0.34 (3.72)
Static ambition	0.19 (0.21)	0.35 (0.20)*	0.13 (0.20)
Progressive ambition	0.03 (0.27)	0.29 (0.25)	0.17 (0.25)
Trustee	–0.12 (0.06)**	0.08 (0.06)	0.02 (0.06)
State orientation	–0.14 (0.07)**	0.05 (0.06)	–0.02 (0.06)
Voter orientation	0.01 (0.06)	–0.06 (0.06)	–0.07 (0.06)
Surrogate orientation	0.01 (0.18)	–0.08 (0.18)	0.21 (0.18)
Rural	0.001 (0.003)	–0.004 (0.003)	–0.001 (0.003)
Contact	0.26 (0.06)***	–0.04 (0.05)	–0.01 (0.05)
Legislator education	0.18 (0.13)	0.17 (0.12)	0.13 (0.12)
Southern states	–0.54 (0.51)	–0.65 (0.49)	–0.69 (0.50)
Gone	–0.51 (0.29)*	–0.73 (0.28)***	–0.36 (0.27)
Party	–0.08 (0.18)	0.05 (0.17)	–0.04 (0.17)
Seniority	0.03 (0.01)**	0.00 (0.01)	–0.02 (0.01)
Female	0.58 (0.24)**	0.70 (0.23)***	0.56 (0.23)**
Party strength	–0.01 (0.02)	–0.00 (0.01)	–0.01 (0.02)
Cut 1	–4.07	–1.84	–1.96
Cut 2	–2.12	3.51	–0.61
Cut 3	0.72	6.23	2.12
R^2	0.08	0.04	0.04
Chi^2 (33)	96.16 ***	53.59**	54.84***
Log likelihood	–526.09	–642.05	–642.11
N	567	546	555

* <= 0.10; ** <= 0.05; *** <= 0.01 (using a two-tailed test).
Description of variables is in text.

and staff may serve as spokespersons for groups. Capacity had greater effects. Generally, but unexpectedly, greater capacity increased legislators' reliance on constituents for information. Legislators in chambers with strong committees and leaders relied more on constituents than did others. For example, legislators in chambers with strong leadership (one standard deviation above the mean) had a 0.42 probability of relaying on constituents (scoring a 4), compared to 0.31 for legislators in chambers with weak leadership (one standard deviation below the mean). For legislators in chambers with weak committees (one standard deviation below the mean) the probability was 0.30 and it was 0.45 for those with strong committees. Legislators in chambers with strong committees, as expected, did rely more on other members for sources of information. The probability for a legislator in a chamber with strong committees (one standard deviation above the mean) of relying heavily on other members was 0.57 and it was 0.50 for those in chambers with weak committees. Also, legislators in states with strong committees relied more heavily on interest groups for information. The probability of legislators with strong committees relying heavily on groups was about 0.07 higher than for those in chambers with weak committees. These findings support two common views about the role of committees: 1) they serve of conduit of information, and 2) they contribute to the iron triangle.

A few of the electoral features were related to the relative use of sources of information by legislators, although not always as predicted. Legislators in states with spending limits, like those in term-limited states, relied less on each source of information, although the only statistically significant relationship was with regard to use of other lawmakers. Legislators in states with limits had a 0.33 probability of relying heavily on legislators (scored a 3) and those without limits had a 0.54 probability. Similarly, legislators who live in states with community redistricting principles were also more independent; the coefficients for use of constituents and lawmakers were significant. Legislators in states with community principles (scoring a 2) had a 0.38 probability of relying heavily on constituents (scoring a 4) and a 0.54 probability of relying heavily on other legislators (scoring a 3). For those in states without community principles the probabilities were 0.50 and 0.59, respectively. In fact, legislators with cohesive districts may need less information to know their districts' interests. The other electorally related features did not have consistent or significant effects on which sources of information legislators relied upon.

There was no evidence that features believed to increase dyadic relationships increased legislators' use of constituent-derived information. However, as expected, legislators in MMDs relied more heavily on members.

The control variables offered a few interesting findings. Legislators with static ambition were more likely to listen to interest groups. This offers some support for the idea that legislators' electoral concerns increase the role of special interests. Those wanting to keep their jobs listen to groups, since groups can offer good information about constituent preferences as well as campaign funding. Legislators with a trustee or state orientation were less likely to use constituent-derived information and those who spent much time on symbolic representation more. Legislators who were leaving office rely less on any source of information, but seniority did not decrease how heavily legislators relied on constituents but rather increased it. Also, women were significantly more likely to use each of the sources of information.

These findings suggest that institutional features can affect which sources of information are used by legislators. However, it is less clear that proximity is the key factor. It appears as though some features, such as office budgets, term limits, community principles, and spending limits simply enhance legislators' independence from the sources of information examined here. Whether independent decision makers are good or bad for policy making is debatable. They have a high risk of being rogue lawmakers, but may also be better positioned to take a longer term or broader perceptive in evaluating policy.

PERCEPTUAL ACCURACY

Legislators need to know their constituents to offer them high levels of substantive representation. Regardless of whether they are more likely to see themselves as delegates or trustees, they need to know their constituents' interests. However, it is unclear how accurate legislators' perceptions are of constituents' interests. Uslaner and Weber (1979), looking at legislators' knowledge of statewide constituency views, found legislators had generally inaccurate perceptions while other research finds legislators able to predict or know outcomes of ballot items (Erikson, Luttbeg, and Holloway 1975). Yet others found legislators' knowledge contextual varying with issue and district traits (Miller and Stokes 1963; Hedlunk and Friesema 1972). What is clear, however, is that there is variation from legislator to legislator in the accuracy of their perceptions. Below I examine whether legislative features account for some of that variation.

There are two conflicting theories about what affects the ability of legislators to know their districts. One is the citizen legislator theory, which generally holds that legislators who live lives similar to their constituents will have the most accurate perceptions. Professional politicians are feared to be separated from the rest of society, without fully understanding what it is like to have real jobs, pay mortgages, and live with the laws politicians write. Thus only citizen legislators can understand their constituents. A legislator from Utah expressed this view: "Before running for office in 2000, I taught high school in my community for thirty-three years. As a result I had name ID, a positive reputation, and shared views about education, family, safe communities, and other values important to this community." The other theory, the professional legislator theory, holds that professional legislators will best understand their districts. It takes a full-time legislator dedicated to learning the policies, to studying and purposively getting to know the district, to really know the district or constituents. This may be particularly true in large heterogeneous districts.

If the professional thesis is correct, then legislators in professional legislatures should have more accurate perceptions than those in amateur legislatures. These legislators have the professional requisites to collect information and be well informed. Conversely, if the citizen legislator thesis is correct, then those in amateur legislatures, with term limits and small districts should have more accurate perceptions. Since term-limited legislators have less time to become distinct from their constituents, it is often assumed they will be more like their constituents. Small districts may also increase understanding, because legislators likely have contact with a greater share of constituents simply by living in the district.

Regardless of whether there are citizen legislators or highly professionalized legislators, specific features may increase or decrease the accuracy of legislators' perceptions. Legislators in MMDs may have more accurate perceptions since they have other legislators they can ask about their constituents. They have an extra resource: a colleague who may have an in-depth understanding of their specific constituents. Also, legislators in states with community-based redistricting principles should have better understanding of their districts. These districts may be easier to know. After all, this principle requires states to try to keep communities together during redistricting.

In addition to affecting legislators' ability to know their constituents, institutional features may increase legislators' incentives to know their district. The expectation here is that term limits and features affecting elections will have such effects. Not only might term limits decrease the resources legislators have to gain information about their constituents, but they might also decrease the value of the information. By shortening the amount of time legislators can represent a district, term limits prevent legislators from seeing long-term value in obtaining the information. Also, the length of legislators' terms could affect their incentives to be informed. Legislators with shorter terms are expected to have better understanding, since they have to consistently pay attention to their district for reelection purposes. Legislators with longer terms who misgauge constituent opinion may better survive, since voters will have more time to forget legislators' mistakes. Campaign finance laws that make campaigns difficult (contribution and spending limits) may also increase legislators' incentives to know their constituents. That is since resources for campaigns are limited legislators may try to reach constituents through their official positions. Features that are associated with incumbent security, such as no pro-incumbent redistricting principles and ballot access laws may decrease their incentives to know their constituents.

Following from the above: If the citizen legislator thesis is correct legislators in professional legislatures (capacity or resources), without term limits and populous districts should have less accurate perceptions of their constituents. Conversely, if the citizen legislator thesis is correct the opposite would be the case. Additional expectations are that large district magnitude, long terms, spending and contribution limits, pro-incumbent redistricting principles, many community-based principles, and few ballot access restrictions should increase accuracy.

The measures of the accuracy of legislators' perceptions of their districts were based on the districts' position on same-sex marriage. This issue was selected because there was a measure of district positions. In each of the legislator's states there had been a ballot item on same-sex marriage since 2004. These ballot items generally put definitions of marriage as a union between one man and one woman in state constitutions. Some items also prevented states from recognizing same-sex marriages from other states or made other clarifications. Although there were differences in the ballot items, measures of accuracy should still be comparable because of the way legislators estimated their districts' positions. Legislators were asked to estimate the district's vote on the item. The district vote was calculated by the author and an assistant using precinct level results for the ballot item.[2] Two variables measured legislators' estimates of their districts' opposition to same-sex marriage. One variable was based on legislators' responses to the question: "What is your best guess as to the percentage of your district that supported your state's ballot item banning same-sex marriage?" A handful of legislators appeared to have misread the question and their answers were treated as missing. Those treated as missing appeared to answer the question as what percentage supported same-sex marriage. For example, the legislator guessed 20 percent when the vote was close to 80 percent. The correlation between legislators' guesses and actual vote was a reasonable 0.42 ($p = 0.00$) when looking at all legislators who responded. This coefficient jumped to 0.49 when I removed cases where legislators seemed to have misread the question. The variable used to measure accuracy was the absolute difference between legislators' guesses and the actual district vote. Larger numbers indicate that legislators had less accurate responses. The mean was 9.79 (standard deviation = 8.48); indicating that the average member's guess was about 10 points off.

Because of their theoretical importance I control for role orientation, ambition, and electoral vulnerability. Hedlund and Friesema (1972) find that those reelected have more accurate perceptions than those who lost and that district characteristics have significant effects on perceptual accuracy. I control for role orientation even though there is little evidence that role orientation affects perceptual accuracy (Hedlund and Friesema 1972; Erikson, Luttbeg, and Holloway 1975), because it is often thought to have such an effect. I also control for seniority (Erikson, Luttbeg, and Holloway 1975), unipolarity of districts' ideology (Clausen, Holmberg, and deHaven-Smith 1983), the size of the same-sex marriage ban vote,[3] and amount of symbolic representation.

The second variable was based on the districts' relative opposition to same-sex marriage. Legislators were asked, "Compared to the voters in the rest of your state, the voters in your district are ________ supportive of state-recognized same-sex marriages." The options were: significantly more (coded 1), somewhat more, about as, somewhat less, and significantly less (coded 5). These responses were compared to the gap between their districts' vote and the state vote. This gap was measured by subtracting the state vote from the district vote. With both variables, a large coefficient means the district was more supportive of same-sex marriage ban or less supportive of same-sex marriage. Since legislators' responses and state-district gap are on a different scale, however, I could not create a simple gap score to measure legislators' accuracy. Instead, I created a series of multiplicative interaction variables by multiplying legislators' estimate of relative support by each institutional feature separately. These variables indicated how closely legislators' estimates approximated their districts' relative vote under different contexts (with different features). Since the dependent variable was in support of same-sex marriage, I used a different set of control variables. These were variables that could affect the size of the districts' support for same-sex marriage and included district education, district race, district ideology,[4] political culture (southern states) and legislators' party.

Table 6.2 reports the findings for the legislator-district gap variable. The model only modestly explained variation. Only about 10 percent of the variance was explained and institutional features had limited effect on the accuracy of state legislators' perceptions of their constituents. One finding supports the professionalism thesis: legislators with staff had better estimates of their districts' support of same-sex marriage. The guesses of legislators with staff were about 6 points closer to the actual vote than the guesses of those without staff. Two other variables had significant findings. Legislators in states with redistricting principles requiring communities to be recognized had less not more accurate perceptions. Legislators in states with tough ballot access laws had at least somewhat less accurate perceptions.

Table 6.2. Institutions and Perceptual Accuracy of District Views

Variable	*B*	*Standard Error*
Leadership strength	0.43	0.32
Committee strength	0.32	0.48
Chamber size	0.02	0.03
Office budget	1.93	2.01
Staff	–6.28	1.79***
Full-time	–0.25	0.59
Term limits	2.59	2.40
District size	0.01	0.01
District magnitude	0.44	2.83
Contribution limits	–0.05	0.90
Spending limits	2.78	4.34
Term length	0.51	1.25
Community principles	1.95	1.10*
Pro-incumbent principles	–0.78	1.57
Petition requirements	–2.81	2.54
Filing fee	–0.004	0.003*
Vote gap	–0.002	0.019
Reelection rate	–15.96	29.76
Progressive ambition	–1.19	1.99
Static ambition	–1.99	1.57
Trustee orientation	–0.74	0.46
State orientation	0.61	0.50
Voter orientation	–0.85	0.45*
Surrogate orientation	–1.81	1.36
Contact	0.22	0.42
Seniority	0.10	0.11
Southern states	5.91	3.93
Gone	–1.42	2.27
Unipolar	0.88	0.79
Female	2.06	1.89
Marriage vote	–1.57	7.71
Party strength	0.13	0.12
Constant	9.16	31.54
R^2	0.11	
Adj. R^2	0.04	
N	465	

* <= 0.10; ** <= 0.05; *** <= 0.01 (using a two-tailed test).
Description of variables is in text.

Examining legislators' perceptions of their districts' relative support of same-sex marriage (table 6.3) also suggests that institutional features had limited effects on legislators' perceptual accuracy. Table 6.3 just reports the relationships between relative support and the interaction variables, as well as the variables comprising the interaction. They do not include the strength of the control variables. Only three features had significant correlations. Again, leg-

Table 6.3. Institutions and Relative Perceptual Accuracy of District Views

Variable	*Term Limits*	*Term Length*	*Office Budget*	*Staff*	*Full Time*	*District Size*	*MMD*	*Committee Strength*
Legislators' estimate	0.013 (0.004)***	0.002 (0.008)	0.01 (0.00)***	0.02 (0.00)***	0.01 (0.00)***	–0.01 (0.00)***	–0.01 (0.00)***	0.01 (0.01)
Term limits	0.02 (0.02)							
Term length		–0.01 (0.01)						
Office budget			0.03 (0.02)					
Staff				0.07 (0.02)***				
Full-time					0.011 (0.004)**			
District size						0.0002 (0.000)**		
District magnitude							–0.05 (0.04)	
Committee strength								–0.002 (0.005)
Interaction	–0.007 (0.005)	0.003 (0.003)	–0.008 (0.005)	–0.01 (0.01)**	–0.002 (0.001)	0.00004 (0.00002)	0.004 (0.010)	0.001 (0.001)
Constant	0.01	0.05	0.01	0.01	0.02	0.01	0.03	0.04
R^2	0.20	0.28	0.28	0.30	0.29	0.29	0.28	0.28
N	595	595	595	595	595	595	595	595

(continued)

Table 6.3. (*continued*)

Variable	*Leadership*	*Chamber Size*	*Community Principle*	*Pro-Incumbent*	*Petition*	*Filing Fee*	*Contribution Limits*
Legislators' estimate	0.01 (0.01)*	0.01 (0.01)*	0.001 (0.001)	0.02 (0.01)***	0.01 (0.00)***	0.01 (0.00)***	0.01 (0.00)**
Leadership strength	0.005 (0.004)						
Chamber size		–0.000 (0.000)					
Community principle			–0.008 (0.011)				
Pro-incumbent				0.03 (0.01)**			
Petition					0.03 (0.02)		
Filing fee						0.0001 (0.0000)***	
Contribution limit							0.006 (0.011)
Interaction	0.001 (0.001)	–0.000 (0.000)	0.004 (0.003)	–0.008 (0.003)***	–0.009 (0.006)	–0.00002 (0.00000)**	–0.001 (0.003)
Constant	–0.04	0.02	0.04	–0.01	0.01	0.01	0.01
R^2	0.28	0.28	0.29	0.29	0.28	0.30	0.28
N	595	595	595	595	595	595	595

* <= 0.10; ** <= 0.05; *** <= 0.01 (using a two-tailed test).
Description of variables is in text.

islators with staff differed from others; here, however, they had less accurate perceptions (the interaction variable was negative). Another feature that had a significant coefficient concerned pro-incumbent redistricting principles. Legislators in states with more pro-incumbent redistricting principles had less accurate perceptions. The other variable that had a significant interaction coefficient was filing fee. Legislators in states requiring a filing fee had less accurate perceptions. These last two findings suggest that safer legislators have less accurate perceptions. There was also some evidence that legislators with smaller districts had more accurate perceptions, although this relationship just neared statistical significance. Also nearing statistical significant were the coefficients for term limits and office budgets. Term-limited legislators and those with office budgets had less accurate perceptions. Perhaps part of the reason these findings do not better match those from table 6.2 is that this indicator of accuracy requires legislators not only to know their districts' position but also the states' position. As Uslaner and Weber (1979) observed legislators have fairly inaccurate perceptions of state preferences.

This section found little support for the professional or citizen legislators theses. The main finding was the legislative features do not have clear meaningful effects on legislators' perceptual accuracy of their constituents. To confirm that institutional features have nominal effects on the accuracy of legislators' perceptions, I replicated these finding but examined demographic traits. The survey also asked legislators' to estimate the percentage of the district that had a college degree and were either black or Latino. To estimate the accuracy of these guesses, I calculated the absolute difference between census measures of these traits and the guesses. These findings (not shown) too indicated that most institutional features do not affect the accuracy of legislators' perceptions of their districts. The significant findings concerning perceptions of the districts' racial make-up were that large chambers, large districts, and community principles increased the gap. The significant finding concerning perceptions of the districts' level of education were strong leadership and filing fees increased the gap. These findings confirm the early conclusions that large districts, filing fees, and community principles limit accurate perceptions.

I was also curious whether sources of information used by legislators' increased the accuracy of their perceptions. Thus I reran the analysis for the legislator-district vote gap and added the variables for the sources of information. Each source had a weak and insignificant positive correlation, indicating the more legislators relied on a source of information the less accurate their perceptions. I confirmed this tendency by running the analysis with the race gap and the education gap variables as dependent variables. The reason that institutional features have limited effect on the accuracy of legislators' perceptions may have to do with the policy preference and demographic traits examined. Levels of education, race, and views on same-sex marriage may be well known and easy to discern. Had it been possible to measure district preferences on less visible policies, greater variation may have been found. However, these results do not indicate very clear or consistent effects of institutional features on legislators' perceptions of their district.

CONCLUSION

This chapter examined the degree to which institutional features affect the sources of information used by legislators and the accuracy of their perception of constituents' preferences. Although legislative features have very little influence on the accuracy of legislators' perceptions, features have greater effects on the information sources used by legislators. These findings, however, offer just modest support for Mooney's proximity thesis; instead they suggest that some legislative features decreased legislators' use of sources of information, or that they were independent. Term-limited legislators, those with spending limits and office budgets, and those in states with community redistricting principles were independent decision makers.

NOTES

1. This is the variable that combines the two measures of symbolic representation.
2. I want to thank Ben Pryor for helping with this detailed and tedious task. There were a handful of cases where county vote totals were used instead of precinct vote totals, because neither the state nor the county could provide precinct level results.
3. I also tried a variable that was how far the vote was from 50 percent since it may be easier to guess at the extremes than in the middle. However, this folded variable was not significant.
4. Missing data coded as mean.

7

Institutional Design and Substantive Representation

It's all about helping and serving people!

I usually know my constituents in need. I go to their house many times. I get very personally involved in their problems.

Substantive representation is the only type of representation that actually requires legislators to act on behalf of constituents' interests and is at the nexus of legislators' legislative and representational responsibilities. As such, it is often seen as the ultimate form of representation. In this chapter I examine how institutional features can affect two types of substantive representation, policy and service. As noted in chapter 1, policy representation concerns the congruence between constituent preferences and policy-makers' actions, and service representation involves legislators helping constituents with specific problems. I will discuss service representation first.

SERVICE REPRESENTATION

Service representation is of a relatively recent vintage. It has only been since the twentieth century that the U.S. government has taken an active role in affecting Americans' daily lives. As such, it has only been since WWII that citizens on a large scale have come to legislators asking for help accessing governmental programs. Although state policies had affected people's daily lives earlier, it has only been since state legislatures became more professionalized that legislators had the resources to help constituents. Today it is a key aspect of the legislators' job. As one legislator said,

"When I ran for office, I was not aware of the extent that I would work as a social worker. I continue to be amazed at what constituents request me to do as their representative in the legislature."

Although conceptually distinct from symbolic representation, the institutional features likely to increase service representation match those of symbolic representation. Features that increase legislators' abilities to act and incentives to be concerned with constituents will increase service representation. Legislators in professionalized institutions with resources to help legislators work on the behalf of individual constituent's demands will do more casework and focus more on service representation (Ellickson and Whistler 2001). Staff can be used either to free legislators' time, so that they can help constituents or can aid legislators by helping solve constituents' problems. Legislators with full-time legislative positions have more time to engage in service representation than those who have jobs or careers in addition to being a state legislator. And those with office budgets may have more resources to solicit requests for help or to help solve constituent problems. Legislators in chambers with greater capacity may also engage in more casework. Legislators in efficient legislatures may have more time for casework and routinized procedures that enhance helping constituents. Strong committees, for example, may help legislators build contacts with bureaucrats and others helpful with casework. It should be noted too that resources and capacity generally (with some variation by specific feature) were associated with the incentives to be responsive to constituents.

Legislators' time in office can also affect their ability to engage in service representation. Term-limited legislators may be less likely to engage in service representation, since they have less time to build relationships with constituents, as constituents are more likely to ask for help from legislators with which they are familiar. Newer legislators are less likely to be familiar to their constituents. Also, junior legislators may have neither the relationships with bureaucrats nor the needed understanding of bureaucratic procedures to help constituents. It takes time to learn how to solve constituents' problems, and more senior legislators should find it easier to be helpful. Not only might term-limited legislators have less time to develop contacts to engage in service representation, but they might also have less incentive to do so. As noted in previous chapters, term-limited legislators will only reap the electoral and policy benefits of having good relations with constituents for a relatively short period of time. Research too finds term-limited legislators spend less time on constituent service than non-term-limited legislators (Carey et al. 2006; Powell, Niemi, and Smith 2007).

The features that increase the dyadic relationship between legislators and constituents are likely to have mixed or muted effects. First, how district magnitude affects service is hard to predict a priori. On the one hand, MMDs may decrease the value legislators see in service representation, since other legislators from the district can free-ride on their work. Voters are likely to improve their views of their legislative delegation if just one legislator helps them with a request. A counter to this argument, however, is that these legislators may have to work harder to get any benefit from service and will work harder at service. The limited literature on the effects of district magnitude on constituent service, finds legislators in MMDs spend more time working on service than those in SMDs (Freeman and Richardson 1996). The effects of district magnitude on legislators' incentives to be responsive too were weak and mixed. Overall then the effects of district magnitude are expected to be weak.

The effects of district size may be clearer. Legislators in small districts likely have greater incentives and ability to engage in service representation. By helping one constituent, they are helping a larger share of their district. And research in a variety of settings finds district size related to service representation. State legislators representing smaller populations spend more time on casework (Ellickson and Whistler 2001). Senators in smaller states are more likely to engage in casework (Johannes 1980). And legislators in Canada and Australia who represent smaller districts (less than 250,000) spend more time on casework than those with larger districts (Halligan et al. 1988).

The effects of election laws on service representation too may be muted and or mixed. Many of the electoral features had mixed effects on legislators' incentives (vulnerability, ambition, and orientation). Also the effects of tough election laws on the value of and ability of legislators to engage in service representation is mixed. On one hand, they offer legislators a way to reach voters and improve reelection prospects (Serra and Moon 1994; Box-Steffensmeier et al. 2003). Legislators too believe that constituency service helps with reelection (Rosenthal 2004, 33). As such, tough campaign laws may increase the electoral value of service representation. For example, legislators who live in states that limit campaign contribution sources or spending may feel a greater need to use casework as a way to reach voters since these laws may limit their ability to campaign. These legislators are limited in their campaign activities and are likely to use the perks of the office to help reach constituents or voters. On the other hand, laws which make campaigning hard also tend to decrease competition which in turn may decrease the electoral need for casework. Also tough election laws may decrease the ability of legislators to work on service representation. Electoral features which make campaigning tasks more difficult may increase the effort legislators need to expend to get reelected and, as a result, may distract them from representational activities. In other words, legislators in these situations may be too busy campaigning to focus on service representation.

Based on the above, the following features are expected to enhance service representation: professionalism (resources and capacity), smaller constituencies, lack of term limits, and short terms. The expectations concerning district magnitude and the other electoral laws are not clear. By making reaching constituents more difficult MMDs may force legislators to be more active, and easy electoral situations may decrease the need to engage in service representation as a means to reach votes but tough electoral situations may divert legislators away from representation.

To measure service representation, respondents were asked: "When the legislature is in session approximately how many hours a week, on average, do you spend on the following activities? If zero leave blank." One of the activities was "Helping constituents with problems with the government."[1] In answering these questions, respondents were given the following options: 1–4 hours (coded 1), 5–8 (coded 2), 9–16 (coded 3), or more than 16 hours (coded 4). Legislators indicating they spend no time helping constituents were coded 0. Legislators were also asked: "When the legislature is NOT in session approximately how many hours a week, on average, do you spend on the following activities? If zero leave blank." They were then given the same options to indicate how much time they spent helping constituents with problems. The means for the variables hovered around 2, indicating fairly high levels of service representation. I used the same control variables used to estimate symbolic representation, but additionally controlled for the amount of contact between legislators and constituents. To do so, I used the index created by combining the symbolic representation variables. Since these data are ordinal I used ordered logistic to estimate the effects of the features on service representation.

The models generally performed well (see table 7.1). Some of the professional features were significantly related to greater service representation. Although relationships between service and the number of legislators were quite small, legislators in chambers with strong leadership spent more time on service, particularly after the session ended. Those in chambers with strong leadership (one standard deviation above the mean) had a 0.19 probability of working 1–4 hours during the session on service compared to 0.33 for those in chambers with weak leaders (one standard deviation below the mean). The probabilities of working more than 16 hours were 0.05 and 0.02, respectively. Legislators in chambers with strong committees engaged in slightly more service, but the relationships were not significant. The effects of resources were more clearly and consistently positive. Legislators with budgets and full-time positions spent significantly more time on service representation after the session ended. Those with budgets had a 0.20 probability of working 1–4 hours during the session while the probability was 0.31 for those without

Table 7.1. Institutional Effects on Service Representation

Variable	*Time In-Session*	*Time Out-of-Session*
Leadership strength	0.06 (0.04)	0.12 (0.04)***
Committee strength	0.04 (0.06)	0.08 (0.06)
Chamber size	0.006 (0.004)	0.000 (0.004)
Office budget	0.19 (0.26)	0.57 (0.26)**
Staff	0.25 (0.24)	–0.28 (0.24)
Full-time	0.17 (0.08)**	0.16 (0.08)*
Contribution limits	0.04 (0.12)	–0.01 (0.12)
Term limits	–0.60 (0.31)*	0.10 (0.31)
District size	–0.001 (0.001)	–0.002 (0.001)*
District magnitude	–0.86 (0.39)**	–0.12 (0.38)
Spending limits	0.11 (0.54)	0.06 (0.56)
Term length	0.19 (0.16)	0.40 (0.16)**
Community principles	–0.14 (0.14)	–0.14 (0.15)
Pro-incumbent principles	0.30 (0.20)	–0.04 (0.21)
Petition requirement	–0.11 (0.33)	–0.41 (0.33)
Filing fee	–0.001 (0.000)***	0.000 (0.000)
Vote gap	0.006 (0.002)**	0.004 (0.002)
Reelection rate	–5.18 (3.83)	–5.48 (3.95)
Progressive ambition	–0.56 (0.28)**	–0.22 (0.22)
Static ambition	–0.37 (0.22)*	–0.18 (0.27)
Trustee	0.04 (0.06)	–0.02 (0.06)
State orientation	–0.09 (0.07)	–0.12 (0.07)**
Voter orientation	–0.09 (0.06)	–0.07 (0.06)
Surrogate	–0.04 (0.19)	0.18 (0.18)
Seniority	0.03 (0.01)**	0.03 (0.01)*
Rural	0.000 (0.003)	0.006 (0.003)*
Time not in-session	0.003 (0.007)	0.05 (0.01)***
Party ID	0.08 (0.18)	–0.26 (0.18)
Southern states	–0.30 (0.50)	0.79 (0.51)
Gone	0.49 (0.30)	0.58 (0.30)*
Legislator education	–0.13 (0.13)	–0.09 (0.13)
District education	–0.02 (0.01)*	–0.01 (0.01)
Previous experience	–0.11 (0.18)	–0.22 (0.18)
Female	0.14 (0.25)	0.20 (0.24)
Party strength	–0.02 (0.02)	–0.003 (0.015)
Contact	0.86 (0.07)***	0.86 (0.07)***
Cut 1	–7.02	–3.41
Cut 2	–1.47	1.14
Cut 3	0.71	3.11
Cut 4	2.35	5.50
Pseudo R^2	0.23	0.29
Chi^2 (DF)	345.29 (36)***	463.65 (36)***
Log likelihood	–563.45	–566.95
N	563	564

*<= 0.10; **<= 0.05; ***<= 0.01 (using a two tailed test). Description of variables is in text.

office budgets. The probabilities were 0.05 and 0.03 for working more than 16 hours a week. Legislators with full-time positions (one standard deviation above the mean) had a 0.20 probability of working 1–4 hours on service during the session and 0.27 after the session. For those with more part-time positions (one standard deviation below the mean) the probabilities were 0.32 and 0.45, respectively. When looking at working more than 16 hours on service the probability for those with full-time positions was 0.05 in session and 0.06 after the session. For those with part-time jobs the probabilities were 0.03 for both time periods. Although office budgets and full-time work were associated with legislators engaging in service representation, legislators with staff did not differ from those without in the time they spent on it. Part of the reason for this is that legislators with staff used staff to engage in service representation. The survey asked legislators to estimate the number of hours their staff spent doing different tasks while in-session using the same 0–4 scale used to measure service. The average score was 2.82 (SD = 1.09) and the most common response was 4, indicating most personal staff spent more time doing casework than did legislators. As a consequence, constituents whose legislator has staff get more service representation from their legislator's office. The legislator does roughly equal amount of service as those without staff but then the staff does as much as the member.

The findings offer some support for the expectation concerning term limits. Although term-limited legislators did not differ from non-term-limited legislators in service representation after the session ended, they engaged in significantly less during the session. Term-limited legislators had a 0.43 probability of working 1–4 hours during the session compared to 0.29 for those not term-limited. The probabilities for working more than 16 hours were 0.03 and 0.05, respectively. This supports the view of term-limited legislators as somewhat disengaged from the district. One might argue that this indicates that term-limited legislators spend more time making laws. But the correlation between the legislating scale used in chapter 5 and term limits was only 0.03 ($p = 0.42$).

There was mixed evidence that features affecting the dyadic relationship increased service representation. Legislators in MMDs were less likely to spend time on service, not more. Legislators in MMDs had a 0.53 probability of working 1–4 hours on service compared to 0.32 for those in SMDs. When looking at the probability of working more than 16 hours the probabilities were 0.02 and 0.04, respectively. When the legislature was not in-session, the difference was quite small. Legislators with smaller constituencies spent at least somewhat more time on service when the session was over. Legislators representing 175,000 constituents had a 0.30 probability of working 1–4 hours and those with 25,000 constituents 0.23. The probabilities for working more than 16 hours were 0.03 and 0.04, respectively.

As was anticipated, electoral laws had little effect on service representation. Only two features had significant effects. Legislators in states with greater filing fees, which increase incumbent security and make campaigning more costly, offered less service representation during the session. The probability of a legislator who has no filing fee working 1–4 hours was 0.30 compared to 0.42 for a legislator with a $500 fee. The probabilities were 0.05 and 0.03 for working 16 hours. Term length was also related to service, legislators with longer terms spent more time on it after the session. A legislator with a two-year term had a 0.31 probability of working 1–4 hours after the session compared to 0.17 for a legislator with four-year terms. When looking at working 16 hours on casework the probabilities were 0.03 and 0.06, respectively. It may be that since most legislators with two-year terms were up for reelection during the year of the survey, they spent less time on service and more on symbolic representation and campaigning. This suggests that these features increased legislators' incentive but, at the same time, decreased their ability to work on service representation.

The results concerning some of the control variables warrant mentioning. As one might expect, those who engaged in more symbolic representation spent more time on service representation. In addition, those who had tougher elections (vote gap), represented rural districts, worked more hours out-of-session, and had more seniority engaged in more service representation. Those with state orientation spent less time on service than those with a district orientation. Surprisingly, those with discrete ambition and those leaving office spent more time on service. It may be that since they are less concerned about reelection, they have more time to engage in these activities.

To summarize, the findings support the general expectation that legislators who are able and have incentives to engage in more service representation do so. Legislators with the resources and capacity to engage in service spend more time on it. Legislators with strong leadership, office budgets, and full-time positions increase their service representation. Also, the value of the work (term limits) was likewise related to the amount of time legislators spent on service representation. However, the findings offer little support for the idea that the features thought to affect electability, such as redistricting principles and campaign funding laws, increase service representation. They are likely to have limited effects since they have mixed effects on incentives and may make it more difficult to campaign.

Interactions

So far I have examined the main effects of the institutional features, that is, I assumed that the effects of each feature would be independent of context: an assumption that may not be wholly true. Here I examine how the effects of legislative resources needed to respond to constituents' demands are affected by factors likely to affect legislators' incentive to respond to constituents. The effects of resources are expected to be greater when accompanied by features that increase, and smaller when accompanied by features that decrease the incentives to be responsive. It may be that the interactions are most noticeable with service representation. Service requires legislators to do something that involves resources and is not an automatic part of the legislative function. The importance of incentives to work in areas that are a less critical part of the job are likely to be more important than in other areas.

In order to test for the interaction of resources and incentives it is helpful to create multiplicative interaction variables. To do so, I multiply Squire's 2007 measure of professionalism by specific institutional features and individual characteristics found to affect service representation. I use the professionalism index in lieu of each of the three resource variables for simplicity; it significantly reduces the number of equations. Also, although the resource variables did not always have the same effect on aspects of representation, resources more uniformly increased service representation.

The factors that might depress the value of resources are those that decreased the time legislators spent on service representation. There were four such features. Term-limited legislators spent less time engaged in service representation during the legislative session. Legislators with shorter terms and those serving MMDs spent less time on service. Finally, legislators in states with filing fees for ballot access, which tend to make legislators safer, were associated with lower levels of service representation. Additionally, legislator's role orientations affected their levels of service representation.

These findings (not shown) offer just modest support for the expectation that features interact to affect representation. First, the interaction variables between resources and term limits failed to have any significant effects on service representation; likewise, the interaction variables for filing fees, district magnitude and role orientation did not have any significant effect. However, there was some evidence that legislators with longer terms and resources were more likely to engage in service representation than those without resources and short terms. Both coefficients for the interaction variables were positive and one (when the session was over) was statistically significant.

Comparing Service and Symbolic Representation

Comparing these findings to those in chapter 5 brings out the similarities and differences between symbolic and service representation. In many ways these forms of representation were similar: They involved direct contact between legislators and at least some of their constituents, they both were measured by time, and they both require some resources. As such, professionalism (capacity and resources) increased the time legislators spend on these activities. Professionalism, also according to chapter 5, generally increased the types of activities legislators use for symbolic representation. Additionally, ballot access requirements (petition and/or filing fees) depressed legislators' engagement in these forms of representation. Although term limits had nominal effects on the amount of time legislators' spent on symbolic representation, they decreased the time legislators spent on service representation and the modes of symbolic representation. There were also some features that affected neither, for example, spending limits and redistricting principles. And some features increased symbolic and decreased service representation, or vice versa. Large districts increased symbolic representation (although the coefficients did not quite reach statistical significance) and depressed service representation. It is likely that legislators can reach a large number of constituents through symbolic representation but reach relatively few with service representation. Thus those who need to reach a large number of constituents specialize in symbolic and others service representations. Long terms depressed symbolic representation and increased service representation. This may be a by-product of those with four-year terms being less likely to be up for reelection in the year of the survey. They simply had more time for service representation since they were not campaigning. Legislators with MMDs generally spent less time on service and symbolic representation, except after the session they spent less time on symbolic representation.

Another similarity between the two types of representation is that in both cases there were few interactions between resources and incentives. This suggests that legislators use their available resources to represent their constituents regardless of extra incentives. As Rosenthal (1998) and others have noted, legislators as a rule believe they have a responsibility to represent constituents and will work to do so.

POLICY REPRESENTATION

One of the topics dominating research on representation in legislatures concerns the degree to which legislators act in accordance with the constituents' interests. While these studies vary in the degree to which they find congruence (Miller and Stokes 1963; Erikson 1978; Herrera, Herrera, and Smith 1992; Hill and Hurley 1999), I am less interested in general levels of policy representation and more interested in whether institutional features affect the degree to which legislators' work on constituents' interests.

The analysis of congruence is best done examining one issue at a time (Jewell 1982, chapter 5). It is of course possible to examine general ideological tendency. That is, one could examine the degree to which legislators of liberal constituencies support liberal policies. But general ideology is so broad that a legislator could support the general ideological preference but differ on most specific policies. In this section I examine the policy area of gay, lesbian, and bisexual (GLB)[2] rights. This is done in large part because there is the measure of constituent preferences noted in chapter 6. That is, I can use district votes on same-sex marriage ballot items as an indicator of district preferences. It is also a good policy to examine because it is salient and visible to constituents. It is also a moralistic issue so constituents are likely to feel qualified to have an opinion. There are, of course, real limits to using a measure of majoritarian preferences for interests on what is essentially a civil rights matter. But every issue and measure has it limitations, and thus I encourage other projects to examine other issue areas.

An advantage to GLB rights is that it is also a policy where legislators' and constituents' preferences could differ. Jewell (1982, chapter 5) has indicated that conflict between legislators' and constituents' preferences is most likely to occur when a policy debate is new. And, with the exception of some action in the early 1970s, gay rights issues have fairly recently made it to the agenda of state legislatures. Legislative activity in GLB rights began in earnest after the Hawaiian Supreme Court ruled in 1993 that denying gay and lesbian couples the right to marry violated the state's constitution. Thus constituents should have a preference, and legislators should have some idea of constituent preferences and still could differ from constituents in those preferences.

Given the general difficulty that legislators can have in knowing constituent preferences, features that make it easier for legislators to know their constituents' interest should increase the congruence between legislators' behavior and constituents' preferences. One such feature is likely size. Smaller constituencies are more homogeneous and simply have fewer constituents to follow.[3] Legislators with smaller districts were also more electorally vulnerable and more likely to have progressive ambition, which should increase responsiveness. Indeed, research on the Senate finds that there is higher congruency in more homogeneous states (Bailey and Brady 1998). Variation in district magnitude may also offer unique challenges, opportunities, and incentives for policy representation, but I was not able to test for these due to methodological issues.[4]

Legislative professionalism may also make it easier for legislators to work on behalf of constituents' interests. They have more time, staff, and money to determine what their constituents' interests are and have the legislative capacity to do so. They may also have greater motivation to work for their constituents. As noted earlier, although they are not more electorally vulnerable, legislators in professional legislatures have greater interest in keeping their job and being reelected. Generally, too, they had role orientations and ambitions likely to lead to responsiveness. All this can conspire to increase the congruence between constituent preferences and legislator behavior.

Term limits may decrease the ability and willingness of legislators to work on behalf of constituents. Assuming term-limited legislators are leaving politics when they reach their limits (see chapter 3), term limits should weaken the electoral connection, thus freeing legislators to behave as they will. Legislators unconcerned about reelection will not feel a need to vote with constituents to gain votes. This may be exacerbated if term-limited legislators are more ideological, which research suggests that they are (Herrick and Thomas 2005; Herrick and Fisher 2007, chapter 4).

The effects of electoral features are likely to be mixed and/or muted. Although campaigning may not have the same distracting effect on policy representation as it does on symbolic or service representation, the effects of tough election laws generally did not result in a pattern of increased or decreased responsiveness. Spending limits increased vulnerability and district orientations, which should increase responsiveness, but also increased discrete ambition, which should decrease responsiveness. Pro-incumbent principles could increase responsiveness because they are associated with greater vulnerability and progressive ambition but could decrease it since it is also associated with state role orientations. And filing fees were not associated with any of the incentives. A few electoral features had more consistent effects on incentives. Campaign contribution limits should decrease responsiveness, as they were associated with decreased vulnerability and discrete ambition. Petition requirement may also be associated with less congruence. Legislators in states with petition requirements were less vulnerable and more likely to have discrete ambition. Short terms should increase responsiveness since they increase the likelihood legislators have progressive ambition and a delegate role orientation. Legislators with short terms are expected to have greater congruence as they are constantly up for reelection. Thus voters do not have time to forget unpopular behaviors early in a term. Kuklinski's (1978) examination of California legislators find that lower house members with their shorter terms were more likely to follow the wishes of constituents than were senators. Research on the U.S. Senate too finds that senators with their six-year terms were more likely to follow constituent wishes as their elections approach (Amacher and Boyes 1978). Community principles may also be associated with greater congruence. Not only may it be easier if these districts are more homogeneous but they were also associated with district orientations.

The features likely to increase policy representation are small districts, professional chambers (resources and capacity), no term limits, short terms, community principles, and few campaign funding limits. The other features are unlikely to have significant effects.

Much of the research on policy representation has examined roll-call voting: by taking an issue estimating the district's interests and then seeing if district interest is related to how legislators vote on legislation concerning that interest. However, it is difficult to find comparable bills across states. Additionally, roll call votes may have less affect on policy outcomes since they occur late in the process after much of the bargaining has taken place. Instead of examining roll call votes I examine bill cosponsorships. Swers (2002) has defined cosponsorships as loud voting, because it is a way of indicating intensity and a true preference on a policy area. To determine bill cosponsorships on gay rights issues, I use a listing of legislation concerning sexual orientation in each state legislature from the Human Rights Campaign Foundation publications for 2007 and 2008. From this list I removed bills that I considered too broad; for example, anti-bullying or hate crime bills that did not include sexual orientation in a list of protected groups. I then used state legislative web pages to determine whether each legislator had cosponsored any of these bills. The bills included both pro- and anti-GLB rights bills. However, there were very few anti-GLB bills and only about 2 percent of the legislators had cosponsored anti-GLB rights bills. Thus I only examine pro-GLB rights bills. Most (85 percent) of the legislators did not cosponsor any pro-GLB bills, 9 percent cosponsored one, 2.5 percent cosponsored two, 2 percent cosponsored three, 1 percent cosponsored four, and one sole legislator cosponsored five. Since the dependent variable was count data, I used negative binomial regression. Since these coefficients are difficult to interpret, I will also report the incidence rate ratios (IRR).

To measure each district's position on same-sex marriage, I use the district vote on the ballot items discussed in chapter 6. I examined whether legislators' views of the districts' position on same-sex marriage or the district vote was more strongly related to cosponsoring pro-GLB legislation. The findings suggest that district vote had the strongest effect. The correlations between legislators' estimate of the vote and cosponsorship was –0.21 ($p = 0.00$), the correlation between legislators' relative estimate (district's support compared to state's support) was –0.24 ($p = 0.00$). And the correlation between district vote and cosponsorship was –0.33 ($p = 0.00$).

To estimate whether legislative features affect policy representation; I created a series of multiplicative interaction variables by multiplying each feature's variable by the district vote on same-sex marriage. I then regressed these variables one at a time on the cosponsorship variable. The strength of this relationship indicates how well district preferences matched legislative behavior under a particular condition. Since the measure of the district's preference indicated opposition to GLB rights and cosponsoring a pro-GLB bill indicated support of GLB rights, the interaction variable would be negative if the feature increased policy representation. In conducting the analysis I controlled for legislators' characteristics that likely would affect legislators' support for GLB rights: legislator ideology,[5] gender, age, and seniority. I also controlled for the number of GLB bills introduced, minority party strength, southern states, and if legislator had left the chamber. I did remove legislators from Idaho since they do not cosponsor legislation.

The results, reported in table 7.2, indicate that professionalism had little positive effect on congruence. Although none of the resource variables reached normal levels of statistical significance, the interaction variable measuring the interaction with staff neared statistical significance and was negative. This offers some modest support for the idea that legislators with staff offer more policy representation than those without staff. The results also indicated that increased capacity does not enhance congruence. Two capacity variables reached normal levels of statistical significance but indicated that legislators in chambers with strong committees and fewer members had lower levels of congruence. The IRR for the interaction was 1.84 (range 0.98–10.14); it was 0.67 for the committee variable and 0.00001 for marriage vote variable. It may be that strong committees get legislators to look beyond district preferences. Also, those in small chambers (more capacity) offered less policy support. The IRR was 0.03 for the interaction variable (range 6.62–160.45).

Constituencies that likely make it easier for legislators to offer policy representation have higher levels of congruence. Legislators with small constituencies offered more policy representation. The IRR for the interaction variable was 1.01 (the district size variable ranges from 6.62–694.28); it was 0.99 for constituent size variable and 0.009 for the vote variable.

The evidence also suggests that elections have little effect on policy representation. The variables measuring the interactions between the vote variable and term length, filing fee, and redistricting principles did not have significant relationships with policy representation. Legislators with contribution limits had somewhat greater policy representation, with the coefficient nearing but not quite reaching normal levels of statistical significance. The IRR for the interaction was 0.33 (range 0–2.44); it was 1.73 for the contribution limit variable and 0.11 for the marriage vote variable. Also legislators in states that required petitions for ballot access (increasing electoral security) offered less policy representation. The IRR for the interaction variables was 11.81 (range 0–0.92); it was 0.25 for the signature variable and 0.01 for the vote variable.

Table 7.2. Institutional Effect on Policy Representation: Bill Cosponsorships

Variable	*Committees*	*Leadership*	*Chamber Size*	*Office Budget*	*Staff*	*Full-time*
District vote	−11.27 (3.83)***	−4.19 (2.25)***	−.78 (1.68)	−3.85 (1.20)***	−2.02 (1.39)	−3.87 (0.77)***
Committee strength	−0.37 (.17)**					
Leadership strength		−0.20 (.21)				
Chamber size			0.02 (0.01)			
Office budget				−421 (0.90)		
Staff					1.58 (1.03)	
Full-time						−0.07 (0.16)
Interaction	0.58 (0.28)**	0.12 (0.33)	−0.03 (0.02)*	56 (1.45)	−1.85 (1.60)	0.43 (0.26)
Constant	7.04***	3.46*	0.17	2.16*	0.89	2.10**
Pseudo R^2	0.23	0.23	0.23	0.22	0.23	0.25
Log likelihood	−278.79	−278.81	−279.78	−281.37	−279.37	−272.99
Chi^2 (11)	166.52***	166.48***	164.54***	161.36***	165.35 ***	178.12***
N	592	592	592	592	592	592

Variable	*Term Limits*	*Term Length*	*Contribution*	*District Size*
District vote	−2.49 (.95)***	−4.20 (2.09)**	−2.37 (1.00)**	−4.84 (.89)***
Term limits	1.53 (.90)*			
Term length		.17 (.46)		
Contribution limits			.50 (.41)	
District size				−.006 (.002)**
Interaction	−2.08 (1.45)	.20 (.73)	−1.01 (.68)	.011 (.004)***
Constant	.91 (1.14)	1.50	1.36	2.58 **
Pseudo R^2	.23	.23	.23	.23
Log likelihood	−279.72	−278.78	−279.97	−278.13
Chi^2 (11)	164.66***	166.55 ***	164.15***	167.84***
N	592	592	592	592

Variable	*Community*	*Pro-Incumbent*	*Petition*	*Filing Fee*	*Trustee*	*State*
District Vote	–4.75 (1.99)**	–2.62 (1.39)*	–4.41 (.91)***	–4.15 (.90)***	–6.37 (1.71)***	–5.99 (1.91)***
Community principle	–.27 (.51)					
Pro-incumbent principle		.85 (.63)				
Petition requirement			–1.47 (.85)*			
Filing fee				–.001 (.001)		
Trustee					–.49 (.26)*	
State orientation						–.44 (.31)
Interaction	.60 (.80)	–.60 (.90)	2.84 (1.42)**	.002 (.002)	.73 (.42)*	.68 (.50)
Constant	2.52*	1.05	2.49**	2.37**	3.54 **	3.58**
R^2	.22	.23	.23	.22	.23	.23
Log likelihood	–280.84	–278.61	–279.42	–280.68	–268.52	–275.95
Chi^2 (DF = 11)	162.422***	166.88***	165.25***	162.74***	160.82***	163.79***
N	592	592	592	592	572	580

* <= 0.10; ** <= 0.05; *** <= 0.01 (using a two-tailed test).
Description of variables is in text.

Term-limited legislators offer their constituents somewhat more policy representation. The interaction coefficient had a negative relationship that neared normal levels of statistical significance. This earlier finding is interesting given the findings that term-limited legislators are generally less engaged with constituents. Apparently, term-limited legislators offer more policy representation without having a clear picture of constituent preferences. This implies that term-limited legislators offer policy representation by acting as trustees.

Although not the topic here, it should be noted that I examined interaction coefficients for ambition (not shown) and role orientation. There was no evidence that legislators' ambition affected their policy representation, but there was some evidence that legislators with state and trustee orientation offered less policy representation. The coefficient was statistically significant for trustees and neared significance for state orientated legislators.

Given the limitations of examining just one policy area, I wanted to try to replicate these findings. To replicate these findings, I examine legislators' cosponsorship of English-only legislation. These pieces of legislation include bills and resolutions that officially designate English as the only language or require governmental documents or examinations to be in English. To determine which legislators had cosponsored such legislation, I examined legislative web pages for 2007–2008 sessions of state legislators. Several states (Arizona, Arkansas, California, Florida, North Dakota, South Dakota, Texas, and Utah) did not have any such legislation and legislators from these states were not examined. Also legislators from Idaho were not examined since they do not cosponsor legislation. I did not have a measure of district preferences but did have a measure of legislators' perceptions of the district preference. The question read, "Compared to the voters in the rest of your state, the voters in your district are ________ supportive of supportive of English-only laws." The options were: significantly more (coded 1), somewhat more, about as, somewhat less, and significantly less (coded 5). Again, interaction variables were created and control variables likely to affect legislators' work on English-only legislation were controlled.

These findings (not shown) generally reinforce the previous findings. The conclusions were the same concerning leadership, office budgets, constituency size, term length, contribution limits, community principles, pro-incumbent principle, filing fee, and state orientation. They also tended to support, albeit with weaker findings, those concerning full-time status, term limits, and signature requirements. The coefficients for three variables changed direction but were not significant: committees, staff, and pro-incumbent principles. Thus the results concerning the relationships of these features are suspect.

CONCLUSION

As with the preceding chapters this chapter demonstrates that institutional features affect how legislators represent their constituents. Several of the institutional features affected service representation: leadership strength, office budgets, full-time positions, term limits, term length, district magnitude, and filing fees. Policy representation was enhanced by small constituencies, weak leaders, contribution limits, and somewhat by staff and term limits. The findings indicate that electoral features have fewer significant effects on substantive representation than resources. This is likely the result of legislators being predisposed to offer high levels of policy representation (Rosenthal 1998). This may be particularly true on the issues examined, same-sex marriage, and English-only laws, on which the public tends to have strong positions. The culture of representation and the presence of elections are sufficient to produce incentives for substantive representation. The findings with regard to policy representation need to be interpreted with a degree of caution since only civil rights policies were examined.

NOTES

1. As with the measures of symbolic representation these questions were modeled after, but are not identical to those used in the 2002 Survey of State Legislators (Carey et al. 2002).

2. It is more common to see the abbreviation GLBT or LGBT. However, I left off the T, which stands for transgender because the measures do not directly affect transgender rights.

3. I do not have the best data to test for the relationship between homogeneity and district size. But district size was related to the district ideological heterogeneity variable ($r = 0.13$, $p = 0.03$) and to a measure of racial homogeneity ($r = -0.25$, $p = 0.00$). Racial homogeneity was measured by folding the percent of district that was black and Latino. Thus large scores indicate racial homogeneity.

4. I considered examining district magnitude but the equation produced very high standard errors when it was in the equation.

5. To increase the number of cases, I used mean substitution for legislators' ideology.

8

Conclusion

> I learned from a veteran legislator that: A successful politician is in front of and behind her constituents all times!

The goal of this book was to estimate the effects of institutional design on how state legislators represent their constituents. The findings indicate that institutional design can affect legislators' incentives to be sensitive to constituents (electoral accountability, representational role orientation, and political ambition); their symbolic, service, and policy representation; and the accuracy of legislators' perceptions of their district, and the sources of information legislators use to make decisions. Although some features (particularly those related to professionalism) had stronger effects than others and some aspects of representation were more affected by institutional features than others, institutional design does affect representation. As a general rule legislators in institutions that provide resources for or otherwise enable legislators to engage in certain activities are more likely to engage in those activities, and legislators with incentives to engage in certain activities are more likely to engage in those activities. However, the effects of many features, particularly electoral features, had conflicting effects on legislators' incentives and abilities to be responsive, and as a result had little effect on representation. In the previous chapters I examined how several legislative features affected legislators' representational styles. Below I offer a quick summary.

Accountability: Legislators were less electorally secure if they

1. were in less professionalized chambers (Except for staff and committee strength),
2. served MMDs,

3. had longer terms,
4. had less populous districts,
5. had campaign spending limits but not contribution limits,
6. were in states with pro-incumbent redistricting principles (this is likely because vulnerability increased the use of pro-incumbent principles), and
7. lacked petition requirements for ballot access.

Political ambition: Legislators' ambitions were affected by

1. their chambers' leadership strength and size,
2. the degree to which their job was full-time,
3. district magnitude,
4. district size,
5. term limits,
6. their states' laws concerning campaign funding,
7. term length,
8. pro-incumbent redistricting principles, and
9. petition requirements for ballot access.

Most of these increased the likelihood legislators had discrete ambition.

Role orientations: Legislators' role orientations were affected by

1. their chamber's leadership strength, committee strength, and size,
2. office budgets and staff,
3. term limits,
4. term length,
5. state laws concerning campaign funding,
6. redistricting principles, and
7. filing fees for ballot access.

Symbolic representation: Legislators spent more time on symbolic representation if they

1. were in chambers with strong leaders, weak committees,
2. greater resources,
3. represented populous districts,
4. had longer terms,
5. were in states with limited campaign contributions but not spending limits, and
6. did not have ballot access laws.

Legislators with resources also engaged in more modes of symbolic representation, and those with term limits engaged in fewer. Those with populous districts also specialized in modes of contact that reached larger numbers of people.

Sources of information: The sources of information legislators used in making decisions were related to

1. the strength of leaders and committees,
2. whether legislators had office budgets and staff,
3. their districts' magnitude,
4. term limits,
5. spending limits, and
6. whether their states had community redistricting principles.

One of the key findings was that office budgets, community principles and term limits produced legislators who were independent in their decision making and relied less on all sources of information.

Accuracy of legislators' perceptions: The accuracy of legislators' perceptions was hampered by

1. office budgets,
2. full-time positions,
3. not having staff (mixed results),
4. populous districts,
5. term limits,
6. redistricting principles, and
7. ballot access laws (mixed results).

Service representation: Legislators working under the following conditions spent more time on service representation:

1. strong leaders,
2. greater resources,
3. SMDs,
4. populous districts,
5. no term limits,
6. longer term lengths, and
7. filing fees.

Policy representation: Legislators working under the following conditions offered their constituents more policy representation:

1. weak committees,
2. large chambers,
3. full-time status and to a lesser extent staff,
4. populous districts,
5. term limits,
6. campaign contribution limits, and
7. no petition requirements for ballot access.

Democratic theory suggests that elections are critical to having legislators responsive and responsible to their constituents. Yet the findings here suggest that election laws and vulnerability have modest effects on representation. Too much should not be made of this. First, vulnerability (measured by individual vote gaps and reelection rates) has some significant effects on representation. Additionally, it is likely that legislators are all running scared, to quote Jacobson. Just the presence of an election is enough to keep legislators interested in serving their constituents. Second, many of the electoral features had conflicting effects on legislators' incentives and ability to be responsive. For example, while features that make reelection tough increase some of legislators' incentives to be responsive, they decrease others and they may also make legislators spend more time campaigning distracting them from active forms of representation.

Next, I will examine each feature discussed in the book and discuss how it affected representation. Table 8.1 gives a brief description of the effects of each feature on different aspects of representation. This provides a somewhat different perspective on the issue at hand. This chapter ends with some overall conclusions from this project.

PROFESSIONALISM

Professionalism refers to a set of changes made to state legislatures during the 1960s and 1970s designed to improve their ability to meet the demands and challenges of the times. The reforms were of two general types: capacity and resources. Capacity refers to changes in the organization of the chambers that increase efficiency, such as strengthening committees, strengthening leadership, and decreasing the size of the chambers. The resources included giving legislators' an office budget, staff, and full-time salaries. Legislatures varied in how they reformed themselves, and some have subsequently weakened these reforms. One of the conclusions of this project is that professionalism did not have uniform effects. While one specific reform might expand an aspect of representation, another reform might depress it. These results bring into question the value of treating professionalism as a single factor, but do indicate that the reforms had significant effects on representation. Another general conclusion is that increased resources increased levels of representation, but capacity did not. Below, I discuss how changes in capacity and resources affected representation.

Capacity, as studied here, includes strong leadership, strong committees and small chambers. The results suggest that capacity, like professionalism, is not a single legislative feature but is made up of different parts that have

Table 8.1. Summary of Significant Effects

	Leadership Strength	*Committee Strength*	*Number of Legislators*	*Office Budget*	*Staff*	*Full-time*
Candidate emergence	No effect	No effect	No effect	Fewer challengers	No effect	Lower quality of challenger
Accountability/ Electoral security	More secure, but lower rates	No effect	More secure	More secure	No effect	Higher reelection rates
Ambition	More progressive, less discrete	No effect	More discrete	No effect	No effect	More progressive, less discrete
Role orientation	Less surrogate, more voter than district	Less surrogate	More delegate and district than state	More trustee than delegate and more district than state, and more district than voter	More delegate than trustee, more district than state	No effect
Symbolic representation	More out-of-session	Less in-session	No effect	More	No effect, but staff spends time on contact	More out-of-session
Modes of contact	Less likely newsletter	Less likely newsletter	More newsletter, less e-contact	More newsletter	More all, at least somewhat	More newsletter and meetings
Use of information	More constituents	More all	No effect	Less all	More groups	No effect
Perceptual accuracy	No effect	No effect	No effect	Somewhat less	Mixed	Somewhat less
Service Representation	More	No effect	No effect	More casework, out-of-session	No effect, but staff does much casework	More casework
Policy representation	No effect	Less	More	No effect	Somewhat more	Somewhat less

(*continued*)

Table 8.1. (*continued*)

	District Magnitude	*District size*	*Term Limits*	*Term Length*	*Spending Limits*	*Contribution Limits*
Candidate emergence	No effect	No effect	No effect	No effect	Higher quality challenge	Somewhat lower quality
Accountability/ Electoral security	Less secure	More secure	No effect	Lower reelection rates	Less secure	More secure
Ambition	Somewhat less discrete	More progressive	More discrete	More discrete/ less progressive	More discrete	More discrete
Role orientation	No effect	No effect	Less voter more district, more surrogate	Less trustee	More district than state, surrogate	Less surrogate
Symbolic representation	Somewhat less time—in-session, more out-of-session	More	No effects	Less	Less—out-of-session	Less—out-of-session
Modes of contact	Somewhat more e-contact	More newsletter	Less newsletter, e-contact	Less all	No effect	Somewhat fewer meetings
Use of information	More lawmaker	No effect	Less all	No effect	Generally, less	No effect
Perceptual accuracy	No effect	Somewhat less accurate	Somewhat less accurate	No effect	No effect	No effect
Service representation	Less	Less	Less—in session	More	No effect	No effect
Policy representation	NA	Less	Somewhat more	No effect	NA	Somewhat more

	Redistricting Principles	*Ballot Access Laws*	*Electoral Vulnerability*	*Ambition*	*Role Orientation*
Candidate emergence	No effect	No effect			
Accountability/ Electoral security	Pro-incumbent less secure	Petition requirements more secure, but lower rates			
Ambition	Pro-incumbent more progressive	Petitions more discrete	Large vote gap somewhat more progressive		
Role orientation	Community principle more district than state; pro-incumbent more state and less surrogate	Filing fees somewhat more state	No effect	Progressive and static more delegate. Static somewhat less state, surrogate	
Symbolic representation	No effect	Both less	No effect	Static more in-session	Trustee less time–surrogate more
Modes of contact	Community principle more newsletter pro-incumbent less	Petition requirement less on all	Reelection rates less all	Static and progressive generally more all	Voter orientation more meetings
Use of information	Community principles generally less	No effect	Vote gap somewhat more constituent, less lawmakers	Static more groups	Trustee and state less on constituents
Perceptual accuracy	Pro-incumbent somewhat more, community mixed	Both mixed	No effect	No effect	Voter more, surrogate somewhat more
Service	No effect	Filing fee less—in-session	Vote gap more, reelection rate somewhat less	Static less, progressive less	State less when out-of-session
Policy representation	No effect	Petition less	No effect	No effect	Trustee less, state somewhat less

Note: "Somewhat" indicates relationships neared but did not reach normal levels of statistical significance.

different effects on representation. First, I will summarize the relationships of leadership strength with issues of representation. Although legislators in chambers with strong leaders were more electorally secure, they also had more voter orientation and progressive ambition. This suggests that this security is caused by legislators wanting to keep their jobs (or at least a political job) and are likely to be responsive. These legislators appear to be responsive by specializing in service and symbolic representation and by relying on constituent-derived information.

The strength of committees had surprisingly little effect on how legislators' represent their constituents. Legislators in chambers with strong committees did not differ from others in accountability, ambition, or—with the exception of surrogate orientation—role orientation. Given that it did not affect factors thought to affect legislators' incentives to engage in representational actions, it is not surprising that it had little effect on behaviors. There were only four significant effects of committee strength on representation. Legislators in chambers with strong committees spend less time on symbolic representation during the session, presumably because they are busy with committee work. They are also more likely to rely on each source of information. Legislators in chambers with strong committees likely get information from many sources during committee work. Legislators in chambers with strong committees were less likely to send newsletters and offered less policy representation—perhaps because they had more sources of information.

The size of legislative chambers was more strongly related to legislators' incentives than actions. Legislators from larger chambers (less capacity) had more discrete ambition; presumably a legislator in a large chamber has limited influence. These legislators also had less accountability or were more electorally secure. Discrete ambition and electoral security are thought to limit legislators' incentives to cater to constituents. However, legislators in large chambers also had orientations that focused on constituents. They were more delegate and district (less state) in their orientations. Thus these legislators' incentives were not consistently favoring or opposing responsiveness; and consequently the effects on representation were modest. Legislators in large chambers were more likely to send newsletters but engaged in fewer modes of e-contacts. More importantly however, legislators in large chambers offered greater policy representation.

To summarize, each individual aspect of capacity had unique effects on the different aspects of representation. Strong leadership appeared to increase responsiveness, but strong committees and small chambers modestly decreased representation. Oddly the only consistent finding across all three features was that greater capacity decreased the likelihood legislators sent out newsletters.

Resources generally had more positive effects on representation than did capacity, but, again, each resource had its own unique set of effects. Generally the effects of resources on legislators' incentives to be sensitive to constituents, such as accountability, ambition, and role orientation, were mixed or weak. And yet, these resources tended to increase legislators' representational activities. This suggests that legislators want to engage with constituents and do not need additional incentives to do so. This is supported too by the lack of significant interaction effects of resources and incentives on symbolic and service representation. Providing legislators greater resources seem to be enough to increase legislators' representational activities.

First, legislators with office budgets appeared to have mixed incentives to be actively engaged in representing their constituents, but they were more active. Although they were more electorally secure than others: facing fewer challengers and winning with larger margins, this is likely a product, not a cause of legislators' sensitivity to constituents. Also, although they also had more of a trustee orientation they also had more of a district than state orientation. Although their incentives may have been mixed, these legislators spent more time keeping in touch with constituents, and did more casework. Although they offered an active form of representation they may have been less sensitive to policy representation: they did not differ in their level of policy representation, had less accurate views of their constituents, and were more independent from others in gaining information. This presents a picture of legislators who specialize in symbolic and service representation. Specializing in these forms of representation may increase the trust constituents have of their legislator and give legislators leeway in policy making weakening policy representation.

The effects of full-time status paint a somewhat muted picture of the above. Legislators with full-time positions faced lower quality challengers and were more electorally secure, but they also had higher levels of progressive ambition and were not unique in their role orientations. As a consequence, they were active in service and symbolic representation but offered somewhat less policy representation.

The effects of providing legislators with staff were among the most interesting. Although legislators with staff did not differ from those without staff in their electoral security or ambition, they had more of a delegate and district (as opposed to state) orientation. Perhaps because of these orientations, legislators with staff offered somewhat more policy representation, but the findings were mixed. Although legislators with staff did not personally spend more or less time on service and symbolic representation, their staff spent much time on these activities resulting in there being overall more symbolic and service representation for constituents. Additionally, legislators with staff were more likely to send newsletters and used more modes of e-communications. The one caveat to the picture of legislators with staff as the most engaged with constituents is that they were not more or less likely to use constituent-derived information. Instead they relied on groups. These groups could, however, provide good accurate information about constituent preferences/interests. Although not discussed earlier, legislators listen to their staff. On a scale from 1 to 5, the average legislator reported a 2.65 on how heavily they relied on staff for information. There was also some, albeit mixed, evidence that legislators with staff offered more accurate perceptions of their districts' preferences.

To conclude, the professionalism reforms changed legislators' relationships with their constituents. However, different reforms had different effects. While giving legislators personal staff did not affect their accountability, it increased their commitment to constituents and levels of representation. Comparatively, giving legislators office budgets or full-time status decreased their accountability, increased their trustee orientation, and had some negative effects on policy representation, although it increased their symbolic and service representation.

TERM LIMITS

Much has been written about the effects of term limits on legislators' relationships with their constituents. Reformers speculated that term limits would produce a closer relationship between constituents and legislators, a more distant relationship, or have no effect at all. Although, this work finds some evidence of all three perspectives, overall term-limited legislators are less sensitive to constituents. Legislators with term limits do not differ from others in their accountability (electoral security or quality of challenger). They are, however, likely to be less interested in reelection as they have more discrete, without more progressive ambition than non-term-limited legislators. Perhaps as a consequence, they have more of a district and less of a voter orientation, and they are more likely to have a surrogate orientation. There is also evidence that they engage less in symbolic (less like to send newsletters or engage in e-communications) and service representation. The fact that they have less accurate perceptions of the district also indicates some disengagement from the district. Term-limited legislators also are more independent in their sources of information, relying less heavily on each source of information. Given this picture of the independent disengaged term-limited legislator, it is surprising that term-limited legislators nevertheless offered somewhat greater policy representation. Interestingly, these effects are almost the mirror image of the effects of giving legislators' office budgets and making their position full-time. This indicates that what increases service and symbolic representation does not necessarily increase policy representation and visa versa. It is also possible that since only GLB issues were examined to measure policy representation these results may not reflect all or even most policy areas.

FEATURES AFFECTING THE DYADIC RELATIONSHIPS

I examined two features thought to affect the one-on-one relationship between legislators and constituents. Small district magnitude and small district size are expected to build a tighter relationship between legislators and constituents. In MMDs, since there is more than one representative, constituents may not feel the same connection with their representatives, and one legislator may free ride on the work of another. In smaller districts there may be a closer relationship, since legislators and constituents are more likely to know each other on a personal basis and the districts may be more homogenous. This suggests that legislators in SMDs and those with smaller districts would be more sensitive. However, there is another possibility. It may be that legislators in MMDs will work more on representation because it is difficult to be seen and heard and those in small districts will work less since they have an easier job. The results offer at least some support for both ideas; which might explain the fairly anemic results.

Legislators in MMDs were less electorally secure than those in SMDs but were somewhat less likely to have discrete ambition. Thus these legislators should be expected to be hypersensitive to their districts. But there was little evidence of this. Legislators in MMDs did not have unique role orientations and spent less time on service representation. They also spent less time on symbolic representation during the session, but somewhat more when the session was over, and they used somewhat more types of e-communications. Legislators in MMDs also did not differ from those in SMDs in policy representation but relied more heavily on other legislators as a source of information.

Constituency size had mixed effects on legislators' incentives. Legislators from smaller districts may have greater incentives because they are less secure, but legislators from larger districts may likewise have greater incentives because they are more likely to have progressive ambition. The effects of constituent size on representation tend to suggest that small constituencies increase representation. Legislators in smaller districts have more accurate perceptions of their constituents, spent somewhat more time on service representation, and offer somewhat more policy representation than those in large districts. Legislators representing more populous districts were more engaged in symbolic representation. However, since there were more constituents to be reached in larger districts, it was not fully apparent that these legislators in larger districts were indeed more visible than those in smaller districts. Although the picture is not completely clear, district size appears to make substantive representation easier and enhance service and policy representation.

ELECTORAL FEATURES

Electoral features that increased legislators' electoral concerns are often expected to increase legislators' sensitivity to constituents' interests and representation. This is based on the idea that elections motivate legislators to represent constituents in order to keep their job. There is some, albeit limited, support for this expectation. Instead, the findings indicate that features that make campaign tasks difficult can also distract legislators from representing constituents. The fact that electoral features can increase incentives but decrease the ability of legislators to represent constituents may help account for the generally muted effects of electoral features on representation. What can also help account for the weak findings are that many features had mixed effects on incentives. Many laws that increased electoral security also increased discrete ambition. It may be that these laws do make campaigning hard and focus legislators on reelection and that is why they win, but this work is draining and encourages legislators to want to leave.

First, term length had mixed effects on legislators' incentives and representation. Legislators with long terms were associated with lower reelection rates, and had less of a trustee and more of a delegate role orientation, but also had more discrete and less progressive ambition. This suggests that legislators with long terms have mixed incentives to be sensitive to constituents. As a consequence, the effects of term length on representation were mixed. Term length had no significant effects on policy representation, perceptual accuracy, or sources of information used. Those with long terms were more active in service, but those with short terms were more active with symbolic representation. It may be that since those with long terms were less likely to be running for reelection during the year of the survey, they simply had more time to work on service.

Second, the effects of campaign finance laws varied greatly depending on whether the law limited funding sources, or limited spending. A word of caution is needed in this discussion. There were only two states in the population that had spending limits. Thus the results could be biased if these states were otherwise unique in the ways that could affect issues of representation. Having said that, spending limits increased incentives and contribution limits decreased incentives for legislators to be sensitive to constituents. While spending limits increase accountability by encouraging higher quality challengers to emerge and spurring more competitive elections, contribution limits somewhat discouraged quality challengers, and increased legislators' security. Those with spending limits and contribution limits were more likely to have more discrete ambition. Those with spending limits were more district focused and less voter focused, and had a surrogate orientation, while contribution limits minimally affected role orientations. Although the effects of spending limits on presumed incentives would suggest somewhat greater sensitivity to constituents, the effects of spending limits were not so clear. Legislators with spending limits spent somewhat less time on symbolic legislation after the session ended and relied less heavily on each source of information. The effects of contribution limits were also mixed. Although legislators with contribution limits spent less time on symbolic representation after the session ended, they offered somewhat more policy representation. Both types of campaign finance laws can make campaign tasks more difficult and result in less symbolic and service representation.

Third, although redistricting principles had some significant effects on legislators' incentives and representational behaviors, their effects were muted and do not form a nice pattern. Consistent with the notion that redistricting principles increase legislators' sensitivity to constituents, legislators in states with pro-incumbent redistricting plans were more electorally vulnerable and had more progressive ambition. As suggested by Forgette, Garner, and Winkle (2007), it is likely that pro-incumbent redistricting principles are enacted where legislators are more insecure. It is insecurity that causes the redistricting principles, not the principles causing the insecurity. This would imply that the principles do not have much effect even if there are relationships. On the other hand, legislators in states with pro-incumbent redistricting principles also had more of a state and less of a district orientation, and were less likely to have a surrogate orientation. Legislators in states with pro-incumbent principles were also less likely to send newsletters, but they had more accurate perceptions of their districts. Legislators in states with community redistricting principles had more of a district than state orientation, sent more newsletters, and relied less heavily on each source of information. This is suggestive of the possibility that these legislators have an easier time knowing their district preferences and thus need less constituent contact and information to make decisions.

Finally, ballot access laws had few effects on issues of representation. Legislators in states with petition requirements had fewer incentives to be responsive. They were more electorally secure and had discrete ambition.

Consequently, they also relied less on each mode of symbolic representation and offered less policy representation. Otherwise, petition requirements had little effect on representation. Legislators in states with filing fees had more of a state orientation and spent less time on symbolic and service representation. The modest findings indicate that ballot access laws increase the costs of holding office and limit legislators' ability to be responsive to constituents.

ELECTORAL VULNERABILITY'S EFFECT ON REPRESENTATION

Although elections are thought to be the tie that binds legislators and constituents, legislators who were more vulnerable differed moderately from others. I used two measures to calculate electoral vulnerability. One was based on the individual legislator's margin of victory in his/her last election, and the other was based on state reelection rates. The first measures legislators' personal vulnerability; the other measures the culture of vulnerability: to what degree do legislators who see their peers lose office feel insecure. The evidence offers modest, but fairly consistent, support for the idea that vulnerability affects issues of representation. Legislators winning by larger margins had somewhat more progressive ambition and did more casework; they also relied more on constituents and less on lawmakers for information. Large reelection rates somewhat decreased service and symbolic representation. These findings suggest that legislators who are active in representation are less vulnerable but that a culture of vulnerability increases representation (at least service and symbolic).

AMBITION'S EFFECT ON REPRESENTATION

Chapter 3 examined whether institutional features affect legislators' ambition, assuming legislators with discrete ambition would be less engaged with constituents and would be less sensitive to constituents' needs. There was at least modest evidence that ambition affected issues of representation. Those with progressive and static ambition had more of a delegate than trustee orientation, and those with static ambition had less of a state orientation and more of a surrogate orientation. Those with static ambition also spent somewhat more time on symbolic representation, and legislators with either static or progressive ambition used more modes of symbolic representation. However, those with static and progressive ambition spent less time on service representation. Also those with static ambition were more likely to rely on group information when making decisions.

ROLE ORIENTATIONS' EFFECT ON REPRESENTATION

In contrast to Eulau and Wahlke (1978), who warned against assuming that trustees would differ from delegates in their relationship with their district, these findings indicate that their warning was somewhat misplaced. Although, as one would expect, legislators with a trustee orientation offered less policy representation, they also were less engaged with constituents. Trustees spent less time on symbolic representation and were less likely to rely on constituent-derived information in making decisions. Legislators with more of a state orientation relied less on constituents for information and engaged in less service representation. Legislators with voter orientations had more accurate perceptions and attended more meetings while those with surrogate orientation had somewhat more accurate perceptions.

OTHER FACTORS

Institutional features do matter, but they are not all that matters. District and legislators' characteristics can matter as well, and they do so often in ways consistent with the expectation that legislators' incentives and abilities affect their actions. Older legislators had more of a delegate orientation, had more discrete ambition, and they did less e-communications. Legislators with more seniority had more discrete ambition, were more likely to have a trustee and a state but less of a surrogate orientation, spent more time on service representation, and relied heavily on constituents for information. Women had more static and progressive ambition, and they were less likely to rely on each source of information. Those who are leaving their chamber had more discrete ambition, less voter orientation, surrogate orientation, relied on each source of information, and spent more time on service representation. Those with previous experience had more district (less state and voter) orientation. Legislators with ideologically heterogeneous districts were more likely to have trustee, state, and voter orientation. Rural legislators had more of a delegate and district (not state) orientation and spent more time on service representation. Southern legislators had more static ambition, had surrogate and district (not state) orientations, and engaged in more symbolic and service representation. Democrats were more likely to be surrogates and engaged in more symbolic representation. Legislators with more educated constituents spent less time on symbolic representation and where the minority party was strong, legislators spent more time on symbolic representation.

CONCLUSION

There are seven broad conclusions based on this research. First, having the resources to engage in representational activities is key. For example, the resources associated with professionalism had strong effects on service and symbolic representation. Resources are important because these forms of representation require a mix of staff, time, and money. Having the resources would not have significant effects, however, if legislators did not want to use them for representation. The cumulative findings here imply that legislators do want to represent their constituents. This is supported too by Jewell (1982) and Rosenthal's (1998) suggestions that legislators want to be good representatives.

Another broad conclusion is that legislators with staff have an advantage at being good delegates. Legislators with staff have role orientations that focus on the district and offer more service and symbolic representation. The evidence about staff effects on policy representation is less clear, but legislators with staff had more accurate views of the districts' vote on same-sex marriage and offered at least somewhat more policy representation on this one issues. Additionally, while other resources tend to increase incumbent security, staff does not. Thus providing legislators with staff does not harm the accountability function of elections and could counter the negative effects of professionalism on policy representation.

A third broad conclusion is that the professionalism reforms should be treated as many things rather than one that can be summed up with a single index. It involves capacity as well as resources. Capacity and resources each have several different components. At times these components work in sync, but often they do not.

Fourth, while the speculation about the effects of term limits have been all over the board, these findings suggest that term-limited legislators are fairly independent, fairly unconcerned about elections, do less symbolic and service representation, and have less accurate perceptions of their district. While these findings paint a fairly consistent picture of legislators disengaged from their constituents, term-limited legislators offered more policy representation. Since only policies concerning civil rights were examined, more research on this issue is called for since types of policy affect policy congruence (Miller and Stokes 1963).

Fifth, the discussions of professional legislatures and term limits can offer some insight into the debate on whether legislators who are professionals differ from citizen legislators in their representational styles. Assuming professional legislators are more likely to be found in professionalized legislatures, there is some evidence that these legislators will offer less policy but more symbolic and service representation. Legislators who are more distant from constituents in their everyday lives try to gain the trust of their constituents by being attentive, however they are not more likely to use constituents as sources of information or offer policy congruence. Whether preferences and interests are interchangeable is of course debatable and this debate is not addressed here. When looking at citizen legislators there does appear to be a different pattern. Assuming term-limited legislators are citizen legislators, these legislators are disengaged from symbolic and service representation but offer higher levels of policy representation, at least on GLB issues. My guess, and it is only a guess, is that term limits increase policy representation not by affecting legislators' incentives, but by affecting the role of elections. In term-limited states electoral dynamics may change. Since open seats are more frequent, the issues that affect elections are more current. Thus legislators first elected in the 2000s may have been more likely to have been elected because of GLB or similar social policies. Where legislators are electorally secure, the incumbency advantage strong, the issues that first helped legislators win the office are no longer a driving controversy.

The findings also suggest some need to refine arguments about surrogate orientation/representation. The evidence here suggests that legislators who are electorally vulnerable or need electoral help are more likely to be surrogates. This leads me to believe that some legislators are surrogate representatives, not so much out of a shared experience with an underrepresented group but to secure electoral support from a key constituency. It is likely that there are two types of surrogates, those who wish to represent a group because they want to help an underrepresented group and may likely feel that way because of shared experiences and those who wish to represent a nongeographically based group for electoral reasons. These types of surrogate orientation are not likely to be mutually exclusive. For example, women legislators may wish to help women because women's interests have been underrepresented but also want to keep the support of women's groups.

Finally, the findings offer a warning to legislative reformers. It is often difficult to predict how a feature will affect representation. This is because any given feature is likely to have multiple effects some effects working together to enhance or harm representation but others at cross-purposes. Additionally, features that enhance one form of representation may have negative effects on others.

This book attempts to do a lot, estimating the effects of many institutional features on many aspects of representation. Unfortunately, by doing so it is almost a preliminary study that needs much follow-up. By taking broad strokes, it does not—and was not intended to—directly test why the features have the effects they have. Further research should look into what causes the relationships identified here. The effects of institutional design could be contextual and greater research on how context affects the influence of institutions is needed.

Appendix A: State Legislators and Their Districts

There are three sections to the survey. Please answer all of the questions in each section by checking the box that corresponds to the best answer, or writing in your response. Please use the margins to elaborate on or clarify any of your answers. Thank you for your help.

Section I. Representational Concerns

1. Which of the following describes how your office handles written communication from constituents?

□ I personally respond to most of the communications
□ My staff and I divide responding to communications
□ My staff responds to most of the communications
□ Other (Please specify ______________________________)

2. How often do you use the following sources of information in considering whether or not to support legislation? If you do not receive a type of information please select never.

	Almost Always	*Often*	*Roughly ½ time*	*Rarely*	*Never*
Constituents	□	□	□	□	□
Other legislators or their staff	□	□	□	□	□
Organized interests	□	□	□	□	□
Your legislative staff	□	□	□	□	□
Your own views	□	□	□	□	□

3. When voting on bills, do you feel you should be more concerned with the needs of the people who voted for you or the needs of your district as a whole?

Always District					*Always Voters*	
1	2	3	4	5	6	7

4. When voting on bills, do you feel you should be more concerned with the needs of the district or the needs of the state as a whole?

Always District					*Always State*	
1	2	3	4	5	6	7

5. When there is a conflict between what you think is best and what you think the people want, do you think you should follow your conscience or follow what the people in your district want?

Always District					*Always Conscience*	
1	2	3	4	5	6	7

6. Please list any constituencies you feel a particular responsibility to represent. If none, please state so.

7. When the legislature is in session approximately how many hours a week, on average, do you spend on the following activities? If zero leave blank.

	1–4	*5–8*	*9–16*	*16+*
Studying or developing legislation	☐	☐	☐	☐
Meeting with group representatives	☐	☐	☐	☐
Meeting with other policy makers	☐	☐	☐	☐
Keeping in touch with constituents	☐	☐	☐	☐
Helping constituents with problems with the government	☐	☐	☐	☐

8. When the legislature is NOT in session approximately how many hours a week, on average, do you spend on the following activities? If zero leave blank.

	1–4	*5–8*	*9–16*	*16+*
Studying or developing legislation	☐	☐	☐	☐
Meeting with group representatives	☐	☐	☐	☐
Meeting with other policy makers	☐	☐	☐	☐
Keeping in touch with constituents	☐	☐	☐	☐

Helping constituents with problems with the government	□	□	□	□

9. Approximately how many hours a week does your staff spend on the following activities? If you do not have personal staff, skip to question 10. If zero leave blank.

	1–4	*5–8*	*9–16*	*16+*
Studying or developing legislation	□	□	□	□
Meeting with group representatives	□	□	□	□
Meeting with other policy makers	□	□	□	□
Keeping in touch with constituents	□	□	□	□
Helping constituents with problems with the government	□	□	□	□

10. When your legislature is in session, approximately how many hours per week do you work on tasks associated with being a legislator?

_________ Number of hours per week

11. When your legislature is NOT in session, approximately how many hours per week do you work on tasks associated with being a legislator?

_________ Number of hours per week

12. Approximately how many communications, such as emails, letters, and phone calls, did you receive a week from individual constituents during the last legislative session?

_________ Number of contacts per week

13. In your average MONTH THIS YEAR, how many local meetings or speaking engagements did you have with groups in your district such as but not limited to: school, business, social service, gender, race/ethnic, or church groups?

_________ Number of meetings per month

14. Approximately how many large mailings to your district did you send THIS YEAR? Do NOT include newsletters or campaign materials.

_________ Number of communications this year

15. Do you have a newsletter you send to your constituents?

□ No (Skip question 16)
□ Yes

16. If yes, how many did you send this year?

________ Number of newsletters

17. Which of the following do you use to communicate with constituents?

	Used	*Did not use*
Legislative web page	☐	☐
Blog	☐	☐
Mass email or text messaging	☐	☐
Facebook or similar site	☐	☐

Section II: Questions about Your District and Its Voters.

18. How would you describe your political views and those of others in your district?

EL = Extremely liberal; L = Liberal; SL = Slightly liberal; M = Moderate, middle of the road; SC = Slightly conservative; C = Conservative; EC = Extremely conservative

	EL	*L*	*SL*	*M*	*SC*	*C*	*EC*
Voters in the district	☐	☐	☐	☐	☐	☐	☐
Democratic primary voters	☐	☐	☐	☐	☐	☐	☐
Republican primary voters	☐	☐	☐	☐	☐	☐	☐
Yourself	☐	☐	☐	☐	☐	☐	☐

19. Compared to the voters in the rest of your state, the voters in your district are

____________ supportive of English-only laws

☐ significantly more
☐ somewhat more
☐ about as
☐ somewhat less
☐ significantly less

____________ supportive of state recognized same-sex marriages

☐ significantly more
☐ somewhat more
☐ about as
☐ somewhat less
☐ significantly less

____________ supportive of placing limitations on the government's ability to tax

- ☐ significantly more
- ☐ somewhat more
- ☐ about as
- ☐ somewhat less
- ☐ significantly less

20. What is your best guess as to the percentage of your district that

Is Latino or black? __________
Identifies with the Democratic Party? __________
Supported your state's ballot item banning same-sex marriage? __________
Supports English only laws? _________
Generally supports bonds to improve education? __________
Has a college degree? __________
Lives in an urban area? __________

21. In your last election bid, which of the following describes your main opponent? If your primary election was more competitive than your general election please answer this question with regard to your opponent in the primary. If you did not have an opponent, go to section III.

	Describes my opponent	*Does not describe my opponent*
Was a lawyer	☐	☐
Had held an elected position	☐	☐
Had held an appointed political position	☐	☐
Was well known prior to election	☐	☐
Campaign was well funded	☐	☐
Was an incumbent	☐	☐

22. What percentage of the vote separated you from your main opponent?

__________ %

23. To what degree did you rely on a political consultant to perform the following tasks?

	Heavily	*Somewhat*	*Very little*	*None*
Polling	☐	☐	☐	☐
Developing strategy	☐	☐	☐	☐
Developing themes	☐	☐	☐	☐
Designing materials	☐	☐	☐	☐
Developing ads	☐	☐	☐	☐

Section III. Questions about You

24. When did you enter your current legislative chamber?

__________ Year

25. Did you hold an elective position in government prior to your current chamber?

□ Yes, please list most recent (__________________________)
□ No

26. What is your sex?

□ Male
□ Female

27. In what year were you born?

__________ Year

28. Which of the following best describes what you plan to be doing five years from now?

□ Hold same or similar office
□ Hold a higher office
□ Hold a lower level office
□ Work for a party or political organization
□ Hold no political office

29. How many years have you lived in your district?

_________ Number of years

If there is anything else you would like to tell me about your experiences with your constituents or your views concerning legislators' roles in representing their districts, please use this page. Thank you for your help. Without your participation this research would not be possible.

Appendix B: Descriptive Statistics of Variables

Variable	*Range*	*Mean*	*SD*	*n*
Accountability				
Uncontested	0–1	0.25	0.43	612
Quality of challenger	0–3	0.96	1.15	612
Safe district	0–1	0.60	0.49	612
Margin of victory	0–100	44.81	36.65	612
Prior vote	0–100	75.69	18.51	610
Reelection rate	1–0.83	0.96	0.04	624
Institutional features				
Leadership strength	6–16.5	13.24	2.95	625
Committee strength	3–11	6.50	2.02	625
Chamber size	29–180	88.67	41.14	624
Office budget	0–1	0.52	0.50	625
Staff	0–1	0.55	0.50	625
Full-time	–1.92–6.36	0.02	1.96	625
Contribution Limits	0–2.5	1.42	0.94	625
Voluntary spending limits	0–1	0.05	0.21	625
Filing fees	0–2,000	191.95	338.03	625
Signature requirements	0–1	0.27	0.44	625
Community principle	0–3	2.11	0.91	625
Pro-incumbent principle	0–3	1.18	0.89	625
Term length	2–4	2.77	0.97	625
Term limits	0–1	0.41	0.49	625
District magnitude	0–1	0.13	0.34	625
Size of district	7.6–975.5	76.97	101.94	625
Control variables				
South	0–1	0.42	0.49	625
% Minority party	20–50	40.37	4.47	625
Female	0–1	0.19	0.39	625
Seniority	0–47	8.13	7.20	625

Variable	*Range*	*Mean*	*SD*	*N*
District education	5–53.9	16.70	8.85	625
Age	29–90	58.08	11.47	625
Gone	0–1	0.11	0.32	625
Squire's professionalism	0.05–0.63	0.15	0.10	625
Majority party	0–1	0.60	0.49	625
Party identification	0–1	0.46	0.50	624
Members' education	0–3	2.27	0.71	625
Previous experience	0–1	0.44	0.50	625
District ideological difference	0–6	2.51	1.31	590
District rural	0–100	35.79	33.1	625
Hours in-session	0–80	22.89	14.26	603
Unipolar	1–4	2.32	0.84	625
Marriage vote folded	0.00–0.48	0.21	0.12	624
District ideology	0–7	4.79	1.36	597
District race	0.6–90.9	18.88	20.14	624
Number of GLB bills	0–12	2.95	3.29	625
Ambition				
Progressive ambition	0–1	0.18	0.39	618
Static ambition	0–1	0.44	0.50	618
Role Orientation				
Trustee	1–6	3.73	1.53	600
State orientation	1–7	3.78	1.45	610
Voter orientation	1–6	2.67	1.52	610
Surrogate	0–1	0.57	0.50	625
Symbolic representation				
In-session time in touch	0–4	2.21	0.96	611
Out-of-session in touch	0–4	2.36	1.09	611
Contact scale	0–8	4.57	1.72	609
Legislating scale	2–16	7.72	2.50	603
Lobbying scale	0–8	3.75	1.48	607
Newspaper	0–1	0.43	0.40	598
Meetings	0–300	11.83	16.18	596
e-communication	0–4	1.40	1.02	589
Information sources				
Use constituents	1–3	2.27	0.65	610
Use interest groups	1–4	2.39	0.85	588
Use legislators	1–4	3.62	0.87	597
Perceptual accuracy				
Member-district gap	0.01–48.30	9.79	8.48	474
State-district gap	–0.39–0.32	0.00	0.10	624
Service representation				
In-session service	1–4	1.95	1.00	610
Out-of-session service	1–4	2.11	1.08	611
Policy representation				
Cosponsor GLB	0–5	0.25	0.72	624

References

Adler, E. S., C. E. Gent, and C. B. Overmeyer. 1998. The Home Style Homepage: Legislator Use of the World Wide Web for Constituency Contact. *Legislative Studies Quarterly* 2: 585–95.

Allebaugh, D., and N. Pinney. 2003. The Real Costs of Term Limits: Comparative Study of Competition and Electoral Costs. Pp. 161–76 in *The Test of Time: Coping with Legislative Term Limits*. Eds. R. Farmer, J. D. Rausch, Jr., and J. C. Green. Lanham, MD: Lexington Books.

Alperin, D. J., and D. Schultz. 2003. E-Democracy: Legislative-Constituent Communications in Minnesota and Wisconsin. *Annual Meeting of the American Political Science Association*. Philadelphia, PA, August 28–31. www.allacademic.com/meta/p62554_index.html.

Amacher, R. C., and W. J. Boyes. 1978. Cycles in Senatorial Voting Behavior: Implications for the Optimal Frequency of Elections. *Public Choice* 33: 5–13.

Arnold, R. D. 1990. *Logic of Congressional Action*. New Haven, CT: Yale University Press.

Ansolabehere, S., and A. Gerber. 1996. The Effects of Filing Fees and Petition Requirements on U.S. House Election. *Legislative Studies Quarterly* 21: 249–64.

Atlas, C. M., R. J. Hendershott, and M. A. Zupan. 1997. Optimal Effort Allocation by U.S. Senators: The Role of Constituency Size. *Public Choice* 92: 221–29.

Bailey, M., and D. W. Brady. 1998. Heterogeneity and Representation: The Senate and Free Trade. *American Journal of Political Science* 42: 524–44.

Bartels, L. M. 1991. Constituency Opinion and Congressional Policy Making: The Reagan Defense Buildup. *American Political Science Review* 85: 457–74.

Berry, W. D., M. B. Berkman, and S. Schneiderman. 2000. Legislative Professionalism and Incumbent Reelection: The Development of Institutional Boundaries. *American Political Science Review* 94: 859–74.

Bickers, K. N., and R. M. Stein. 1996. The Electoral Dynamics of the Federal Pork Barrel. *American Journal of Political Science* 40: 1300–1326.

Black, G. S. 1972. A Theory of Political Ambition: Career Choices and the Role of Structural Incentives. *American Political Science Review* 66: 144–59.

Bond, J. R. 1985. Dimensions of District Attention over Time. *American Journal of Political Science* 29: 330–47.

Box-Steffensmeier, J. M., D. C. Kimball, S. R. Meinke, and K. Tate. 2003. The Effects of Political Representation on the Electoral Advantage of House Incumbents. *Political Research Quarterly* 56: 259–70.

Bowman, A. O'M., and R. C. Kearney. 1988. Dimensions of State Government Capability. *Western Political Quarterly* 41: 341–62.

Burden, B. C. 2007. *Personal Roots of Representation*. Princeton, NJ: Princeton University Press.

Carey, J. M., R. G. Niemi, and L.W. Powell. 2000a. *Term Limits: In the State Legislatures*. Ann Arbor: University of Michigan Press.

———. 2000b. Incumbency and the Probability of Reelection in State Legislative Races. *Journal of Politics* 62: 671–700.

Carey, J. M., R. G. Niemi, L. W. Powell, and G. Moncrief. 2002. State Legislative Survey [computer file]. ICPSR 20960-v1. Rochester, NY: University of Rochester [producer], 2002. Ann Arbor, MI: Inter-university Consortium for Political and Social Research [distributor], 2008-03-25. doi: 10.3886/ICPSR 20960.

———. 2006. The Effects of Term Limits on State Legislatures: A New Survey of the 50 States. *Legislative Studies Quarterly* 31: 105–134.

Carroll, S. J. 2002. Representing Women: Congresswomen's Perceptions of Their Representational Roles. Pp. 50–68 in *Women Transforming Congress*. Ed. C. S. Rosenthal. Norman: Oklahoma University Press.

Clausen, A. R., S. Holmberg, and L. deHaven-Smith. 1983. Contextual Factors in the Accuracy of Leader Perceptions of Constituents' Views. *Journal of Politics* 45: 449–72.

Council of State Governments. 2006. *The Book of the States*. Lexington, KY: Council of State Governments.

Cooper, C. A., and L. E. Richardson. 2006. Institutions and Representational Roles in American State Legislatures. *State Politics and Policy Quarterly* 6: 174–94.

Cox, G. W., and S. Morgenstern. 1993. The Increasing Advantage of Incumbency in the U.S. States. *Legislative Studies Quarterly* 18: 495–514.

———. 1995. The Incumbency Advantage in the Multimember Districts: Evidence from the U.S. States. *Legislative Studies Quarterly* 20: 329–49.

Daniel, K., and J. R. Lott, Jr. 1997. Term Limits and Electoral Competitiveness: Evidence from California's State Legislative Races. *Public Choice* 90: 165–84.

Davidson, R. H., and W. J. Oleszek. 2004. *Congress and Its Members*. 9th ed. Washington, DC: CQ Press.

Dillman, D. A. 2007. *Mail and Internet Surveys: The Tailored Design Method*. Hoboken, NY: John Wiley and Sons.

Ellickson, M. C., and D. E. Whistler. 2001. Explaining State Legislators' Casework and Public Resource Allocation. *Political Research Quarterly*. 54: 553–69.

Erikson, R. S. 1978. Constituency Opinion and Congressional Behavior: A Reexamination of the Miller-Stokes Representation Data. *American Journal of Political Science* 22: 511–35.

Erikson, R. S., N. R. Luttbeg, and W. V. Holloway. 1975. Knowing One's District: How Legislators Predict Referendum Voting. *American Journal of Political Science* 19: 231–46.

Eulau, H., and P. Karps. 1978. The Puzzle of Representation: Specifying Components of Responsiveness. Pp. 55–72 in *The Politics of Representation: Continuities in Theory and Research*. Eds. H. Eulau and J. Wahlke. Beverly Hills, CA: Sage Publications.

Eulau, H., and J. Wahlke, eds. 1978. *The Politics of Representation: Continuities in Theory and Research*. Beverly Hills, CA: Sage Publications.

Eulau, H., J. Wahlke, W. Buchanan, and L. C. Ferguson. 1978. The Role of the Representative: Some Empirical Observations on the Theory of Edmund Burke. Pp. 111–26 in *The Politics of Representation: Continuities in Theory and Research*. Eds. H. Eulau and J. Wahlke. Beverly Hills, CA: Sage Publications.

Fenno, R. F., Jr. 1977. U.S. House Members in Their Constituencies: An Exploration. *American Political Science Review* 71: 883–917.

Forgette, R., A. Garner, and J. Winkle. 2009. Do Redistricting Principles and Practices Affect U.S. State Legislative Electoral Competition? *State Politics and Policy Quarterly* 9: 151–75.

Freeman, P. K., and L. E. Richardson, Jr. 1996. Explaining Variation in Casework among State Legislators. *Legislative Studies Quarterly* 21: 41–56.

Gartzke, E., and J. M. Wrighton. 1998. Thinking Globally or Acting Locally? Determinants of the GATT Vote in Congress. *Legislative Studies Quarterly* 23: 33–55.

Gross, D. A. 1978. Representative Styles and Legislative Behavior. *Western Political Quarterly* 31: 359–71.

Hain, P. L. 1974. Age, Ambitions, and Political Careers: The Middle-Aged Crisis. *Western Political Quarterly* 27: 265–74.

Halligan, J., R. Krause, R. Williams, and G. Hawker. 1988. Constituency Service among Sub-National Legislators in Australia and Canada. *Legislative Studies Quarterly* 13: 49–63.

Hamm, K. E., and R. E. Hogan. 2009. Campaign Finance Laws and Candidacy Decisions in State Legislative Elections. *Political Research Quarterly* 61: 458–67.

Hedlund, R. D., and P. Friesema. 1972. Representatives' Perceptions of Constituency Opinion. *Journal of Politics* 34: 730–52.

Herrera, C. L., R. Herrera, and E. R. A. N. Smith. 1992. Public Opinion and Congressional Representation. *Public Opinion Quarterly* 56: 185–205.

Herrick, R. 2000. Who Will Survive? An Exploration of Factors Contributing to the Removal of Unethical House Members. *American Politics Quarterly* 28: 96–109.

———. 2009. The Effects of Sexual Orientation on State Legislators' Behavior and Priorities. *Journal of Homosexuality* 56: 1117–33.

Herrick, R., and S. H. Fisher III. 2007. *Representing America: The Citizen and the Professional Legislator in the House of Representatives*. Lanham, MD: Lexington Books.

Herrick, R., and M. K. Moore. 1993. Political Ambition's Effect on legislative Behavior: Schlesinger's Typology Reconsidered and Revised. *Journal of Politics* 55: 765–76.

Herrick, R., M. K. Moore, and J. R. Hibbing. 1994. Unfastening the Electoral Connection: The Behavior of U.S. Representatives when Reelection Is No Longer a Factor. *Journal of Politics* 56: 214–27.

Herrick, R., and S. Thomas. 2005. Do Term Limits Make a Difference? Ambition and Motivations among U.S. State Legislators. *American Politics Research* 33: 726–47.

Hibbing, J. R. 1984. The Liberal Hour: Electoral Pressures and Transfer Payment Voting in the United States Congress. *Journal of Politics* 46: 846–65.

Hibbing, J. R., and J. R. Alford. 1990. Constituency Population and Representation in the U.S. Senate. *Legislative Studies Quarterly* 15: 581–98.

Hibbing, J. R., and S. L. Brandes. 1983. State Population and the Electoral Success of U.S. Senators. *American Journal of Political Science* 27: 808–19.

Hibbing, J. R., and E. Theiss-Morse. 1995. *Congress as Public Enemy: Public Attitudes toward American Political Institutions*. New York: Cambridge University Press.

Hill, K. Q., and P. A. Hurley. 1999. Dyadic Representation Reappraised. *American Journal of Politics* 43: 109–37.

———. 2002. Symbolic Speeches in the U.S. Senate and Their Representational Implications. *Journal of Politics* 64: 219–31.

Hogan, R. E. 2001. Campaign War Chests and Challenger Emergence in State Legislative Elections. *Political Research Quarterly* 54: 815–30.

———. 2004. Challenger Emergence, Incumbent Success, and Electoral Accountability in State Legislative Elections. *Journal of Politics* 66: 1283–1303.

Holbrook, T. M., and C. M. Tidmarch. 1991. Sophomore Surge in State Legislative Elections, 1968–1986. *Legislative Studies Quarterly* 16: 49–63.

Holian, D. B., T. B. Krebs, and M. H. Walsh. 1997. Constituency Opinion, Ross Perot, and Roll-Call Behavior in the U.S. House: The Case of the NAFTA. *Legislative Studies Quarterly* 22: 369–92.

Human Rights Campaign Foundation. 2008. *Equality from State to State: A Review of State Legislation in 2008*. www.hrc.org/documents/HRC_States_Report_08.pdf.

Jacobson, G. C. 1987. The Marginals Never Vanished: Incumbency and Competition in Elections to the U.S. House of Representatives, 1952–1982. *American Journal of Political Science* 31: 126–41.

———. 2004. *The Politics of Congressional Elections*. 6th ed. New York: Pearson Longman.

Jewell, M. E. 1982. *Representation in State Legislators*. Lexington: University Press of Kentucky.

———. 1983. Legislator-Constituency Relations and the Representative Process. *Legislative Studies Quarterly* 8: 303–37.

Johannes, J. R. 1980. The distribution of Casework in the U.S. Congress: An Uneven Burden. *Legislative Studies Quarterly* 5: 517–44.

———. 1983. Explaining Congressional Casework Styles. *American Journal of Politics* 27: 530–47.

Jones, B. D. 1973. Competitiveness, Role Orientations, and Legislative Responsiveness. *Journal of Politics* 35: 924–47.

Katz, R. S. 1997. Representational Roles. *European Journal of Political Research* 32: 211–26.

Kiewiet, D. R., and L. Zeng. 1993. An Analysis of Congressional Career Decisions, 1947–1986. *American Political Science Review* 87: 928–41.

Kingdon, J. W. 1989. *Congressmen's Voting Decisions*. 3rd ed. Ann Arbor, MI: University of Michigan Press.
Kousser, T. 2005. *Term Limits and the Dismantling of State Legislative Professionalism*. New York: Cambridge University Press.
Kuklinski, J. H. 1978. Representativeness and Elections: A Policy Analysis. *American Political Science Review* 72: 165–77.
Kuklinski, J. H., and R. C. Elling. 1977. Representational Role, Constituency Opinion, and Legislative Roll-Call Behavior. *American Journal of Political Science* 21: 135–47.
Kurtz, K. T., B. Cain, and R. G. Niemi. 2007. *The Case of Term Limits: Institutional Change in American Politics*. Ann Arbor: University of Michigan Press.
Lee, F. E., and B. I. Oppenheimer. 1997. Senate Apportionment: Competitiveness and Partisan Advantage. *Legislative Studies Quarterly* 22: 3–24.
LeLoup, L. T. 1978. Reassessing the Mediating Impact of Legislative Capability. *American Political Science Review* 72: 616–21.
Lilley, W. III, L. J. DeFranco, M. F. Bernstein, and K. L. Ramsby, eds. 2007. *Almanac of State Legislative Elections: Voting Patterns and Demographics, 2000–2006*. 3rd ed. Washington, DC: CQ Press.
Little, T. H., and D. B. Ogle. 2006. *The Legislative Branch of State Government: People, Process and Politics*. Santa Barbara, CA: ABC-CLIO.
Madison, J. 2001. Federalist Paper 52. In *The Federalists*. Eds. G. Carey and J. McClellan. Indianapolis, IN: Liberty Fund.
Maestas, C. 2000. Professional Legislatures and Ambitious Politicians: Policy Responsiveness of State Institutions. *Legislative Studies Quarterly* 25: 663–90.
———. 2003. The Incentive to Listen: Progressive Ambition, Resources, and Opinion Monitoring among State Legislators. *Journal of Politics* 65: 439–57.
Mansbridge, J. 1999. Should Blacks Represent Blacks and Women Represent Women? A Contingent "Yes." *Journal of Politics* 61: 628–57.
———. 2003. Rethinking Representation. *American Political Science Review* 97: 515–28.
Martorano, N. 2004. Distributing Power: Exploring the Relative Powers of Speakers and Committees in the State Legislative Process. *Annual Meeting of the American Political Science Association*. Chicago, IL, Sept. 2–5.
Mayer, K. R., and J. M. Wood. 1995. The Impact of Public Financing on Electoral Competitiveness: Evidence from Wisconsin, 1964–1990. *Legislative Studies Quarterly* 20: 69–88.
Mayhew, D. R. 1974. *Congress: The Electoral Connection*. New Haven, CT: Yale University Press.
McAdams, J. C., and J. R. Johannes. 1985. Constituent Attentiveness in the House: 1977–1982. *Journal of Politics* 47: 1108–39.
Miler, K. C. 2007. The View from the Hill: Legislative Perceptions of the District. *Legislative Studies Quarterly* 32: 597–628.
Miller, W. E., and D. E. Stokes. 1963. Constituency Influence in Congress. *American Political Science Review* 57: 45–56.
Moncrief, G. F., J. A. Thompson, and W. Cassie. 1996. Revisiting the State of U.S. State Legislative Research. *Legislative Studies Quarterly* 21: 301–335.

Moncrief, G. F., J. A. Thompson, and K. T. Kurtz. 1996. This Old State House: It Ain't What It Used to Be. *Legislative Studies Quarterly* 21: 57–72.
Moncrief, G. F., L. W. Powell, and T. Storey. 2007. Composition of Legislature. Pp. 22–37 in *The Case of Term Limits: Institutional Change in American Politics*. Eds. K. T. Kurtz, B. Cain, and R. G. Niemi. Ann Arbor: University of Michigan Press.
Mooney, C. Z. 1991a. Information Sources in State Legislative Decision Making. *Legislative Studies Quarterly* 16: 445–55.
———. 1991b. Peddling Information in the State Legislature: Closeness Counts. *Western Political Quarterly* 44: 433–44.
———. 1994. Measuring U.S. State Legislative Professionalism: An Evaluation of Five Indices. *State and Local Government Review* 26: 70–8.
———. 1995. Citizens, Structures, and Sister States: Influences on State Legislative Professionalism. *Legislative Studies Quarterly* 20: 47–67.
National Conference of State Legislatures. www.NCSL.org.
Niemi, R. G., S. Jackman, and L. Winsky. 1991. Candidacies and Competitiveness in Multimember Districts. *Legislative Studies Quarterly* 16: 91–109.
Niemi, R. G., and L.W. Powell. 2003. Limited Citizenship? Knowing and Contacting State Legislators after Term Limits. Pp. 193–209 in *The Test of Time: Coping with Legislative Term Limits*. Eds. R. Farmer, J. D. Rausch, Jr., and J. C. Green. Lanham, MD: Lexington Books.
Oppenheimer, B. I. 1996. The Representational Experience: The Effects of State Population on Senator-Constituency Linkages. *American Journal of Political Science* 40: 1280–99.
Parker, G. R. 1980. Sources of Change in Congressional District Attentiveness. *American Journal of Political Science* 24 (1): 115–124.
Parker, G. R., and S. L. Parker. 1985. Correlates and Effects of Attention to District by U.S. House Members. *Legislative Studies Quarterly* 10: 223–42.
Parker, S. L., and G. R. Parker. 1993. Why Do We Trust our Congressman? *Journal of Politics* 55: 442–52.
Parker, D. C. W., and C. Goodman. 2009. Making a Good Impression: Resource Allocation, Home Styles and Washington Work. *Legislative Studies Quarterly* 34: 493–524.
Payne, J. L. 1984. *The Motivation of Politicians*. Chicago: Nelson-Hall Publishers.
Peters, B. G. 1996. Political Institutions, Old and New. Pp. 205–20 in *A New Handbook of Political Science*. Eds. R. E. Gooding and H. D. Klingemann. New York: Oxford University Press.
Pew Research Center for People and the Press. 2007. Trends in Political Values and Core Attitudes: 1987–2007. http://people-press.org/reports/pdf/312.pdf.
———. 2009. Budget Woes Take Toll on Views of State Government. http://people-press.org/reports/pdf/534.pdf.
Pitkin, H. F. 1967. *The Concept of Representation*. Berkeley: University of California Press.
Powell, L.W., R. G. Niemi, and M. Smith. 2007. Constituent Attention and Interest Representation. Pp. 38–54 in *Institutional Change in American Politics: The Case of Term Limits*. Eds. K. T. Kurtz, B. E. Cain, and R. G. Niemi. Ann Arbor: University of Michigan Press.

Powell, R. J. 2000. The Impact of Term Limits on the Candidacy Decisions of State Legislators in U.S. House Elections. *Legislative Studies Quarterly* 25: 645–61.

Prewitt, K., and W. Nowlin. 1969. Political Ambitions and the Behavior of Incumbent Politicians. *Western Political Quarterly* 22: 298–308.

Rohde, D. W. 1979. Risk-Bearing and Progressive Ambition: The Case of the United States House of Representatives. *American Journal of Political Science* 23: 1–26.

Rosenthal, A. 1981. *Legislative Life: People, Process, and Performance in the States*. New York: Harper and Row.

———. 1998. *The Decline of Representative Democracy: Process, Participation, and Power in State Legislatures*. Washington, DC: CQ Press.

———. 2004. *Heavy Lifting: The Job of the American Legislature*. Washington, DC: CQ Press.

Rothenberg, L. S., and M. S. Sanders. 2000a. Lame-Duck Politics: Impending Departure and the Votes on Impeachment. *Political Research Quarterly* 53: 523–36.

———. 2000b. Severing the Electoral Connection: Shirking in the Contemporary Congress. *American Journal of Political Science* 44: 316–25.

Sarbaugh-Thompson, M., L. Thompson, C. D. Elder, J. Strate, and R. C. Elling. 2006. *The Political and Institutional Effects of Term Limits*. New York: Palgrave Macmillan.

Schlesinger, J. A. 1966. *Ambition and Politics*. Chicago: Rand McNally.

Serra, G., and D. Moon. 1994. Casework, Issue Positions, and Voting in Congressional Elections: A District Analysis. *Journal of Politics* 56: 200–213.

Smith, M. A. 2003. *Bringing Representation Home: State Legislators among Their Constituents*. Columbia: University of Missouri Press.

Snyder, J. M., Jr. and M. Ueda. 2007. Do Multimember Districts Lead to Free-Riding? *Legislative Studies Quarterly* 32: 649–79.

Soule, J. W. 1969. Future Political Ambitions and the Behavior of Incumbent State Legislators. *Midwest Journal of Political Science* 13: 439–54.

Squire, P. 1993a. Professionalization and Public Opinion of State Legislatures. *Journal of Politics* 55: 479–91.

———. 1993b. State Legislative Careers. Pp. 145–66 in *Ambition and Beyond: Career Paths of American Politicians*. Eds. S. Williams and E. L. Lascher, Jr. Berkeley, CA: Institute of Governmental Studies Press.

———. 2000. Uncontested Seats in State Legislative Elections. *Legislative Studies Quarterly* 25: 131–46.

———. 2007. Measuring State Legislative Professionalism: The Squire Index Revisited. *State Politics and Policy Quarterly* 7: 211–27.

Squire, P., and K. E. Hamm. 2005. *101 Chambers: Congress, State Legislatures, and the Future of Legislative Studies*. Columbus: Ohio State University Press.

Stata. 2009. Stata Annotated Output Negative Binomial Regression. www.ats.ucla.edu/stat/Stata/output/stata_nbreg_output.htm

Stratmann, T. 2005. Ballot Access Restrictions and Candidate Entry in Elections. *European Journal of Political Economy* 21: 59–71.

Studlar, D. T., and I. McAllister. 1996. Constituency Activity and Representational Roles among Australian Legislators. *Journal of Politics* 58: 69–90.

Sulkin, T. 2005. *Issue Politics in Congress*. New York: Cambridge University Press.

Sullivan, J. L., and E. M. Uslaner. 1978. Congressional Behavior and Electoral Marginality. *American Journal of Political Science* 22: 536–53.

Swers, M. L. 2002. *The Difference Women Make: The Policy Impact of Women in Congress*. Chicago: University of Chicago Press.

Thomas, S. 1992. The Effects of Race and Gender on Constituency Service. *Western Political Quarterly* 45: 169–80.

Thompson, J. A. 1986. State Legislative Reform: Another Look, One More Time, Again. *Polity* 19: 27–41.

Thompson, J. A., and G. F. Moncrief. 1992. The Evolution of the State Legislature: Institutional Change and Legislative Careers. Pp. 195–206 in *Changing Patterns in State Legislative Careers*. Eds. G. F. Moncrief and J. A. Thompson, Ann Arbor: University of Michigan Press.

Uslaner, E. M., and R. E. Weber. 1979. U.S. State Legislators' Opinions and Perceptions of Constituency Attitudes. *Legislative Studies Quarterly* 4: 563–85.

Van Der Slik, J. R., and S. J. Pernacciaro. 1979. Office Ambitions and Voting Behavior in the U.S. Senate. *American Politics Quarterly* 7: 198–224.

Van Dunk, E., and R. E. Weber. 1997. Constituency-Level Competition in the U.S. States, 1968–1988: A Pooled Analysis. *Legislative Studies Quarterly* 22: 141–59.

Wahlke, J. C. 1978a. Policy Demands and System Support: The Role of the Represented. Pp. 55–72 in *The Politics of Representation: Continuities in Theory and Research*. Eds. H. Eulau and J. C. Wahlke. Beverly Hills, CA: Sage Publications.

———. 1978b. The Problem of a Legislative Model. Pp. 23–30 in *The Politics of Representation: Continuities in Theory and Research*. Eds. H. Eulau and J. C. Wahlke. Beverly Hills, CA: Sage Publications.

Wahlke, J. C., H. Eulau, W. Buchanan, and L. C. Ferguson. 1962. *The Legislative System: Explorations in Legislative Behavior*. New York: Wiley.

Weber, R. E., H. J. Tucker, and P. Brace. 1991. Vanishing Marginals in State Legislative Elections. *Legislative Studies Quarterly* 16: 29–47.

Weissberg, R. 1978. Collective vs. Dyadic Representation in Congress. *American Political Science Review* 72: 535–47.

Welch, S., and J. R. Hibbing. 1997. The Effects of Charges of Corruption on Voting Behavior in Congressional Elections, 1982–1990. *Journal of Politics* 59: 226–39.

Will, G. F. 1993. *Restoration: Congress, Term Limits and the Recovery of Deliberative Democracy*. New York: Free Press.

Winburn, J. 2008. *The Realities of Redistricting: Following the Rules and Limiting Gerrymandering in State Legislative Redistricting*. Lanham, MD: Lexington Books.

Wright, G. C., and M. B. Berkman. 1986. Candidates and Policy in United States Senate Elections. *American Political Science Review* 80: 567–88.

Index

accountability, 7, 21, 27, 41, 133–34, 140–42, 148. *See also* elections
Adler, E. Scott, 9, 26, 84
Alabama, 19
Alford, John R., 17, 30, 82
Allebaugh, Darlene, 31
allocation representation, 23n2
Alperin, Davida J., 91
Amacher, Ryan C., 125
ambition, 7–8, 12, 18, 21, 43–55, 62, 65, 68, 70, 73, 84, 87, 103, 109, 125, 130, 133–34, 140–41, 144, 146–47; discrete, 7, 14, 43–55, 56, 79–82, 121, 125, 142, 143–45, 147; progressive, 6–7, 13, 15–16, 43–55, 65, 79–80, 82, 92, 95–6, 125, 140–45, 147; static, 7, 14, 16–17, 43–55, 62, 65, 73, 87, 92, 95–6, 105–6, 147
Arizona, 19, 33–34, 90, 130
Arkansas, 19, 130
Arnold, R. Douglas, 2
Ansolabehere, Stephen, 28
Atlas, Cary M., 81–82
Australia, 59
Bailey, Michael, 124
ballot access laws, 13–14, 28, 31, 34, 38, 40, 48, 53–54, 60–61, 65–66, 68–69, 71–72, 75, 80–81, 83, 87, 92, 102, 108–9, 123, 135, 145. *See also* filing fees, signature requirements, and election laws
Ballot Access News, 23n10
Bartels, Larry M., 26
Berkman, Michael B., 7, 12, 27
Berry, William D., 12, 27
Bickers, Kenneth N., 7, 26
Black, Gordon S., 44
blogs, 91. *See also* e-communication
Bond, Jon R., 26
Boyes, William J., 125
Bowman, Ann O'M., 11
Box-Steffensmeier, David C., 78, 117
Brace, Paul, 12, 27, 29–30
Brady, David W., 124
Brandes, Sara L., 30
Buchanan, William, 6
Buckley v. Veleo, 23n9
Burden, Barry C., 4

California, 10, 17, 19, 130
campaign finance laws, 13, 28, 31, 33, 38–39, 41, 53, 60, 65–66, 69, 87, 108, 126, 134–35, 144–45. *See also* spending limits, contribution limits and election laws
Canada, 59
candidate emergence. *See* challengers
campaign contribution limits, 13, 28, 33, 37–38, 41, 48–49, 53–54, 60–61, 67–69, 71–72, 74–75, 79–80, 83, 87, 102, 108, 117, 125, 127, 130–31, 134–35
Carey, John M., 9, 12, 16, 20, 27, 29–31, 45–46, 60, 76n3, 76nn6–7, 81, 97, 116, 131
Carroll, Susan J., 6
casework, 6, 26, 59. *See also* service representation
Cassie, William, 47
challengers, 25, 27–33, 35–37, 141, 145. *See also* electoral vulnerability
chamber size, 11, 13, 23n7, 33, 38, 41, 47, 52, 55n3, 65–66, 68, 71, 74–75, 83, 86, 95, 105, 113, 118, 127, 134–35. *See also* legislative capability and professionalism
citizen legislator. *See* legislator, professional v. armature
Clausen, Aage R., 109
Colorado, 13, 19, 79
committee strength, 11, 13, 33, 38, 40, 47, 65, 71–72, 74–75, 83, 86–87, 88, 95, 101–2, 105, 116, 118, 127, 130, 134–35, 140
constituent size. *See* district size
constituent interests, 5, 99–100, 106, 123. *See also* policy representation
contact, 43, 59, 81–82, 84, 90–91, 100, 118; modes of contact, 89–96. *See also* e-communication, meetings, symbolic representation
Cooper, Christopher A., 6, 59–61
Cox, Gary W., 12, 27, 30

Daniel, Kermit, 31
Davidson, Roger H., 2
deHaven-Smith, Lance, 109
delegate. *See* role orientation
Dillman, Don A., 19
district: education, 35, 62, 76n2, 84, 109, 113, 147; homogeneity, 8, 62, 65, 68, 76n2, 107, 109, 122, 131n3, 147; ideology, 109, 131n5; magnitude, 16–17, 30–31, 34, 37, 39, 41, 47, 49, 61, 66, 68–69, 71–72, 75, 81, 87–88, 102–3, 105, 107–8, 116–18, 120, 124, 131, 131n4; race, 109, 113; rural, 62, 65, 68, 76n2, 84, 91, 103, 121, 147; size, 8, 16–17, 30–31, 34–35, 37, 39, 41, 46–47, 49, 51–52, 54, 61, 68–69, 71–72, 75, 81–82, 87–92, 96–97, 102, 107, 113, 117–18, 120, 123, 124, 126–27, 130, 131, 131n4, 134–35, 143–44; views same-sex marriage, 108–114, 124–31
dyadic relationships, 16–19, 30, 45–47, 49, 51–52, 54, 65–66, 69, 72, 75, 76n4, 81, 83, 87, 102, 105, 116–17, 120, 143–44; defined, 16. *See also* district magnitude, and district size

e-communication, 90–92, 95–97, 142–43, 147
Elder, Charles D., 9
electoral vulnerability, 4, 7, 12, 14–15, 18, 21, 25–42, 44, 48, 62, 68–71, 73, 78–82, 84, 87, 92, 96, 103, 109, 121, 125, 136, 140–46, 149
elections, 2, 7, 25–42, 68–71, 78; features, 13–15, 22, 27–30, 38–39, 48–49, 53–54, 60–61, 72, 75, 76n4, 79, 87, 102, 105, 117, 121, 125, 127–28, 131, 144–46. *See also* accountability, ballot access, campaign finance, redistricting, term length
Ellickson, Mark C., 6, 9, 26, 43, 59, 84, 116–17, 123

Elling, Richard C., 9, 26, 58–59
English-only laws, 130
Erikson, Robert S., 99, 106, 109
Eulau, Heinz, 2, 3–6, 23n2, 57–59, 147

Facebook, 91. *See also* e-communication
Fenno, Richard F., Jr., 3, 6–8, 26, 66, 78, 83
filing fees, 13–14, 34, 38, 40, 49, 53, 74–75, 87, 89, 102, 113, 121–23, 125, 127, 130–31, 134–35
Fisher III, Samuel H., 9, 43, 45, 84, 125
Florida, 19, 130
Forgette, Richard, 14, 27, 29–31, 34, 39, 70, 145
Freeman, Patricia K., 9, 84, 117
Friesema, Paul, 59, 99, 106, 109

Garner, Andrew, 14, 27, 31, 70
Gartzke, Erik, 4, 26
gay rights, 124, 126–27, 143. *See also* same-sex marriage, district views same-sex marriage
Gent, Chariti E., 9, 26, 84
Georgia, 19
Gerber, Alan, 28
Goodman, Craig, 78
Gross, Donald A., 4, 58, 62

Hain, Paul L., 48
Halligan, John, 6, 59, 117
Hamm, Keith E., 10–11, 15–16, 28, 31
Hawker, Geoffrey, 6
Hedlund, Ronald D., 99, 106, 109
Hendershott, Robert J., 81, 82
Herrera, Cheryl Lyn, 123
Herrera, Richard, 123
Herrick, Rebekah, 8–9, 16, 25, 43–46, 59, 70, 84, 125
Hibbing, John R., 3, 8, 17, 25–26, 30, 44, 82
Hill, Kim Quaile, 3, 7, 123
Hawaii, 124
Hogan, Robert E., 27–28, 30–31
Holbrook, Thomas M., 12, 27, 29
Holian, David B., 4, 26
Holloway, William V., 99, 106, 109
Holmberg, Sören, 109
homestyles. *See* contact
Human Rights Campaign, 126
Hurley, Patricia A., 3, 7, 123

Idaho, 19, 34, 127, 130
incumbency advantage. *See* electoral vulnerability
institutional design, xii, 9–19, 21–22, 41, 44–45, 54, 57–58, 71, 73–74, 77, 79, 89, 96–97, 100, 106, 114, 126, 131, 133; defined, 9. *See also* dyadic representation, electoral laws, professionalism, term limits
interest groups, 100–6, 142. *See also* lobbyists

Jackman, Simon, 30
Jacobs, Paul, 46
Jacobson, Gary C., 2, 7, 26, 136
Jewell, Malcolm E., 2, 5, 8–10, 17, 23n2, 26, 58–59, 61–63, 77–78, 82–84, 90, 100, 148
Johannes, John R., 8, 26, 84, 117
Jones, Bryan D., 58

Kansas, 19, 40, 42n7, 78–79
Karps, Paul, 2, 5, 23n7, 58
Katz, Richard S., 59, 62
Kearney, Richard C., 11
Kentucky, 19, 91
Kiewiet, D. R., 44, 48
Kimball, Scott, 78
Kingdon, John W., 100
Kousser, Thad, 9–10
Krause, Robert, 6
Krebs, Timothy B., 4, 26
Kuklinski, James H., 26, 58–59, 125
Kurtz, Karl T., 9, 11

leadership strength, 11, 13, 33, 38, 40, 47, 51–52, 65, 70, 72, 74, 83, 86, 95, 105, 113, 118, 121, 131–31, 134–35, 140. *See also* legislative capability and professionalism
Lee, Frances, E., 30
legislation: introduction, 8; co-sponsorships, 126–131
legislative capacity, 23n6, 33, 37, 47, 49, 52, 54, 61, 65, 82–83, 86–87, 92–95, 101–2, 105, 116, 123, 127, 136–141, 148. *See also* chamber size, committee strength leadership strength, professionalism
legislative design. *See* institutional design
legislative staff, 11, 13, 33, 37–38, 40, 65–66, 68, 73, 82, 86, 90–92, 95–97, 103, 109–13, 116, 118–20, 127, 131–31, 134–35, 141–42, 148. *See also* resources and professionalism
legislator: ability to represent, 4, 8, 10, 15–16, 18–19, 21–22, 75, 80, 97, 116–17, 121, 133; age, 48, 54, 55n6, 62, 92, 127, 147; behavior, 8; education, 62, 76n1, 84
full time, 11, 13, 33, 37–38, 49, 53–54, 86, 92, 96, 116, 118–21, 130–31, 134–35, 141–42. *See also* resources and professionalism; gender, 35, 48, 54, 55n6, 62, 68, 84, 103, 106, 127, 147; goals, 7, 78–79; incentives to represent, xii, 4, 8, 10, 14–15, 17–19, 21–22, 74–75, 77–80, 89, 92, 96–97, 116–17, 121–23, 131, 133; party identification, 48, 54, 55n6, 62, 68, 76n1, 84, 103, 109, 147–48; pay, 33. *See also* legislator full-time; perceptions of constituents, 21, 59, 77, 106–114, 133, 135, 141–45, 147–48; previous experience, 62, 76n1, 84, 99–100, 147; professional v. amateur, 12, 106–9, 113, 149; time legislating, 88, 120. *See also* office budget
legislatures, state variation, 10
LeLoup, Lance T., 23n10
Little, Thomas H., 2–3, 10, 17, 23n4, 33
lobbyists, 78, 88, 102. *See also* interest groups
Lott, Jr., John R., 31
Louisiana, 19
Luttbeg, Norman R., 99, 106, 109

Madison, James, 7
Maine, 23n12
Maestas, Cherie, 8–9, 43–44, 47, 83–84
Mansbridge, Jane, 6, 66, 70
Martorano, Nancy, 33, 49
Mayer, Kenneth R., 28
Mayhew, David R., 83
McAdams, John C., 8
McAllister, Ian, 6, 59
media, 78
Meinke, Scott, 78
meetings, 90, 95–96, 97nn3–4
Michigan, 19
Miler, Kristina C., 7, 58, 78, 100
Miller, Warren E., 4, 99, 106, 123, 148
Minnesota, 91
Mississippi, 19, 42n4
Missouri, 2, 13, 19
Moncrief, Gary, 10–12, 16, 20, 46–47, 81, 116
Montana, 10
Moon, David, 78, 117
Mooney, Christopher Z., 11, 58, 100–1, 114
Moore, Michael K., 8, 44
Morgenstern, Scott, 12, 27, 30
multimember districts. *See* district magnitude and dyadic relationships

National Conference of State Legislatures (NCSL), 20, 33–35, 40, 55n6
NCSL. *See* National Conference of State Legislatures
neo-institutionalism, 22

New Hampshire, 13
New Mexico, 40
newsletters, 89–97, 140, 142, 145
Niemi, Richard G., 9, 12, 16, 20, 27, 29–31, 46, 60, 66
norms, 9, 22, 23n4
North Dakota, 13, 18, 34, 130
Nowlin, William, 8

office budgets, 11, 13, 33, 35–37, 40–41, 65–66, 68, 70, 82, 86, 89, 91–92, 96, 103, 106, 113–14, 116, 118–21, 130–31, 134–35, 141–42. *See also* professionalism and resources
Ogle, David B., 2–3, 10, 17, 23n5, 33
Ohio, 19
Oklahoma, 19, 55n1
Oleszek, Walter J., 2
Oppenheimer, Bruce I., 30
Oregon, 19
Overmeyer, Cary B., 9, 26, 84

Parker, David C. W., 78
Parker, Glenn R., 9, 43, 78, 83–84
Parker, Suzanne L., 9, 43, 78–84
party strength, 35, 48, 62, 68, 84, 103, 127, 147
Pernacciaro. Samuel J., 8
Peters, B. Guy, 22
petition requirements. *See* ballot access and signature requirements
Pew Research Center for People and the Press, 1
Pinney, Neil, 31
Pitkin, Hanna F., 1–2, 23n1
policy congruence 4, 11, 26. *See also* policy representation
policy representation, xi–xii, 1–2, 8, 18–19, 123–31, 133, 135, 140–49
political ambition. *See* ambition
politico, 59
pork barreling, 26
Powell, Lynda W., 9, 12, 16, 20, 27, 29–31, 46, 66, 81, 116
Powell, Richard J., 46
Prewitt, Kenneth, 8
professionalism, 10–13, 15, 27, 31–33, 39, 41, 47, 52, 57, 61, 66, 69–73, 82–83, 90, 95, 97, 101, 103–5, 107–8, 115–16, 118, 120, 122–27, 133, 136–42. *See also* chamber size, committee strength, full time, leadership strength, legislative capability, legislative staff, office budgets, resources
public opinion, 1, 3

redistricting, 13, 29–31, 34, 37, 39–40, 48–49, 54, 60–61, 65–67, 69–72, 74–75, 76n4, 80, 83, 87, 92, 96, 102, 105–9, 113, 125–27, 130, 134–35, 145. *See also* electoral features
representation, xi–xii, 1–9, 13, 15, 18–19, 21–22, 25–27, 43, 54, 57, 76n8, 99–100, 106, 133; defined, 1; collective v. dyadic, 3–4. *See also* allocation representation, policy representation, service representation, symbolic representation
resources, 8, 27, 33, 41, 47, 49, 54, 61–65, 82, 86, 88–89, 92, 96–97, 101, 116, 122–23, 127, 131, 136, 141–142, 148. *See also* legislative staff, legislator full time, office budget, professionalism
responsiveness. *See* representation
retirement, 62, 84, 103, 106, 121, 127, 147. *See also* discrete ambition
Richardson. Lilliard E., 6, 9, 26, 59–61, 84, 117
Rohde, David W., 44–45
role orientation, 4–7, 12, 15, 17–18, 21, 57–76, 84, 87–88, 103, 109, 122, 125, 130, 133–34, 140–41, 143, 147–48; defined, 57; trustee/delegate, 4–6, 16, 58–66, 68, 72, 79, 82, 87, 89, 106–7, 125, 130, 141–42, 144, 146–48; foci, 57, 66–73; state/district, 6, 16, 66–68, 72, 80, 88, 106, 121, 125, 130, 141, 146–47; voter/district, 6,

68–70, 72, 81–82, 140, 142, 145, 147–48; surrogate, 6–7, 70–73, 76n8, 81, 89–89, 140, 142, 145, 147, 149. *See also* politico
roll-call votes, 126
Rosenthal, Alan, 3, 7, 9–12, 26, 43–44, 47, 63, 69, 90–91, 99, 101, 117, 123, 131, 148
Rothenberg, Lawrence S., 8

same-sex marriage, 124; ballot items, 23n12, 108. *See also* district views same-sex marriage
Sanders, Mitchell S., 8, 43–44
Sarbaugh-Thompson, Marjorie, 9
Schlesinger, James A., 7, 43–44
Schneiderman, Stuart, 12, 27
Schultz, David, 91
seniority, 31, 35, 48, 54, 55n6, 68, 73, 84, 103, 106, 109, 121, 127, 147. *See also* term limits
Serra, George, 78, 117
service representation, xi–xii, 2, 8, 17–19, 115–123, 133, 135, 140–49. *See also* representation
session length, 33. *See also* legislator full time
signature requirements, 13–14, 34, 38, 49, 53–54, 72, 75, 80–81, 87–89, 92, 95–96, 102, 123, 125, 127, 130, 134–35, 145–46
Smith, E. R. A. N., 123
Smith, Michael A., 6, 8, 26, 60, 66, 68
Snyder Jr., James M., 81
Soule, John W., 8
sources of information, 21, 99–106, 113–14, 133, 135, 140–47, 149
South Carolina, 19, 40
South Dakota, 10, 13, 19, 34, 130
Southern legislators, 35, 49, 54, 62, 84, 103, 109, 127, 147
spending limits, 13–14, 33, 37–38, 40–41, 48–49, 53–54, 60–61, 66–67, 69, 71–72, 74, 80, 83, 87, 102, 105–6, 108, 114, 117, 123, 125, 134–35, 144–45. *See also* campaign finance laws
Squire, Peverill, 10–11, 15–16, 20, 23n13, 27, 29–31, 44, 122
staff. *See* legislator staff
Stein, Robert M., 7, 26
Stokes, Donald E., 4, 99, 106, 123, 148
Storey, Tim, 46
Strate, John, 9
Stratmann, Thomas, 28, 31
substantive representation. *See* service representation, policy representation
Studlar, Donley T., 6, 59
Sulkin, Tracy, 7, 26
Sullivan, John L., 26
surrogate representation, 76n6. *See also* role orientation, surrogate
Swers, Michele L., 70, 126
symbolic representation, xi–xii, 2–3, 8, 17–19, 77–97, 103, 106, 109, 116, 118, 121–23, 133–34, 140–49

Tate, Katherine, 78
Tennessee, 19
term length, 13, 28–29, 31, 34, 37, 39–41, 48–49, 53, 55n5, 60–61, 66, 68–71, 74–75, 79, 83, 87, 89, 92, 96, 102, 107–8, 118, 121–22, 125–27, 130–31, 134, 144. *See also* electoral features
term limits, 15–16, 30–31, 34, 37, 39–41, 44–46, 49–51, 54, 55n1, 59, 61, 65–66, 68–75, 81, 83, 92, 95–96, 101, 103, 106–8, 113–14, 116, 118, 120–23, 125–26, 130–31, 142–43, 148–49
Texas, 17, 19, 130
Theiss-Morse, Elizabeth, 3
Thomas, Sue, 16, 46, 59, 88, 125
Thompson, Joel A., 10–12, 47
Thompson, Lyke, 9
Tidmarch, Charles M., 12, 27, 29
trustee. *See* role orientation
Tucker, Harvey J., 12, 27, 29–30

Ueda, Michiko, 81
uncontested elections. *See* challengers
Uslaner, Eric M., 26, 99, 106, 113
Utah, 19, 107, 130

Van Der Slik, Jack R., 8
Van Dunk, Emily, 12, 27, 30
Virginia, 19, 42n4

Wahlke, John C., 4–7, 57–59. 62, 66, 147
Walsh, Michael H., 4, 26
Weber, Ronald E., 12, 27, 29–30, 32, 99, 106, 113
web pages, 91. *See also* e-communication
Weissberg, Robert, 3–4
Welch, Susan, 25
Whistler, Donald E., 6, 9, 26, 43, 59, 84, 116–17
Will, George F., 60
Williams, Robert, 6
Winburn, Jonathan, 14
Winger, Richard, 23n10
Winkle, John, 14, 27, 31, 70
Winsky, Laura, 30
Wisconsin, 19, 33
Wood, John M., 28
Wright, Gerald C., 7
Wrighton, J. Mark, 4, 26

Zeng, Langche, 44–45, 48
Zupan, Mark, 8

Breinigsville, PA USA
22 March 2011
258195BV00004B/14/P

9 780739 150672

* conceptual definitions
("security" vs. "accountability")

* generalizeability
— limits of scope of legislation in federal system, etc.
– electoral systems

* policy (state level) vs. individual legislators' votes on policy

* bad interpretation of significance of interactive relationships where two non-dichotomous variables are used

* term-limited vs. in last term

NO "independence" in chapter 6
* measure of perceptions

* table 6.3
No easy to distinguish between symbolic representation and campaigning?